Faith-Based Development

Faith-Based Development

*How Christian Organizations
Can Make a Difference*

Bob Mitchell

ORBIS BOOKS
Maryknoll, New York 10545

ORBIS BOOKS
Maryknoll, New York 10545

Fathers and Brothers
MARYKNOLL™

Founded in 1970, Orbis Books endeavors to publish works that enlighten the mind, nourish the spirit, and challenge the conscience. The publishing arm of the Maryknoll Fathers and Brothers, Orbis seeks to explore the global dimensions of the Christian faith and mission, to invite dialogue with diverse cultures and religious traditions, and to serve the cause of reconciliation and peace. The books published reflect the views of their authors and do not represent the official position of the Maryknoll Society. To learn more about Maryknoll and Orbis Books, please visit our website at www.maryknollsociety.org.

Library of Congress Cataloging-in-Publication Data

Names: Mitchell, Bob (Robert Bradley) author.
Title: Faith-based development : how Christian organizations can make a
    difference / by Bob Mitchell.
Description: Maryknoll : Orbis Books, [2017] | Includes bibliographical
    references and index.
Identifiers: LCCN 2016036390 (print) | LCCN 2016054082 (ebook) | ISBN
    9781626982147 (pbk.) | ISBN 9781608336791 (ebook)
Subjects: LCSH: Religious institutions. | Church and social problems.
Classification: LCC BV900 .M58 2017 (print) | LCC BV900 (ebook) | DDC
    361.7/5—dc23
LC record available at https://lccn.loc.gov/2016036390

For Jessie Clark and my friends at BUC

CONTENTS

FOREWORD
By Bryant L. Myers *ix*

ACKNOWLEDGMENTS *xiii*

INTRODUCTION *xv*

LIST OF KEY ABBREVIATIONS *xxv*

PART ONE:
CHRISTIAN HEART, SECULAR PROFESSION

CHAPTER 1
The Secularized Nature of the Development Profession   3

CHAPTER 2
Some High-Level Theological Motivations
for International Development Work   12

PART TWO:
CHRISTIAN MOTIFS AND THEIR IMPACT ON DEVELOPMENT WORK

CHAPTER 3
Theological Reflection on Prevalent Theories of Change   25

CHAPTER 4
The Big Picture Narratives   37

CHAPTER 5
A Spiritual Worldview—Meeting Communities Where They're At   46

CHAPTER 6
Living for the Kingdom: The Now!   54

CHAPTER 7
Work as Ministry   64

CHAPTER 8
A Devotional, Reflective Culture   73

CHAPTER 9
Standing against Evil   81

CHAPTER 10
The Imperative of Inner Transformation   90

CHAPTER 11
Prayer and Spiritual Disciplines   98

CHAPTER 12
A Special Relationship with the Church   106

CHAPTER 13
Implications   119

PART THREE:
FAITH, DEVELOPMENT, AND ACCOUNTABILITY

CHAPTER 14
Accountability for Faith-Based Development Organizations   135

CHAPTER 15
Accountability for Crosscutting Themes   144

CHAPTER 16
Becoming a Faithfully Based Organization   155

EPILOGUE
Getting to Know Your City   175

APPENDIX
List of World Vision Evaluation Reports   181

NOTES   183

SELECTED BIBLIOGRAPHY   211

INDEX   223

FOREWORD

Expanding Our Horizons

As I was reading the manuscript of *Faith-Based Development* in preparation for writing this foreword, I was reminded of a chapter I wrote for a book on holistic mission as part of the Regnum Edinburgh 2010 books series. I had been asked to write a chapter reflecting on the evangelical conversation on holistic mission. After briefly outlining the evangelical re-engagement with social action within the Lausanne Movement beginning in 1974, I posed these questions: Where are the frontiers of holistic mission in 2010? What is the new work that needs to be done? As a preamble, my response began with the following statement:

> We need to begin by noting what has not happened. No new volumes of case studies have been published in the last ten years. There are very few new books on transformational development (holistic or integral mission). There are very few serious program evaluations that are genuinely holistic. There is very little, if any, serious research by Christian practitioners—very few PhD studies, almost no academic research into transformational development. There is very little new theological reflection; we are resting on the excellent work done in the 1980s. There is no new ecclesiology, and yet the question of the relationship between the Christian relief and development agency and local churches remains unclear. The bottom line is this: For the last twenty years, evangelical holistic mission activists have acted. They've gone out and done transformational development. Doing is good. But there is more to doing than just acting.[1]

I then closed the chapter with a list of eight areas for which I believed new work was required.

1. The need to be more intentional and deliberate in the formation of holistic practitioners.

2. The need to better understand where local churches fit into the holistic mission theology and practice of Christian NGOs (non-governmental organizations).

3. The need to recover a Christian account for why development technology is effective.

4. The need for faith-based development organizations to adopt a transformational development approach to their own organizational development.

5. The need to integrate advocacy into our practice of transformational development.

6. The importance of professionalizing without secularizing.

7. The need to provide evidence of the effectiveness of our work.

8. The need to engage the secular development world with confidence.

A mere six years later, Robert Mitchell, currently the CEO of Anglican Overseas Aid and a former senior leader with World Vision Australia, has written an important book that sheds new light and fresh thinking on many of these issues. Mitchell does this by providing the first systematic field-based academic research on the theory and practices of faith-based development done by a Christian organization. In addition to Mitchell's very good theological engagement, the Christian relief and development community finally has some evidence from work on the ground with which to hone our thinking.

The breadth of research locations—two in Central Asia, two in post-Communist Eastern Europe, one in the Middle East and three in Africa—is very helpful in creating nuance where most prior conversations have been either theoretical or drawn in overly simple black-and-white generalizations. For example, Mitchell's comparisons of doing Christian faith-based development in Christian East Africa in contrast to work in Muslim West Africa provokes a new kind of conversation about the relationship of Christian NGOs, churches, and local mosques. Mitchell's findings shift the focus from one of fear and difficult relationships to the possibility of potentially critical cooperation in service of the poor. Recent work—part of the World Faith's Development Dialogue—by Katherine Marshall on the West Africa Ebola epidemic is a highly relevant example of this interfaith potential.[2]

Mitchell has written his book from an Anglican and mainline Protestant perspective, thus adding voices from outside the evangelical Lausanne Movement, the context of my work on integral mission or transformational development. Thus, alongside Catholic Social Teaching and the recent investigations into neo-Pentecostal churches and their development efforts in the global South,[3] we now have a richer and deeper conversation about the theology and practice of development done within the Christian tradition. I am quite sure this will lead to new questions and insights down the road.

Mitchell pays a lot of attention to worldviews. Each development organization is captive to one, he points out, whether this is stated or implicit. This sets the stage for insisting that differences in thinking about or practicing development may find their roots in different sets of assumptions about how the world works and how it came to be as it is. This is an important foundational element to any dialogue between secular and faith-based development frames and practices.

This leads me to Mitchell's point of departure, which is intriguing and important. He begins his investigation by noting the growing interest on the part of the secular development studies community in faith-based development—both its theory/theology and practice. His engagement with the secular development conversation is refreshingly neither defensive nor apologetic. While he acknowledges that faith-based organizations have much to learn from their secular counterparts and are too often not as professional as one might prefer, he also asserts that the faith perspective fills in some glaring gaps in the secular account of the causes and nature of poverty and what constitutes a sustainable response. For example, a Christian perspective offers a conceptual (theological) framework for why and how human beings are creative and seem compelled to improve the world, as well as an account of why human beings also act unjustly and selfishly. The secular development proposal addresses only the former with any substance.

In another example of how Christian development practice may add to the development conversation, Mitchell's chapter on "The Imperative of Inner Transformation" brings personal transformation into the center of the discussion about social transformation. Intriguingly, this is also the conclusion of secular anthropologist Dena Freeman of the London School of Economics. Based on her research into neo-Pentecostal churches doing development in five African cities, she bravely declares that "while Pentecostals seek to bring about personal transformation, NGOs (including Catholic and many main-line Protestant NGOs), tend to think more of the community (social) level. When it comes to bringing about social and economic change, it seems that approaches that focus on individuals are rather more effective."[4]

Mitchell's book is infused with a pastoral tone, which he freely acknowledges. He reflects on his findings with the intent of encouraging faith-based organizations to own their faith commitments as an asset and to work harder at more deeply integrating Christian theology and the values of the kingdom of God into their thinking and practice. He offers a compelling case for the religious identity of faith-based development organizations actually making a difference. This is an important call for the leadership of faith-based agencies to recover their confidence in their own faith traditions in the aftermath of the corrosive effect of two hundred years or so of modernity and its secular faith commitments.

Mitchell has made a significant new contribution to the holistic mission or transformational development conversation. Reconnecting ourselves to our secular friends in the same business is an important new proposal. It opens doors to follow-on investigation, research, and theological reflection. May God encourage others to follow in Mitchell's footsteps.

Bryant L. Myers, PhD
Professor of International Development
School of Intercultural Studies
Fuller Theological Seminary

ACKNOWLEDGMENTS

I particularly want to acknowledge the wisdom and erudition of the staff at Anglican Overseas Aid, especially Nils von Kalm and Brian Holmes. The application of their skills has refined and shaped the manuscript. Professor Dorothy Lee from Trinity College Theological School and Emeritus Archdeacon Alan Nichols, AM, offered many helpful suggestions and comments. World Vision Australia generously gave permission to use their reports and data, thus allowing some key insights to be shared. Finally, this book would not have been brought to completion without the constant encouragement of my wife Anita.

INTRODUCTION

The underlying conflict

A core tenet of Christian faith is social transformation. Many Christians are attracted to work in the international development field for that reason. For them, development work is a way of exercising compassion, pursuing human dignity, and seeking a better world for all. The New Testament is replete with references to the socially transforming quality of Christian discipleship embodying elements of social responsibility, good works, and justice. For example, in Matthew's gospel, those doing God's work in this way are pictured collectively as a light in the world. They are described as a city built high on a hill, a city whose light cannot be hidden.[1]

While the challenge of international development is attractive to many Christians, the development profession is a predominantly secular, modern discipline that has historically distanced itself from any serious consideration of the role of faith in achieving its purposes. Some Christians can end up feeling conflicted, seeing development work as an important opportunity for social transformation, yet being discouraged by a professional ethos that is largely dismissive of religious viewpoints, including their own.

The faith of Christians working for secular development organizations will often be confined to a personal motivating factor. However, many Christians work for Christian faith-based development organizations—some very large and well respected—that do take their underpinning faith very seriously. This book is especially interested in these organizations. They represent an opportunity to unpack how Christian belief can inform development work and day-to-day practice.

Mapping these connections in an explicit way is vitally important. In my experience, even in the most committed faith-based organizations (FBOs) Christians do not always appreciate the range of connections between the faith they uphold and the important work they do. Sometimes they work from the hunch or the feeling that their faith does—or should—make a difference, but they may struggle to say exactly how. In part this is because people can become too enmeshed in their own daily experience. Much of the analysis that follows comes from reports prepared by people with the benefit of an outsider's view. A goal of this book is to help Christian development practitioners explicitly tease out those connections that make faith-based development both distinctive and effective.

Perhaps the most surprising learning from writing this book is that it has not been written already. I find it astonishing that so little attention has been paid to the role of faith in doing international development work, especially given its historical associations with the sector and the large number of faith-based organizations operating within it. Para-church organizations have been major players in international development work for as long as international development has been recognized as an academic discipline and profession. Despite this long involvement, there has been very little attempt to reflect critically on how the beliefs and practices adopted by faith-based development organizations affect their work. Unhelpfully, they have been viewed with a level of condescension and curiosity by the mainstream, being labeled as "interesting or irritating marginal players in the struggle for human emancipation from poverty."[2] This dismissive view contrasts with their status as some of the world's largest development organizations.[3] It is certainly time for a deeper examination.

Who should read this book?

This book is being written with multiple audiences in mind.

My belief is that many governors and leaders of faith-based development organizations do not fully appreciate how the faith they hold dear contributes to the work they oversee. Surprisingly, there is very little written about this subject. In many cases it is simply assumed that Christian faith contributes in a positive but unspecified way to the work of their organizations. This book seeks to make explicit connections between Christian faith and international development work. It is contended that Christian faith not only inspires development activity, but it can deeply inform the way it is carried out.

In an increasingly secularized Western world the faith identity of many faith-based development organizations is at a crossroads. Leaders grapple with questions of how and why to maintain the vitality of faith in organizational life. This book will offer important information on these topics.

Another key audience is Christian development practitioners working in faith-based development organizations. This book is especially directed at those workers who want to better understand how Christian faith connects with the vital work they are engaged in. It does this by describing some of the key Christian motifs typical of many faith-based development organizations and then explores their impact on development work. There are, of course, many committed Christians working in secular development non-governmental organizations (NGOs) who will also be interested in the insights discussed in this book. These insights will provide personal encouragement and challenge even if they do not speak directly into their organizational context.

Lastly, this book will be of interest to the development sector and a range of stakeholders more generally. It will assist scholars and practitioners interested in knowing more about faith-based development organizations and what they can bring to the task of international development. It will raise important questions for Western governments, for other NGOs, and for churches as participants in development. This contribution is timely given the renaissance of interest in faith-based development. The analysis will reveal ways of working that are highly resonant with poor communities and that provide a solid basis for comparative advantage in a number of settings.

Approach

A leading development organization, World Vision, is taken as an example. The resulting analysis enables Christian development practitioners to see how the faith they uphold intersects with development work and practice. In short, it unpacks how an organization's theologically informed worldview affects what it does.

There are many faith-based development organizations that are vastly different from World Vision in scale, style, and particular culture. Notwithstanding, a great many of the insights unpacked about World Vision are still highly relevant to other Christian development organizations. I have concluded that there remains a strong benefit in sharing these insights, confident that readers will be able to make their own contextualization.

What kind of organizations is this book about?

Throughout this book I refer to "faith-based development organizations" or sometimes more briefly "FBOs." I do this for convenience only, acknowledging that I really have a large sub-species of organization in mind. I am concerned with those international Christian development organizations standing in the broad Protestant tradition that take their religious identity seriously. Rather than invent yet another tortured acronym, I have opted to use a general term, delineating what I mean by it. I acknowledge too that there are some aid and development organizations that operate from entirely different religious traditions and that do very fine work. I am not, however, qualified to talk about them.

It is relevant to note at the outset that there is a statistical over-representation of Christian organizations in the aid and development sector, partly because of the rich theological motivations that Christian faith brings to this area of work. This means there are a good many organizations that will readily identify with the chapters that follow.

For completeness, I add that I am less concerned with liberal Catholic organizations because they tend to operate with far more open systems. It has been said that Catholic identity has never defined itself in sectarian terms as over against all other human or secular reality. Catholic always includes catholic with a small 'c.' The catholic understanding involves and touches all reality. The Catholic theological tradition has always insisted on the basic goodness of the human and has seen the divine mediated in and through the human.[4]

This means there is a propensity within Roman Catholicism to work comfortably with more open systems, including using non-Catholic partners, resources, and personnel. This is possible because "much of what is distinctive about Catholic identity can be accepted by others and is not necessarily unique."[5] The result is that liberal Catholic organizations tend not to embody the kind of distinctive organizational culture and praxis that I want to explore.

As stated, one organization squarely in view is World Vision. This international partnership is the largest among all humanitarian and development aid NGOs.[6] World Vision was the subject of my doctoral research, which examined the impact of the organization's theology upon its work. There are many other development organizations with an outlook similar to that of World Vision, and this book will be of general interest to them. This book should therefore not be seen as being "about World Vision."

Hard data...

World Vision Australia has consented to the use of a series of internally produced research reports and interviews to illustrate many of the points made in this book. This important research covers eight different country contexts: Albania, Bosnia and Herzegovina, Lebanon, Georgia, Armenia, Senegal, Rwanda, and Tanzania.[7] The thrust of the research was to examine the role of faith within the development practice in each location. About 250 records of interviews supported the research reports in the form of Key Informant Interviews ("KIIs") and Focus Group Discussions ("FGDs"). When I refer to "the data," this is what I am talking about.

These materials offered some exceptional insights into faith-based development practice and raised many important questions about faith identity and principles. I believe there is a benefit in sharing these insights because so much of what was learned was capable of a more general application. Having said that, no dataset can speak to every context, especially different religious contexts. In some areas, readers will have to make their own translations for the settings they know best.

...With devotional possibilities

The data certainly provides a strong empirical basis for the connections made in describing faith-based development. However, in places the book will take a more reflective tone. Occasionally, I will talk paradigmatically about what faith-based development *should* be like. I am content with this because I hope this book will encourage FBOs, and the practitioners who work in them, to live out fully what their religious identity can bring to the development task.

The title of this book—"Faith-Based Development"—reflects a deliberate ambiguity. At one level the book is mainly descriptive. It talks in a robust and hopefully scholarly way about what faith contributes in the work of FBOs. At another level, however, it expresses my positive personal opinion that having faith in faith-based development is well justified because of the many unique contributions faith can make. If the resulting analysis has a devotional value for some readers, then I rejoice!

The mystery of faith-based development organizations

Before the early 2000s, the idea of religious faith having a positive role in development was downplayed in academic circles or even seen as anathema.[8] Since then, research in this area has gained momentum, although there are still major gaps. One gap exists because the potential contribution of religion tends to be viewed in narrow, instrumental ways. This has led to the superficial labeling of actors in the sector according to their donor constituencies, rather than to addressing religious identity in terms of its distinctive development models and contributions. To be meaningful, a religious identity should tell us "how religion *actually functions* in religiously motivated relief and development."[9] In a similar vein, other researchers regret the paucity of information about "the different ways in which faith or religion is signified and practiced within these organizations."[10]

Researchers in related areas of social science point out that "multiple studies conclude that faith-based services are effective, yet relatively few aim to identify the specific faith components related to successful outcomes."[11] In international development there is a parallel need to define which elements of faith-based operational practice contribute to and sometimes impede its goals. This book aims to show

how the religious identity of faith-based development organizations actually makes a difference. This will move the discourse beyond viewing religion as merely a private motivation for a cohort of staff or a donor category.

Locating myself in the narrative

I have been a board member of several organizations concerned with international aid and development, and have been employed in senior positions by two others. I am also an ordained Anglican minister. These roles have provided many occasions to reflect on the distinctive contribution that Christian faith can make to international development work.

Over the years, a range of views has been expressed to me by development sector colleagues about the integration of faith in development. A common perspective is that faith-based development organizations do essentially the same "stuff" as secular ones, and there is no real difference. At a superficial level, faith-based development agencies look very similar to other development NGOs. They are represented in all the usual sectors—community health, HIV and AIDS, literacy, microfinance, water and sanitation, and agriculture—and they share the common objective of uplifting communities on a sustainable basis.

Others locate the distinctive contribution of faith-based agencies in the area of personal motivation. This may mean that while development work is inspired by faith convictions, it is not materially different from that of other organizations in terms of its execution. A few colleagues have argued that Christian faith influences both the motivation and the execution of development work. More ambitiously, some have posited that faith-based approaches must inform the understandings of what "development" is, claiming that such approaches speak to a more comprehensive notion of personhood, one that takes spiritual life seriously.

Some detractors of faith-based approaches see them as introducing far too many ethical problems, especially when mixed with an evangelical agenda. Another group describes faith-based approaches as well-meaning but sometimes amateurish, pointing out that faith-based actors occasionally transgress accepted norms of development practice and divert attention from more important ideas about universal human rights.

This multiplicity of perspectives has been exercising my critical faculties for several years. It has instilled a desire in me to unpack the meaning of faith in development for that group of Christian organizations that try to embed their religious identity in their work in a serious way. These organizations provide the best opportunity to see what faith can distinctively bring to development work both in terms of benefit and sometimes risk.

Broader implications

This book addresses an important topic because, while international development has discovered religion, "it has yet to investigate its diverse meanings for faith-based organizations."[12] It is hoped that the transparency of faith-based development organizations will be improved by what is shared. This book responds to calls for research that will promote greater "faith literacy" for donors and other stakeholders.[13] Unless more is known about faith-based approaches, it will not be possible to optimize their benefits or mitigate their risks. Accordingly, this type of enquiry is of fundamental concern to both the development profession and the world's poor.

Analysis of the data can lead to well-grounded observations that have a more general application for the sector as a whole, as well as other stakeholders. Some very important questions are raised. How can Christian theology be reimagined as a development asset? Is a more enlightened type of secularism appropriate, so that Western governments can better engage with faith institutions? How can governments mitigate the risks of faith-based development? What do faith-based approaches say about the meaning of "development"? Are new faith-based techniques and methodologies warranted? These and many other questions are thrown open by the data.

What this book is not trying to do

This book does *not* seek to show that Christian faith-based approaches are superior to all other development approaches. This would be arrogant and problematic on several levels. As stated, the intent is to illustrate how faith actually works within the operational life of faith-based development organizations. My sincere hope is that this will benefit those organizations, the Christians who work in them, and others who want to know more about faith-based approaches. Without over-reaching, it is important to focus critical attention on those aspects that do point to comparative advantage. The qualitative data relied on is very helpful in this regard.

The structure of this book

This book is structured in three parts. Part 1, "Christian Heart, Secular Profession," introduces the conflicted experience of many Christians working in the development sector. Chapter 1 explains the deeply secular underpinning of international development as a profession. Chapter 2 locates development work within the broader trajectory of social initiatives by which Christians have sought to bless the world and outlines the rich Christian theological traditions that partly account for the over-representation of faith-based development organizations.

Part 2 is the largest section of the book. Chapters 3 to 13 are a thematic exploration of how Christian beliefs or motifs in the life of faith-based development organizations can affect international development work. This will show that faith-based approaches offer strong advantages in some contexts. This is followed by an overview of some of the implications that flow from the analysis.

Having established that faith-based development organizations have something distinctive and valuable to offer, the book in part 3 looks at the notion of Christian accountability in international development and what can be done to maintain faith in organizational life.

The book concludes with an epilogue that provides a brief final reflection.

Themes you will encounter

Throughout the book, some key themes and arguments are reiterated. It may be helpful to introduce these here.

All organizations have a worldview. It is contended that every NGO working in international development has a worldview, whether that worldview is explicitly stated or not. Worldviews have advantages or disadvantages depending on context. It is a mistake to think that Western modernist views of development can be easily and happily transposed to the setting of any developing country.

"Development" is a contested term. "Development" means different things to different people and groups. Many would accept that the objective of development is "to advance human dignity, freedom, social equity and self-determination"[14] and that a lack of development involves "social exclusion, poverty, ill-health, powerlessness and a shortened life-expectancy."[15] However, there is a strong rationalistic overlay that frequently imbues Western concepts of international development with a much narrower economic focus. This book will show that a more holistic approach to development, one that takes religious beliefs of communities seriously, can offer a broader vision of human flourishing. In this process, understandings of "development" will be challenged.

There is an arrogance associated with Western models of development. It is a shocking conceit to think that development of any kind can or should take place without engaging with the primary source of meaning of the vast majority of communities in developing countries. That primary source of meaning is their religious worldview. While that may seem obvious, and is statistically incontrovertible, that is exactly what the development profession has tried to do since its inception. Because faith-based development organizations take human spirituality seriously, they will have comparative advantages and a much greater resonance in some contexts.

Instrumental approaches to religious institutions are far from ideal. The nascent interest in religion by the development sector has been superficial. It leaves mainstream conceptions of development completely unchallenged and reduces the relationship with churches and other faith-based institutions to one of convenience as a delivery channel. Questions of faith, if they are viewed at all, tend to be viewed strictly *from the outside.* This book is fundamentally different. It looks at faith from within, from the perspective of those for whom it matters. It asks what difference Christian faith makes in doing development work, not how religious institutions can best assist pre-existing development agendas. It looks back at the sector and poses some important questions that the mainstream may not ask itself. How does the sector need to change so that the interests of the world's poor are better served?

Faith tends to be suppressed in organizational life. There are many factors, some subtle and some overt, that operate to subdue the religious identity of faith-based development organizations. These must be countered in a very intentional way to maintain the unique and integrated-values base of faith-based approaches.

Development is also an interior human challenge. Faith-based development recognizes the inextricable link between people's interior and exterior worlds in a way that is both motivating and powerful. Some of the most difficult development challenges are those that lie within the human heart.

Poverty is not just a deficit of things. Poverty can also include deficits of many kinds: community support, human rights, civic voice, and spiritual and social participation. While they may be materially poor, so-called developing communities may be rich in many other ways, and learning from them can help Western communities address their own poverty.

My preferred approach to development

As will become obvious at different points, I believe strongly in participatory approaches to development. These approaches treat the local community with dignity and respect through a more cooperative engagement. This ensures that the community has agency in decisions that affect it, reducing the risk of "development" being seen as something "done" to it by outsiders. I also prefer strengths-based approaches because they are more sustainable, building on assets, capacities, and visions already present. This type of approach is consistent with my belief that God is already at work in every community.

Part 1 now introduces the tension that sometimes comes with Christian participation in a highly secularized profession.

LIST OF KEY ABBREVIATIONS

ADP Area Development Program (the suite of development activities facilitated by World Vision within a particular geographic area, typically with a population ranging from 20,000 to 100,000; the ADP is World Vision's characteristic development model and each ADP has a lifespan of twelve to fifteen years)

ATR African Traditional Religion

CEDC Children in Especially Difficult Circumstances

The data the World Vision Evaluation Reports listed in the Appendix and the KIIs and FGDs supporting them

DFID Department for International Development (UK)

FBO Faith-based organization

FGD Focus Group Discussion

FGM female genital mutilation

HEA Humanitarian and emergency assistance

HIV/AIDS Human Immunodeficiency Virus/Acquired Immune Deficiency

KII Key Informant Interview

NGO Non-governmental organization

PNG Papua New Guinea

RDT Resource Dependency Theory

UN United Nations

WHO World Health Organization

Christian Heart, Secular Profession

CHAPTER 1

The Secularized Nature
of the Development Profession

There is an under-representation in academic study of the role of religion in international development work. The main reason proposed to explain this deficit is the influence of modernity and secularism in shaping development studies as an academic discipline. While this may be historically true, there has been a resurgent interest in examining the role of faith within development studies since the early 2000s.

A brief, sad history

For most of the twentieth century, the academy was set firmly against religion. The period in which development studies emerged as an academic discipline began after World War II, at a time when the social sciences were largely shaped by the narratives of modernization and secularization. These narratives "saw religion as a conservative and traditional force, destined to withdraw and disappear from public life as part of societal progress towards an increasingly modern society."[1] Some commentators were even blunter: "The evolutionary future of religion is extinction... Belief in supernatural powers is doomed to die out, all over the world, as a result of the increasing adequacy and diffusion of scientific knowledge."[2] The impact of modernity was to relegate religion to the private sphere. Religious beliefs were seen as superstitious and unscientific. In addition, the academic discourse saw itself striving against an old world order of European elites and repressive economic and political structures that were often associated with and defended by the churches. The sociological literature reflected that contest.

At times there has been pressure to disavow or disassociate from any religious position in public scholarship:

> In our Western academic philosophy, religious belief is commonly disregarded as unreasonable and is viewed with condescension or even contempt. It is said that religion is a refuge for those who,

3

because of weakness of intellect or character, are unable to confront the stern realities of the world. The objective, mature, strong attitude is to hold beliefs solely on the basis of evidence.[3]

Those who have the nerve to own up to their religious convictions in scholarship can be "given the appearance of deviance within the scholarly consensus."[4] The end result has been to conflate *disbelief* with taking an *objective* or scientific stance.

Marginalization of faith within development studies

In terms of development practice specifically, it was Kurt ver Beek's study that brought the issue of systemic bias to prominence in 2000. His research examined three of the world's leading development journals for the period 1982 to 1998 and looked for keyword references to religion and spirituality, compared with other themes. His results are summarized in the table below.

The analysis shows that while development journals contained many references to issues affecting worldview and social structures, there was a conspicuous absence of articles dealing with the role of religion or spirituality within development.[5] Ironically, ver Beek described this failure as "anti-developmental" because it weakened "the individuals' and communities' capacity to determine their own values and priorities," thereby devaluing "the very thing which may give people the strength and hope they need..."[6] He observed that this failure reduced the effectiveness of development interventions.[7]

Some organizations claim that they avoid the topics of religion and spiritual belief because these topics are inherently sensitive and have the

NUMBER OF ARTICLES WITH REFERENCE TO LISTED KEYWORDS, BY JOURNAL					
Journals 1982–1998	Environment	Gender	Population	Spiritual, spirituality	Religions, religious
World Development	83	85	89	0	5
Journal of Development Studies	19	46	38	0	1
Journal of Developing Areas	18	32	43	0	10

potential to be conflictual or sectarian. However, ver Beek counters this reasoning by noting that the same organizations do not fear equally sensitive topics such as land reform or violence against women. In these areas, difference of opinion is seen not only as acceptable, but as necessary and healthy.[8]

In 2004, research was published describing religion as "the forgotten factor" in development.[9] This research focused on the web pages for the United Nations (UN), the UK Department for International Development (DFID), and the World Bank. It concluded that there was very little content addressing the role of spirituality or religion in development.[10] Importantly, the published material tended to "avoid religion in the construction and critique of development strategy."[11] The tendency to view religion instrumentally, as a convenient vehicle to deliver development programs, is a recurring theme in this book.

Within a few years momentum was building to revisit the role of religion, spirituality, and faith in international development work. In a critical overview published in 2009 the conclusion was reached that the marginalization of these areas within the academic literature has lasted six decades.[12] This neglect was claimed to represent a risk to the world's poor.[13]

More recently, the focus has turned to the normative assumptions that define the mainstream development industry. These assumptions offer no substantive role for a consideration of religion.[14] An important contribution was made in 2011, this time commenting on the way development work is reported. The reporting invariably excludes religious elements or the significance of religious issues. It deals only with the familiar, looking at that which is field focused, practical, and more easily measurable.[15] The purpose of reporting then becomes merely "to report quantifiable results in industry approved language."[16] The result is a mechanistic and perfunctory exercise that has the effect of excluding any deeper consideration of the interplay between religious beliefs and development practice or outcomes. By default, this kind of reporting helps to define what "development" is.

The influence of modernity on development discourse

The root cause of the marginalization of religion in development studies is the Western idea of modernity. This way of understanding dates back to the European Enlightenment and the first scientific and industrial revolutions.[17] It involves a high level of confidence in "objective" science and the human capacity to overcome social problems. The dominance of economics and a mechanistic conception of nature and the universe are paradigmatic aspects of modernity. The rise of modernity has left little room for the transcendent. Against this background, religion can be seen as a "quaint, purely private and personal affair,"[18] a view "apparently widespread in Western academia."[19]

Such rationalistic conceptions of development have excluded the role of religious faiths in responding to the complex phenomenon of global poverty. Multi-dimensional problems require multi-dimensional solutions, but they are seldom offered.[20] Western scholars are trapped by their modernist views and remain "very uncomfortable about talking in public about belief and spirituality, which they view as private and personal."[21] Leading development theorist Robert Chambers agrees: "[development] academics affect to abhor moralising and reward appearances of dispassionate scientific detachment and objectivity."[22] The result has been a separation of religion from Western development scholarship. While sometimes this is presented as being an expression of "respect" for local culture, "the silent conviction [is] that science and development ultimately will allow people to leave behind their spiritual and 'unscientific' beliefs."[23]

In the academic literature religion has been less significant sociologically since the 1920s. A more rationalistic worldview has taken its place. One consequence of this shift is the persistent focus on economic growth as *the* defining factor in "development." There can be no clearer indication of this shift than the ubiquitous definition of poverty as those living on less than US$1.50 per day.

Sociologists such as Max Weber indirectly contributed to the marginalization of religion. Weber defined the role of Christian religion as a private motivating force in terms of personal ethics.[24] The so-called "Protestant work ethic," for example, was conceived as a helpful impetus or condition for economic growth within capitalistic systems. This allowed a place for religion, albeit a marginal one, within an overall rationalistic framework that placed material gain at the center.[25]

The persistent exclusion of the role of religion from development studies has implied that it is an illegitimate subject for serious academic study. This exclusion has influenced thinking within the sector among key stakeholders, donors, and governments. Foucault's theory of the dominant discourse is particularly relevant here. The theory posits that "power is created and transferred through unwritten belief systems (so called discourses), which define 'truth' and 'knowledge.'"[26] A discourse is a broad term referring to a rubric of ideas, concepts, and categories that explain a given phenomenon.

In terms of development theory, the discourse becomes powerful and self-legitimating, and it may discourage faith-based approaches and research. The unwritten rules that make up the dominant discourse may "pressure FBOs [faith-based organizations] to modify their behaviour in order to adapt it to be consistent with the dominant discourse."[27]

Secular donors from high-income countries have tended to avoid close engagement with FBOs and have in some cases been "FBO-phobic." Research suggests that multilateral organizations, such as the UN and the World Health Organization (WHO), have difficulty engaging with FBOs because of their own profoundly secular identities:

> They have Westphalian ideals which relegate faith to the private domain. The treaty of Westphalia stated that international politics would no longer be examined from a theological standpoint... The Westphalian ethos claimed that "logic" and "reason" would replace religion in providing order to world affairs ... These secularist underpinnings of the UN and the WHO created an environment where it was antithetical for them to substantively engage with the faith element of FBOs.[28]

Where they did so, pressure was exerted to conform to the dominant discourse of the donor. In practice, this meant minimizing or removing faith elements. Organizations such as the WHO operate according to strictly rational post-Enlightenment principles that must "reduce the world to what can be perceived and controlled through reason, science, technology, and bureaucratic rationality."[29] To gain credibility, legitimacy, or funding in the secular development world, FBOs must operate in a way that is consistent with its secular discourse.[30] Within the dominant discourse, "faith-affected approaches are often considered unprofessional"[31] and "consideration of the religious, the spiritual, or the sacred are perceived as non-scientific or even irrational."[32] In response to these perceptions, FBOs working in the field of development out of religious conviction may over time downplay the role of religion as a constitutive force in their own work.[33]

The resurgent interest in faith and development

Since the 2000s, there has been renewed interest in the role that religion can play in responding to global poverty. The World Bank, under the presidency of James Wolfensohn, followed up on this interest by setting up a small research directorate, the Development Dialogue on Values and Ethics. Katherine Marshall,[34] who headed up the directorate, has written extensively on the essential role that religious faith can play in overcoming world poverty, working closely with the World Faiths Development Dialogue.

On a global scale, Marshall notes that religious belief is more widespread and more intensely held than ever before. The predicted secularization of the world during the modern era has simply not occurred. It is commonly estimated that 80 percent of the world's population has a religious affiliation and worldview—with even higher percentages in developing countries.[35] The most recent data places the figure as high as 88 percent.[36] It has been noted that "99.5% of people in Africa have some religious connection."[37] There is a "general realization that faith is a primary source of meaning for most communities in developing countries..."[38] and that this should be respected.

Rowan Williams has critiqued the tardiness of the development sector in facing up to this reality: "There has been a very belated recognition that the majority of the world's population does have religious convictions and that to ignore these is to push against the grain..."[39] While many countries in the West have become increasingly secularized, that is not the case in the developing world. Others have pointedly blamed the failure of previous development efforts on their narrow economic focus. For example, a key contributor "in explaining the failure of development is the absence of the recognition of culture, and more specifically religion, in development theory and practice."[40] The persistent failure of development projects has encouraged a new level of openness to explore whether there is a more positive role for religion.

Another realization has been that churches (and other kinds of religious institutions) offer exceptional reach within developing communities. Religious institutions are located in every community, offer unrivalled rural access, and are present in many of the world's poorest contexts. Taken together, they represent the world's largest distribution system.[41] They are also often the only institutions that are left to survive in conflict-affected countries.[42] In a triumphal tone, The World Conference on Religion and Peace in 2001 claimed that "Religious communities are without question the largest and best organized civil institutions in the world today, claiming the allegiance of billions of believers and bridging the divides of race, class and nationality."[43] It is clear that the scale of religious infrastructure represents a unique opportunity. For example, it has been reported that "one third of all AIDS patients in the world are served under the auspices of the Catholic Church,"[44] and that faith-based hospitals in Africa number over 50 percent of all hospitals there.[45] Accurate percentages are very hard to pin down. A figure of 40 percent of health services in developing countries being delivered through faith-based institutions is commonly bandied about. This may be exaggerated. But whatever the exact figure is, it is a significant proportion of total services.

Research suggests that religious institutions offer advantages not only in terms of reach, but also *trust*. A vast World Bank–sponsored study by Narayan, with over sixty-thousand respondents, concluded that "religious leaders and institutions were often the most trusted institutions in developing countries."[46] For example, it has been reported that "approximately 75% of Africans trust their religious leaders."[47]

One reason for this is that religious institutions have values that are grounded in community, and local people are therefore more likely to trust FBOs than state bodies and non-governmental organizations (NGOs).[48] Religious institutions "are perceived to work for the public good and, in comparison with government agencies, it is believed that they are more sensitive to people in times of catastrophe, chaos, or conflict, are responsive to people's needs and flexible in their provision, act with honesty and take distribution seriously."[49]

These factors have caused some development academics to question the more traditional siloed approach to religion in development.[50]

Utilitarian and instrumental perspectives about religion

There is a tendency to see religion in a highly compartmentalized fashion —that is, as one of several dimensions comprising society. When we do this, "we risk misunderstanding the global resurgence of religion if we apply a *modern* concept of religion to non-Western societies."[51] It is naive and perhaps arrogant to ask non-Western societies to compartmentalize their lives and remove religion from the public sphere, which a Western view of development often requires. It has been pointed out that religion is inherently social and always embedded in wider contexts. It is a phenomenon experienced in the social domain or lived within communities, not simply a matter of individual belief.[52] This suggests that religion cannot be conveniently manipulated for externally imposed development goals.

The tendency to compartmentalize or box religion leads to it being seen as something that stands apart from development. This normative assumption causes the sector to see religion in instrumental ways.[53] It "most often simply uses religion as an instrumental addition to its current agenda."[54] This kind of thinking in turn sees religious institutions as a delivery channel. With this mindset, the type of dealings experienced by faith leaders and religious institutions will be highly transactional. Some researchers argue for more nuanced, open-ended, and thoughtful ways of thinking about the role of religion in development work, noting the difficulty the development sector has experienced in grappling with its complexities. That said, it appears the general approach to religion in development is still largely utilitarian.[55]

The literature identifies a number of reasons why religious identity is suppressed in the life of development organizations. First, the historic marginalization of religion within Western scholarship has led some organizations to be somewhat reticent about this aspect.[56] Another possibility is a "world culture" perspective. The observation has been made that "as international NGOs come increasingly into contact with governments, international bodies, and one another, they exhibit a general homogenization of language, practice and organization. The resulting culture is highly rationalized, production-orientated, and professionalized."[57] This manifests in a general trend toward shared secularization.

A third perspective is that FBOs voluntarily suppress their religious identity. There is a taboo in talking about the subject that reflects not only a desire to fit in with professional environments but a also a concern that a visible faith identity may put off some donors.[58] Most governments, multilateral funders, and corporate donors regard development as a secular project. This is a great challenge that must be overcome through education, with the aim of helping donors achieve a positive engagement with FBOs—without them fearing or being dismissive of the spiritual dimensions of their work.[59]

Explaining and maintaining an integrated values base

Narayan's research shows that one area of potential advantage for FBOs is that they hold faith and development together in a way that is especially resonant in many developing communities. This is particularly significant, as the position of numerous Western governments and secular agencies is that there should be a strict separation between "faith" and "development."[60] Such a separation undermines the advantages of FBOs at their core.

The strict separation required by donors—a separation that tries to divorce religious elements from "real" development—may force agencies to deny their very foundation. Separating faith from life is theoretical and unworkable, and ultimately subversive of the unique strength of faith-based development organizations.

While there may be a comparative advantage in using a faith-based development model in some contexts, most Western governments want to see faith elements quarantined and sidelined to the maximum extent possible. They want to "engage with the institutional forms of faith (the religious institution), but remain suspicious about the spiritual dimensions of faith (belief in God)."[61] Not surprisingly, secular donors also seek a neat clinical separation between "pure" development and spiritual elements. One helpful suggestion is to reconcile these tensions by calling for greater education and faith literacy among donors so that an impasse is avoided. This will eliminate the need to carve up an integrated values base in order to accommodate a Western, dichotomized view of reality. Rather than tear apart that integrated values base, a more effective way forward may be to explain it better.

There is virtually no academic literature that seeks to explore the links between religious beliefs or theology and development work at the level of field practice. Donors need to constructively engage with FBOs without being put off by spiritual elements. In short, "they need to become faith literate."[62] To assist this process, faith-based development organizations need to accept the responsibility of articulating for themselves and others what their faith identity is and the way in which it will be operationalized in development work. It is my hope this book will provide a helpful impetus in this process.

This work is important because the kind of enforced dichotomy that many governments and donors seek is impractical.[63] It may also be difficult for local communities to understand separations that are alien to their psyche. Religion in some cultures is not about a set of abstract doctrinal or theological arguments that can be neatly quarantined. Rather, it is experienced as permeating and influencing everyday life: "The . . . religious and non-religious worlds are deeply inter-penetrated, to the point of being hardly distinguishable."[64]

The next chapter looks at some of the higher-level motivations for Christian involvement in development work. The socially transformative nature of Christian faith partly explains the over-representation of Christian organizations within the sector.

CHAPTER 2

Some High-Level Theological Motivations for International Development Work

Former archbishop of Canterbury William Temple once quipped that "the Church is the only society that exists for the benefit of those who are not its members." The same sentiment applies to faith-based development organizations. Like the church itself, they exist to serve the world.

There has been a very long history of Christian involvement in socially transformative initiatives. For this reason the real history of faith-based development organizations stretches back two millennia. Even the greatest detractors of the Christian faith concede its many transformative impacts.[1] A frequent pattern is religiously motivated persons pioneering responses in areas of social need, with secular NGOs and government then entering the field.[2] It has been observed that "actions on issues relating to soup kitchens, shelters for the homeless, care of battered women and children, counseling for families under siege, child care, and international efforts to curb hunger and provide disaster relief were not initiated by government but to a large extent by people in congregations."[3]

The Christian scriptures themselves provide the first descriptions of organized food distributions and care for the vulnerable under the auspices of the church.[4] During Roman times, especially after official recognition of the Christian faith, the contributions of Christianity included: the elimination of infanticide, the end of gladiatorial sports, improving the rights of women, providing burials for paupers, promoting humane treatment for slaves, and establishment of public healthcare. The First Council of Nicaea in 325 CE urged the church to provide for the poor, sick, widows, and strangers, and it began a program of construction of a hospital in every cathedral town.[5]

In the Middle Ages, the Christian church made startling contributions to music and the arts. The monastic orders had a pioneering role in providing care for the aged and infirm, in establishing teaching institutions, and in providing places of refuge for the persecuted. Christianity encouraged scientific exploration, believing that new discoveries brought ever-greater glory to God as the creator of all. Importantly, this attitude emphasized contemplation and intellectual discovery as goods in themselves. It is important to debunk the popular but mistaken view, based mainly on the individual treatment of Galileo, that Christian faith somehow stood in opposition to the development of scientific thought. The general charge of anti-intellectualism cannot be sustained.[6] More recently, advances in biblical scholarship have provided a renewed appreciation of genre in the understanding of individual texts. Poetry is respected as poetry, and allegory as allegory. This has promoted the authority of scripture by applying a more sensitive hermeneutic. It has also prevented false conflicts with science arising from an uncritical literalism.

In the industrial age, Christians had a prominent role in reforming social ills, such as child labor, debtors' prisons, and unsafe industrial conditions. Christians led the campaign for the abolition of slavery. The Sunday School movement was established, not primarily to promote the Christian faith, but to provide basic literacy for children in industrial slums who might otherwise be trapped by circumstance. Toward the end of the nineteenth century, in the face of glaring social inequities, Christians had a major role in the emergence of Christian socialism and labor movements. Great social reformers like John Wesley[7] and William Booth championed the rights of the underprivileged and laid the groundwork for Archbishop William Temple and others in formulating the idea of the welfare state.

In more recent times, Christians have continued the tradition of social activism in campaigning for civil rights and in helping to frame the Universal Declaration of Human Rights. Christians also have had a long involvement in pacifist and environmental causes. Most recently, Christians have provided a key voice on issues of global poverty and climate justice through such campaigns as the Jubilee movement and Micah Challenge.[8] Former English Prime Minister Gordon Brown has described Jubilee 2000 as the most important church-led social movement in Britain since the campaign for the abolition of slavery two hundred years earlier.[9]

It may seem tendentious to omit reference to the Inquisition, the Crusades, the various sectarian purges, the Salem witch trials, and perhaps more topically, the many cases of institutionalized child sex abuse. These episodes are shocking and egregious, but they do not reflect in any intrinsic way on the Christian faith. The vitality of Christian faith is based on sacrifice in the service of others—that was the way of Jesus himself. Any coercive or selfish use of power is entirely abhorrent to that faith. For this reason it would be unfair to allow those who have misused position or authority to obscure the many positive contributions made by the Christian faith to the transformation of Western society over the last two millennia.

It appears that Christian development organizations are significantly overrepresented among the world's religious NGOs.[10] Even in highly secular Australia, about one-third of the members of the national peak body for development NGOs are Christian FBOs, and over one half of publicly donated funds flow to such organizations.

Theological literature reveals a rich variety of theological reasons why Christians are involved in undertaking international development work. These are overlapping and inter-related rather than discrete categories— and they equally provide a motivation for Christians to be involved in other areas of social justice. This chapter will explore some of the theological reasons why Christians become involved in development work, highlighting the ways in which religious motivation can draw Christians into a highly secularized profession.

The kingdom to come

One powerful motif is that Christians have a role in working for the coming kingdom of God.[11] The notion of kingdom is replete with a rich collation of ideas that look forward to a time when God will reign fully in all things and the heavens and earth will be renewed. The corresponding Old Testament notion of *shalom* pictures the whole of creation taking its right order and relationship before God. In this new kingdom, the sinful and selfish exercise of power by humans over others will give way to godly relationships, and the whole of creation will be reconciled with its Creator and with itself.

In terms of human relationships, important biblical metaphors associated with the idea of the coming kingdom include the nations streaming to Mount Zion to learn of God's ways and the beating of instruments of war into ploughshares.[12]

The renewal of the world is alluded to in St. Paul's writing, which speaks of all of creation groaning, awaiting its rebirth.[13] There are other images that point to a time when the existing enmities within creation will be removed. In Isaiah, a striking picture is given of a new era of peace associated with the messianic descendant of David: "The wolf shall live with the lamb, the leopard shall lie down with the kid, the calf and the lion and the fatling together, and a little child shall lead them. The cow and the bear shall graze, their young shall lie down together; and the lion shall eat straw like the ox."[14]

Establishing the kingdom of God is seen by Christians as a global task requiring a fundamental transfiguring of relationships within creation. The coming of God's kingdom is foreshadowed by the resurrection of Christ from the dead, and it is usually understood to reach fulfillment with the return of Christ to earth. Theologians such as N. T. Wright believe that the physical resurrection of Jesus Christ is emblematic of the Christian call to work for this kingdom.[15] Most Christians believe that they exist in the in-between time, sometimes described as a "now-but-not-yet" period of history. This refers to a time when Christians look for signs of God's in-breaking rule while holding firm to a vision of the ultimate fulfillment of his purposes. Development work is conceived by many Christians as a way to help communities experience a more abundant life in the present as a foretaste of this coming kingdom.[16]

While the kingdom of God is seen as the sovereign work of God alone, Christians are invited by God to live in anticipation of what he is doing. In this sense, God's people may be seen as having an active role in joining in the expression of the Creator's redemptive purposes. According to one view, God's people may be seen as co-creators with God in a joint enterprise of restoring the world. International development work—which has an emphasis on social equity, health and prosperity, peace and reconciliation, and care for the environment—has many points of resonance with the motif of global restoration contained in the idea of the coming kingdom.

Jürgen Moltmann, a theologian in the Reformed tradition, sees the kingdom as a future event, but one that comprehensively informs the present. In his view, Christian eschatology is a vital area of doctrine because it should comprehensively shape the way that followers of Jesus live in the present. Christians are said to comprise an eschatological community of salvation: "This eschatological orientation is seen in everything from which and for which the Church lives."[17] In this analysis, "mission is not carried out within the horizon of expectation provided by the social roles which society concedes to the Church, but it takes place within its own peculiar horizon of the eschatological expectation of the coming kingdom of God, of the coming righteousness and the coming peace, and of the coming freedom and dignity of man."[18]

For Moltmann, the first intercession in the Lord's Prayer—"Your kingdom come, your will be done on earth as it is in heaven"[19]—is highly significant. It enlists disciples in God's service, and is as much a statement of call as it is of invocation. As Christ's disciples orient themselves toward this future vision, they will actively seek God's rule within their communities and the world. Development work is one way to give expression to this Christian hope of a renewed world.

Social Trinitarianism

Another theological basis for undertaking international development work is Social Trinitarianism. Miroslav Volf is one example of a contemporary theologian who has explored the social implications of the

Trinity in human affairs.[20] Broadly, Social Trinitarianism highlights the relationship between the members of the eternal Godhead as being prototypical of God's aspirations for humans. The Trinity is seen as a community that is the paradigmatic example of self-giving love. The Father's love is made manifest in the costly surrender of the Son. The Son's love for the Father is demonstrated through faithful obedience and service. The Holy Spirit is also imbued with these qualities, indwelling the Godhead in a living social relationship known as *perichoresis*.[21]

Social Trinitarianism contends that humans were made in this social or relational image of God. They are intended to emulate the kind of self-giving and faithful community displayed within the Godhead. International development work is one way for humans to express relational solidarity with each other—through mutuality and service, and by seeking to build true community. This understanding that all humans are made in the image of God also lays an important foundation for Christians in understanding and promoting human rights.

The prophetic call

Christian development work responds to the prophetic call to defend vulnerable communities. The public commencement of Jesus' own ministry echoes the prophetic call of Isaiah. Jesus described his mission in Luke's gospel in these terms: "The Spirit of the Lord is upon me, because he has anointed me to bring good news to the poor. He has sent me to proclaim release to the captives and recovery of sight to the blind, to let the oppressed free, to proclaim the year of the Lord's favor."[22]

Development work focuses on impoverished communities, and often communities that have experienced some kind of oppression or trauma. A key thrust of development work is to move beyond a merely compassionate response to sustainable improvements and justice. The prophetic call throughout scripture to defend the widow and the orphan[23] may at times imbue development work with a more political character.[24] Important aspects of development practice are concerned with ensuring that vulnerable groups obtain justice and their human rights are respected. This resonates with the ancient injunction to ensure justice in the gate.[25]

The work of Christian coalitions that speak out on issues of justice —like the Jubilee movement or the Micah Network—stand very much in this prophetic tradition.

Liberation theology

The focus on justice and rights has received attention in recent decades with the emergence of liberation theology. This is a form of political theology emanating from Latin America in the 1960s and 1970s. It interpreted the teachings of Jesus as calling for active liberation from unjust social economic and political conditions, and it is sometimes associated with the application of a Marxist pedagogy to Christian scriptures. International development work and liberation theology share a common impetus in that both respond to circumstances in which oppressed or impoverished peoples seek liberation. The emphasis on community empowerment and participation, which is a consistent feature of development theory, has strong resonance with liberation theology. As well as addressing similar contexts, both liberation theology and development work recognize the important role of political advocacy and social mobilization in bringing about change.

Christian social ethics

More generally, Christian social ethics suggest that the followers of Jesus should be willing to carry each other's burdens. This reflects the second great command to love neighbor as self.[26] Theologians like Dietrich Bonhoeffer emphasize that compassionate action and mutuality underpin real community and are based on the unity and reconciliation humans can experience in Jesus Christ.[27]

Jesus also disabuses attempts to narrowly circumscribe our personal responsibilities. In an acclaimed exegesis of the parable of the Good Samaritan, theologian Ken Bailey adopts a cultural critical hermeneutic. He points out that the victim in the parable is set up by Jesus to be an anonymous, generic person. The removal of the victim's clothes by the robbers deprives the passers-by of the opportunity to determine his ethnicity based on traditional dress.[28] The fact that he is beaten to unconsciousness means that his identity cannot be established by accent, language, or direct questioning. The parable illustrates that responding to the needs of a fellow human constitutes true neighborliness and transcends narrower formal categories.

Holistic missiology

Another reason for Christian engagement in international development work is a broad missiology based on an understanding of God's universal presence within communities. This view acknowledges the self-bestowal by God on all of creation. According to theologians like Leonardo Boff, the Holy Spirit is the first missionary in every community. While recognizing that humans are sinful and broken, God nonetheless provides signs of his life and presence, witnessing to himself within every human context.

The self-bestowal of God on all communities means that development work can be based on the notion of human reciprocity. Because all people are made in the image of God, they will reflect, albeit imperfectly, something of his goodness expressed within their own community life. This provides a firm and positive foundation in seeking to carry out development based on existing community strengths.

A contrast can be drawn with the self-understanding of many Christian missionaries in the colonial era. The idea of the self-bestowal of God on all creation was not well understood or accepted. Such missionaries have been caricatured as seeking to "bring God in their suitcase" in their attempts to "reach" various "unregenerate" people groups. If God is already present in developing communities, then it becomes possible to discern what God is already doing, or perhaps seeking, within those settings. Ways of building up and strengthening communities can then be identified and leveraged. These can be understood as authentic expressions of God's grace. It also becomes possible to learn from communities rather than instructing communities in an asymmetric way.

If God is understood as already at work in the world, then this can lead to a richer and fuller understanding of his redemptive agenda. Typically, faith-based development work may see salvation as less about the afterlife and more about seeking to give expression to the fullness of life in the present. This may involve affirming human life through programs that are holistic, temporal, broad-based, and inclusive. There are resonances here with the Christian understanding of the in-breaking kingdom of God. However, these emphases also help to shape the idea of salvation itself. In particular, a broader understanding of salvation can emerge, one that is neither primarily individualistic nor deferred. The British development agency Christian Aid once captured this well in its by-line "We believe in life *before* death."

Catholic Social Teaching

So-called Catholic Social Teaching provides a rich tradition supporting engagement in international development efforts. God's "preferential option for the poor" and ideas about the global "human family" lie at the heart of this teaching. God's affinity with the poor and outcast is so deep that to neglect the poor is to neglect our human obligation toward God. This line of teaching was clearly articulated through papal encyclicals in the nineteenth and twentieth centuries. It is also very holistic in its approach. Most recently, Pope Benedict XVI has reiterated that "love for widows and orphans, prisoners, and the sick and needy of every kind, is as essential as the ministry of the sacraments and preaching of the Gospel."[29] Séverine Deneulin explains: "A Christian vision of development does not separate the material from the spiritual dimensions of life. Christians believe that humans are made in the image of God and only reach their fulfillment in God. Development, working for social justice and protection of the environment goes hand in hand with conversion of the heart."[30]

Catholic teaching is nuanced when it comes to international development, which is not seen as an end in itself. Ludovic Bertina has traced its evolution to a careful doctrine of "integrated human development" resting upon the three pillars of social consideration, moral behavior, and reconciliation with God.[31] Earlier papal encyclicals had embraced the potential of technology and trade as means of social uplift, but later reflections note the incipient dangers of technocracy and utilitarian absolutism.[32]

While holistic, Catholic teaching makes plain that the idea of development is always subordinated to the pursuit of historical reconciliation between humanity and God.[33] According to Deneulin, "Christians believe that humans become more human when they are closer to God. To reflect this reality, Catholic social teaching refers to integral human development. The development of the whole person is not complete without spiritual considerations."[34] Therefore, the secular "religion of development" practiced by some institutions is seen as idolatry. Progress is possible only because God has decided from the beginning to make humans a sharer of his glory.[35] Bertina states: "It is hoped that humanity's wholehearted recognition of the human family and pursuit of its realization—aspects of the divine plan—will prefigure the advent of the Kingdom of God."[36]

An appreciation of the broad human family, seeking the common good, and promoting economic justice are all elements of the Catholic understanding of integral human development. So are expressing solidarity, promoting civic and social participation, and upholding the principle of subsidiarity (by which decision-making is devolved locally to those impacted).

Practical theology

It can be argued that all theology should involve an iterative dialogue between the theoretical and the practical. This can prevent theology from becoming too abstract or divorced from reality. Theologians such as Friedrich Schleiermacher recognized that the teleological goal and crown of theology as a discipline is to be found in practical concerns.[37] Like most theologians, he argued from theory to practice and examined how theology was applied in given settings. More recent theologians, such as Don Browning,[38] argue for the analysis to proceed in the reverse direction, seeing all theology as fundamentally practical. Browning argues that a consideration of real-life issues provides the necessary hermeneutic to construct and (re)appraise theological thought. This is especially helpful when looking at theological belief in doing development. A two-way process can not only look for evidence of pre-defined themes but also create a dialogue about how field data poses risks and challenges. This may call for a reappraisal in some areas.

Rediscovery of diaconal ministry

The last fifty years have witnessed a growing appreciation of the diaconate in the life of the church. For a long time the role of the deacon was either moribund or diminished by being typecast as that of a liturgical helper. The role of deacon has undergone a comprehensive reappraisal and renewal in several Christian denominations, including the Roman Catholic, Anglican, and Methodist churches, resulting in the establishment of a permanent diaconate. Diaconal ministry was originally conceived as being focused on the scattered community—often people experiencing injustice or disadvantage in some way—a ministry reflecting the life of Christ, which was lived in firm solidarity with people on the margins.

Deacons have a vital role in talking about issues of justice in the established church, thus providing valuable service in challenging institutional structures that can become too easily accommodated to the surrounding society. Diaconal ministry has a strong resonance with international development work, which requires transformation both in the world at large and in the church itself.

New Testament resonance

Although international aid tends to be understood very much as a modern concept, there are fleeting references in the New Testament that bear some resemblance to humanitarian response work. One is the story in Paul's second letter to the Corinthians of the assistance offered by the Macedonian church to the struggling poor church in Jerusalem.[39] While the Macedonian church was itself wracked by poverty, it gave in a generous and sacrificial way to help the Jerusalem church. Paul was involved with Titus in the oversight and remittance of the funds. In another instance, the church in Antioch provided material support for the church in Judea to relieve the suffering caused by famine.[40] Elsewhere in the Book of Acts the example is given of church-based non-discriminatory food distributions, anticipating later humanitarian principles.[41] These brief references build on ancient traditions in the Old Testament in which the people of God are called to live justly.[42]

Overview

This quick overview suggests there is a wide variety of theological reasons for why Christians may be motivated to undertake development work. These motivations help explain the large number of different Christian organizations and traditions operating in the sector. It is certainly the case that many Christians are attracted to a profession that can be highly secular in its outlook, which can be discouraging and dispiriting for some. My hope is that this can be countered by helping Christians to see more clearly how their Christian beliefs can bring a powerful and distinctive approach to the task of international development. I also hope that the development sector as a whole as well as other stakeholders might learn more about the value that faith-based approaches can bring.

The next part of this book pursues these aims by drilling down below high-level theological motivations and looking at how Christian beliefs and practices impact more concretely the day-to-day development work of faith-based organizations.[43] The discussion addresses many connections of foundational importance, such as gaining access to communities, motivation and sustaining of staff, building hope and resilience, mobilizing against the causes of systemic impoverishment, changing the way people relate with one another, leveraging spiritual goodwill, the inculcation of values and ethics, reliance on spiritual disciplines, and working more effectively with faith-based institutions. These are not peripheral matters and speak of a distinctive approach.

Before beginning our analysis, however, it is appropriate to review some of the main theories of change that exist in the sector today and consider how they may relate to the Christian faith.

PART TWO

Christian Motifs and Their Impact on Development Work

CHAPTER 3

Theological Reflection
on Prevalent Theories of Change

This chapter outlines four of the theories of change used by organizations in the international development sector. It illustrates that the difference between faith-based and other approaches to development does not lie in their selection of a theory or theories of change. In fact, all of the theories of change outlined below can be adopted by faith-based development organizations. It is posited that it is other factors that lead to a distinctive praxis.

The theories examined form the basis of practice for many development organizations. The difference between them is found in their approach, which may

1. view change from a scientific rationalist or technocratic perspective;

2. emphasize community participation and empowerment;

3. focus on human rights; or

4. conceive of change as a non-linear process that requires a highly contextualized, fluid, and multi-disciplinary approach.[1]

Faith-based development organizations can use all or any of these approaches. That said, these theories can be critiqued from a Christian faith perspective, and a diverse range of literature from the disciplines of theology, missiology, and development studies will be discussed in doing so.

It is also argued that none of these common theories of change is definitive in terms of how social transformation happens when development work is undertaken. There are additional factors that affect every organization as it caries out its work. The effectiveness of any theory of change will depend in part on commitment of staff, their mode of interaction, levels of trust within the community, acceptance of the organization itself, and community confidence in the development process. A faith-based development praxis can have an impact on a number of these other factors, as demonstrated in later chapters.

Theories that emphasize rationality, science, and technology as drivers of change

The first group of theories may be broadly labeled as scientific or technical approaches. These insist on careful analysis of the development context using scientific principles. Methodologies from both the pure sciences and the social sciences can be called upon. The proposed solutions to development problems will involve the application of particular technologies or scientific methods so that predicted effects can be achieved. Careful measurement, planning, and controls are necessary, and there is a strong emphasis on measurement and evaluation to validate results.

It is trite to observe that modern science has done much to help humankind. Achievements in public health, medical science, access to water and sanitation, and agricultural production have all been significant. It follows that Christians, who are commanded to love their neighbor,[2] must be alert to the good that science can do. A suspicious or anti-intellectual approach will be unhelpful in discharging the fundamental obligation of a Christian. Accordingly, the Christian development theorist Bryant Myers asserts that "any Christian understanding of transformational development must have space for the good that science and technology offer."[3]

Having said that, Christian scripture commands that God's people are to give him primacy in terms of their allegiance and obedience.[4] For this reason, science and technology represent gifts from God that can be used to serve him in the world, rather than to provide an alternative source of hope and confidence. The placing of uncritical faith in science or technology, or indeed any particular theory, to overcome all development challenges would for a Christian development organization be a form of idolatry.[5]

The understanding of development as a discipline within the social sciences has brought many benefits. These have included the establishment of collegial networks, academic rigor and discipline in program design, the sharing of research, an emphasis on assessment and evaluation, and, in general, an appetite for empirically supported field investment. This healthy suite of professional norms is to be commended. That said, Christians may have a number of reservations about a scientific or technocratic approach as the primary driver of development. The first is that the basic assumption that science is "objective" or "neutral" appears doubtful.

The Enlightenment claimed to offer a new plausibility structure based on "objective" science. It was argued that scientific knowledge was factual, value-free, and neutral. This perspective has been contested. As Harold Brown, author of *Perception, Theory and Commitment: The New Philosophy of Science*, notes:

> Science consists of a series of research projects structured by accepted presuppositions which determine what observations are to be made, how they are to be interpreted, what phenomena are problematic, and how these problems are to be dealt with. When the presuppositions of a scientific discipline change, both the structure of the discipline and the scientist's picture of reality are changed.[6]

Philosophers such as Thomas Kuhn and Michael Polanyi have also critiqued the notion of "objective" science, and it has been observed that "what theories are accepted or rejected, what facts are considered relevant or irrelevant, or what studies are deemed important or ignored are dependent on one's presuppositions, perspectives and values—on one's worldview or mindset."[7]

A second criticism is that the claims made for science have been overreaching. Extravagant claims have been made about the ability of science to solve development problems.[8] The underpinning belief has been "that by the power of scientific reason humans could conquer nature and enjoy happiness and health as if heaven was on earth."[9] Yet the results of scientific approaches, viewed as a development paradigm, have been mixed. According to Christian missiologist David Bosch, repeated studies over a twenty-five-year period failed to reveal any real progress: "The Enlightenment was supposed to create a world in which all people were equal, in which the soundness of human reason would show the way to happiness and abundance for all. This did not materialize. Instead people have become victims of fear and frustrations as never before."[10] The task for faith-based development organizations is to consider how to harness the substantial potential benefits of scientific and technical approaches while seeing through the hubris.

One of the problems of scientific and technical approaches is that interventions may occur in a way that are not sensitive to local culture or appropriate for a given context. While the efficiency of science may suggest one path, Ed Dayton has pointed out that this may be contradicted by the "hundreds of rusting tractors and broken water pumps that give their mute testimony."[11] It is posited that faith-based development organizations should go about their work being especially mindful of the culture and capacities of the local communities where they work. When interventions occur in an isolated way, without a thorough and thoughtful consideration of the broader context, their success is least assured.

This criticism alludes to the tendency of science to be narrow and deterministic. In the words of Bryant Myers: "Science helps us figure out how things work, but not why they work or what they are for."[12] It can be argued that *purpose* must be reintroduced as a category that is as basic to human development as clean water and nutritious food. Bosch argues that a new epistemology is needed such that technology is "confronted by a reality outside itself which does not depend on its canons of rationality and which therefore will not be subservient to its deterministic power."[13] The basic complaint is that technology can be a false god that speaks of power and efficiency rather than of care or responsibility.[14] In short, many Christians argue that the linear application of cause and effect must be tempered by a spiritual worldview that includes the responsible use of power, sensitivity to culture and the human condition, and critical ethical overlays.

A related criticism is that science does not offer any self-contained moral framework. It is for this reason that universities and hospitals have ethics committees. The moral framework of faith-based development efforts will be informed by scripture, faith, and theology. Not everything that is scientifically possible is good or desirable.[15] For example, should a faith-based development organization plant genetically modified crops, promote particular reproductive technologies, or support certain high-tech interventions? Scientific data can influence but not determine the answers to these questions.

Finally, there are areas where science and the religious views held by the majority of the world's population simply reach an *impasse*. Science and technology, as a theory of change, needs to find a constructive place within the broader frame of reference of the community. This is not always possible. Science cannot comprehend concepts like evil or love or compassion. It cannot address the unseen world. It cannot penetrate the mysteries of faith, such as prayer. It remains resolutely skeptical about revelation and miracles. It does not acknowledge God's providence in history. It requires evidence to believe in the kingdom to come, and it balks at the notion of an afterlife or resurrection.

On the other hand, science can help to grow food and improve health and sanitation. Yet it does so without necessarily cherishing life. It can help explain the physical world in astonishing detail, but not its meaning. For this reason, Pope Benedict XVI counseled that science should be carefully mentored by faith: "From God's standpoint, faith liberates reason from its blind spots and therefore helps it to be ever more fully itself. Faith enables reason to do its work more effectively and to see its proper object more clearly."[16] Christians involved in development should continue to love God with all their mind, but on occasions that love may demand that science be reproached or tempered.

Theories that emphasize that social change occurs through participation and empowerment

A second theoretical perspective emphasizes that social change occurs through contestation and negotiation. Proponents of this perspective support changes of structures, institutions, and power relations that perpetuate poverty and social injustices. Change strategies employed include mostly participatory approaches that allow community members to take ownership of the change process.

The work of South American educational theorist Paulo Freire has been influential in shaping empowerment approaches. Freire coined the term "conscientization" to describe the process whereby people become aware of and address the power relations that oppress them.[17] This work caused a major shift in emphasis directed at securing far greater empowerment for local communities. One intention was to help these communities break free from models that produced an entrenched dependency. Dewi Hughes summarizes: "To be effective, the education of the poor must ... be a means of empowerment as well as a simple transference of skills. Self-reliance must be the goal from the beginning. What this means for development is that much more attention is given to what the poor want rather than what they are perceived to need."[18] Using this approach, the field worker is more a catalyst than service deliverer.

Development organizations have been slow to appreciate that authentic development cannot take place without a transfer of power.[19] Freire, the pioneer of this type of thinking, saw it very much as an outworking of his Catholic faith.[20]

Theologically, participatory approaches sit well with the Christian ethos. Leonardo Boff has pointed out that when the poor are not involved in decisions that affect them, the final result is "eternalizing relations of dependency, and preventing the impoverished from becoming the subjects, the agents, of their own history."[21] Christian development workers are likely to recognize the intrinsic good of approaches that get "community members to participate more fully in all that it means to be human."[22] This kind of participatory community engagement may also help overcome the colonial legacy of "non-recognition of the other as other."[23]

Although this theory may sound compelling, there has been enormous difficulty in practice in terms of getting development organizations to cede power to the communities they purport to serve. Robert

Chambers laments the dogged persistence of Western hegemony in development practice. He sees the reluctance to transfer power to communities as a matter of personal choice:

> We are so trapped in search for universals which fit normal concepts and criteria, and which are part of our professional tools of trade, that we can easily not notice or discuss what stares us most in the face, the fact that individual personal choice of what to do mediates every action and every change. What is done and not done depends on what people choose to do and not to do, especially those with more power.[24]

This observation underscores the need for openness to personal transformation in undertaking meaningful development work.

Culturally, participatory approaches may be seen as less condescending. They assume that the poor may know something about what needs to happen to secure their own longer-term interests. Development agencies may proceed from the Western assumption that they know best. Brian McLaren, speaking from a North American church context, is alert to this risk. He warns: "The US can so easily become an echo chamber. Western voices arguing with other Western voices about Western topics from a Western perspective."[25] A development pedagogy that involves the development agency and the community in a true dialogue is one where there will be significant learning on both sides. Truly participatory approaches will move beyond the asymmetrical flow of information that has helped perpetuate an unhelpful hegemony. Anna Wrigley notes that faith-based organizations (FBOs) have an especially important role to play in this regard because they are inclined to see people as "subjects of their own lives" rather than "objects of development."[26]

Appreciative Inquiry (AI) is not a theory of change, but it is a methodology that can be usefully deployed with participatory approaches. A development worker using this method engages with the community to try and identify those things that have worked well in its experience. The methodology is concerned with trying to identify past successes and strengths that can be built upon. This approach also resonates well with many Christians. Boff celebrates that, inescapably, "in every culture there will be buds, shoots of the reign, sacraments of grace, signs of the presence of the Word, and accents of the activity of the Spirit."[27] Steve Corbett and Brian Fikkert note that the tool of AI enables Christians "to identify the good gifts that God has placed in a community and to dream about how to use those gifts to fix what is wrong, thereby bringing greater witness to the realities of the coming kingdom."[28]

When entering a new community, Christians may look for signs of God's activity and presence: "The first missionary is the Holy Trinity [who is] always involved in self-bestowal on creation..."[29] Looking for the good things God has already done for others may also help Christians abandon their own cultural insularity.

Communities may, however, be less willing to identify for themselves those things that have been unsuccessful or unhelpful. Every culture is at once the "locus of the fervent acceptance of God's self-communication, as well as the refusal of the same."[30] Every community will reflect responses —positive, negative, or ambiguous—to God's prior initiatives. There will be elements requiring respectful challenge in all cultures, including the development organization's own. Truly participatory approaches do not mean remaining silent in order to avoid causing offense; they call for an open, honest, and at times hard dialogue. Rowan Williams asserts: "It is not an option simply to accept the specificities of a culture (religious or otherwise) that may actually be responsible for reducing the liberties or options that are available for other human beings."[31]

What participatory processes can guarantee, when undertaken in a genuine way, is treating humans with dignity. For this reason, participatory approaches will appeal to those faith-based development organizations that seek inspiration from the unconditional love of Christ. What participatory approaches cannot guarantee, however, is success. Corbett and Fikkert caution that "participation does not have the capacity to overcome the basic corruption in the human condition. Individuals and groups make bad decisions all the time!"[32] Human freedom includes the freedom to make mistakes—mistakes made with sincerity or with selfish intent. While greater levels of civic participation are welcomed, participation itself will not overcome broader moral failings: "Rarely do empowerment strategies make the links that could generate shifts in inner values strong enough to ensure that improvements in one area are not bought at the cost of damage done elsewhere."[33]

Human rights–based theories of change

Efforts to empower communities have often promoted communities' awareness about their universal human rights, and they have involved working with communities to mobilize them in order to claim those rights. This approach was generally introduced by development organizations in the late 1990s. It posits that when human rights are understood and asserted at a local level, with a corresponding holding to account of duty-bearers, lasting change will result from a change in power dynamics. This approach has quickly gained traction. For example, Department for International Development (DFID) in the UK has mandated a "rights-based approach" in all its programming.

Perhaps the most powerful critique though, is that a rights-based approach is a largely Western construct that, despite its stated objective of empowerment, seldom takes into account the views of developing communities. A Western view often sees human rights through a positivistic legal framework, reflecting personal rather than community entitlements. Rowan Williams, among others, sees this as an imposition that has insufficient regard for local frames of reference.[34]

In summarizing the responses to a rights-based approach, the International Policy Network (in a report prepared using DFID's own materials) concluded that "the approach does not appear to have resulted in an improvement of the condition of the poor."[35] Elsewhere, the observation has been made that "there is no consistent correlation between the ratification of human rights treaties and improved health or social outcomes."[36] Some think the time has come for a more fundamental reassessment. One critic argues that "there is clearly an urgent need, particularly among development assistance agencies, to broaden, deepen and nuance the understanding of rights themselves and of rights-based approaches, particularly at the level of action strategies. There are no magic bullets or fast tracks to social justice. It is time to move away from formulas and rhetoric."[37]

There is a range of opinions within Christian communities about human rights approaches, extending from cautious skepticism to optimistic embrace. A great strength of human rights approaches is that they are directed at moving beyond charity and looking toward just and lasting improvements in the life of the poor. The vision of the realization of universal human rights sits sympathetically with the vision of the coming kingdom of God, where justice and dignity are finally achieved for all people.[38]

Christian development organizations will affirm God's vision of justice, including protection of the vulnerable and celebrating human freedoms. Human rights are a part of this vision. However, the motivation for Christians comes from a fundamentally different place from that of those advocating that purely secular human rights constructs be applied in social and political life, even if the latter do have some positive effects. Rowan Williams believes that a more enlightened approach entails

> a readiness to question the kind of secular rhetoric around development which would reduce the whole question to one of securing the formal liberties that can be spelled out in terms of human rights; to question some of the unexamined assumptions about power (political and ideological) that attach themselves to this rhetoric; and to enlarge the definition of human well-being to take in the possibility of relation with the transcendent.[39]

Most Christians assert that all human rights derive from the fact that all people are made and loved by God. They are stamped with God's image,[40] which instills in everyone an intrinsic dignity. This is a crucial and foundational difference between a Christian and a secular worldview. It is this underpinning belief in a shared humanity, derived from God, that leads to a sense of mutuality and obligation. From earliest times, Judeo-Christian ethics have reinforced the idea of upholding the rights of the vulnerable. In the Old Testament, there are repeated injunctions to God's people to respect the rights of the widow, the orphan, the alien, the debtor, the poor, and the oppressed, among others. This is reflected in express commandments in the Deuteronomic law, in the constant refrain of God's prophets, and in the proverbs, psalms, and wisdom literature. It is a common theme right throughout both Old and New Testament.

Many faith-based development organizations acknowledge that a Christian approach to the promotion of human rights will not be grounded in a secular, political agenda but in the life of Christ. There are some instances where Jesus seems to encourage the claiming of individual rights, for example, in the parable of the persistent widow.[41] However, overall there is a greater emphasis on the call to his followers to live justly. The prophetic tradition is one example where duty-bearers are consistently held to account.

Julia Berger explains that, "in contrast with the rights-based approach of many secular NGOs, the starting point for religious NGOs is the duty-orientated language of religion characterised by obligations towards the divine and towards others, by a belief in transformative capacities, and a concern for justice and reconciliation."[42] In this way, religious NGOs "are more directly able to raise moral issues and tap into religious discourse, thereby fuelling a sense of moral duty, indignation or outrage, which makes change possible."[43]

This emphasis can flow from an understanding that humans are also made in the *relational* image of God. This is a central point of difference to the mainly legalistic interpretation of rights that a secular Western worldview promulgates. The Trinitarian Godhead – the very being of God—is understood by many Christians as an eternal and intimate community of self-giving and service. Biblical human rights are about fairness and right relationships. Humans are made in the image of God in order that they may serve others, and, according to Jürgen Moltmann, participate with the Trinity in a kind of open system that extends to serving the whole world.[44]

While Christians seek the rights of others, their own personal responses are open-ended. Christians will have an inherent bias toward preferring the needs of others. They are called to live sacrificially. Jesus Christ came to bring Good News to the poor and disenfranchised.[45] A biblical framework of human rights is therefore partially about a rescuing justice, which can be personally costly. Jesus illustrated this by *not* asserting his human rights on the cross. He abandoned them in what Christians believe is the ultimate act of service for others. All followers of Jesus are likewise called to die to self[46] and to go the extra mile.[47] Richard Amesbury and George M. Newlands recall that one of the paradoxes of Christian faith is that "in Christ...God invests human life with dignity precisely by sharing in the suffering that human beings inflict on one another."[48]

A final observation is that there is an empty formalism that is sometimes associated with a more secular human rights agenda, which is unable to look beyond itself. That agenda is supposed to offer the rubric for discussing, and ultimately mediating, human rights. In theory, human rights will be realized by activities such as awareness raising, promotion, and advocacy. In contrast, a distinctly Christian approach to human rights will be seen as animated and inspired by the loving Spirit of God. Ideally, it will unfold in power, prayer, and love, with humility and with the firmness of a servant heart. Some Christians also argue for a greater understanding of an ultimate human right: for each person to know that he or she is loved, valued, created, and gifted uniquely by God.

Theories that conceive of change as an emergent, complex process

The fourth theoretical perspective conceives of change as "an emergent, complex, multi-directional, non-linear, fragmented and discontinuous process that is difficult to control, manage, or comprehensively understand from a particular vantage point...Change strategies emphasize the need for change agents to become 'searchers' with communities, rather than 'planners' for communities."[49]

This perspective demands a more tentative approach to planning for and managing development processes. It challenges the idea that a development context can be comprehensively analyzed and sufficiently understood to confidently map out a five-year development plan. Lucia Boxelaar recognizes that development issues are often "wicked," which means that the science on how to address these is contested, and solutions to problems require the input of a very diverse range of actors who often do not have a shared view of the nature of the problem, or how to address it.

This perspective highlights that a development context can be only partially understood prior to acting on it, and it therefore needs constant learning and adaptation to find a way through. Overall, development is recognized as a complex endeavor that demands the collective knowledge and initiative of a wide group. Accordingly, this understanding favors multi-stakeholder and partnering approaches. Participatory action research and action learning methods are vital in this perspective.

A Christian theology echoes the fact that there is much that is complex and multi-directional. There is a brokenness, both within the world and within the human heart, that impacts every aspect of life, especially our relationships. Christians await the consummation of the whole of creation that will take place at the final renewal of all things. Until then, "all change is partial and incomplete—part of our journey toward God's redemption of all things."[50] The gospels do speak into the non-linear, complex nature of all of life by articulating a specific worldview that provides purpose and hope for the work of development.

The story of God coming into the world—the Incarnation—also provides the direction to work as "searchers" with communities, to work together with people rather than "for" them in a way that affirms their dignity as image-bearers of a relational God. This requires a posture of humility that values the insights of many. Wendy Tyndale notes that "if poverty itself is a multi-dimensional phenomenon, then the solution to it must also be multi-dimensional, and it is here that the faiths can make a contribution... by demonstrating some of the ingredients of dignity and hope... self-esteem, and a sense of purpose."[51] Complex theories appreciate that knowledge does not rest with any one group but that contributions may come from anywhere. No one has all the answers. As many Christians would say, the opposite of faith is not doubt but certainty. Christians believe in a God who empowers and invites his followers on a daily, contextualized journey of faith in which they receive and incarnate hope. Through humble seeking and attentive listening, the Christian works for the kingdom to come on earth as it is in heaven.

The kingdom of God has a "now-and-not-yet" nature to it. The "now" has been manifested in the life, death, and resurrection of Jesus. There are glimpses of it in the outbreaks of justice, peace, and renewal throughout the world, which stir up rumors of hope. These glimpses instill renewed faith that God is at work and they point to new directions. Christian theology recognizes that human efforts alone will never build the kingdom of God. Yet, with the empowering Spirit of God, there is confidence that provisional human efforts will be transformed in a world where there is justice for all.[52] This is the "not-yet" nature of the kingdom.

Overview

This brief overview has shown that faith-based development organizations are able to adopt any of the main theories of change. There are no fundamental conflicts. The central ideas of all these theories could be incorporated into and deployed within their operational praxis. Some organizations will recognize various limitations, or will nuance and re-frame certain theories within their own understanding of Christian theology and scripture. Importantly, the difference between faith-based and other types of development organizations does not lie in their choice of a theory of change.[53]

Christian beliefs and motifs will set them apart, and we now begin to unpack what some of those beliefs are, and how they affect development work.

CHAPTER 4

The Big Picture Narratives

A visionary picture of salvation

When the life of Christ is examined, a holistic vision of ministry emerges. The biblical picture of salvation is as "coherent, broad and deep as the exigencies of human existence."[1] The restoration of *human community*[2] is one foundational aspect: "In contrast to Western society's emphasis on the autonomous individual, Christianity sees each human life as profoundly inter-connected with others in a series of overlapping relationships."[3] When salvation is viewed only in personal, individualistic terms, a narrow, anemic, and unbiblical picture emerges. Missiologist David Bosch explains:

> In a world where people are dependent on each other and every individual exists within a web of inter-human relationships, it is totally untenable to limit salvation to the individual and his or her personal relationship with God. Hatred, injustice, oppression, war, and other forms of violence are manifestations of evil; concern for humanness, for the conquering of famine, illness and meaninglessness is part of the salvation for which we hope and labour.[4]

Salvation involves the restoration of relationships and communities, even nations. Going even further, scripture indicates that God's plan of salvation also extends to the physical world and non-human elements of creation. The apostle Paul explicitly teaches that all of creation is groaning with anticipation, waiting for the time when it will be renewed.[5]

Faith-based organizations will understand that it is "a false anthropology and sociology to divorce the spiritual or personal sphere from the material and social."[6] Jesus never made such distinctions. In his ministry there is no demarcation between saving from sin and saving from physical affliction. One constant reminder of this is the frequent use of the same verb in the New Testament texts to describe both occurrences.[7] Development theorist Bryant Myers complains that it is only a deep-seated captivity to a Western worldview that tries to force such a separation.[8] Writing in a Latin American context, theologian Leonardo Boff links the physical and spiritual even more bluntly. In speaking about the material deprivation of poor communities he warns: "Unless we attack this kind of poverty directly, in the name of Jesus and the apostles, as a challenge to evangelization, we shall be mocking the poor, by handing them an opiate religion, a religion which answers their cry for help with cynicism."[9]

What we learn from this brief reflection is that salvation is a much bigger narrative than the message we more frequently hear. The doctrine of salvation needs salvation! The biblical picture invokes the future of communities and of the whole world, and it has strong practical dimensions to it. Too often salvation is passed off as some kind of a theological abstraction concerning concepts about the afterlife. It must also speak to the here and now. What are the manifold realities that encumber human flourishing in the present? What do we need to be saved from? Salvation in its fullness addresses not only salvation from sin but the consequences of that sin. Those consequences are too easy for all to see for those living with poverty and oppression. This state of affairs shames us all.

What can sometimes flow from a slimmed down doctrine of salvation is the temptation to make false choices. The recurring discourse about whether verbal proclamation of the gospel trumps good works done in the name of Christ is facile. Both are important. My present purpose is simply to say that those involved in practical expressions of the love of God, such as through international development work, should not feel that their ministry is inferior to other ministries or lacking in legitimacy in any way. Followers of Christ are expressly commanded to love their neighbor.[10] That is enough. This is a good and sufficient warrant to justify obedience to their call. End of story.

Those who insist on blending development work with other agendas may not understand that development *is* a work of salvation, albeit on a broader scale. When programmatic evangelism is forcibly tied to development or relief work an unholy alliance can result. This can undermine the gospel rather than promoting it. The example of so-called "rice Christians" comes to mind. It may be possible to coerce or manipulate people into the Christian faith, but it is deeply offensive to try. To do so may produce a harvest of insincerity, and will certainly constitute a repugnant betrayal of a worldview that rests on unconditional love. It has been said that "if people or power must be manipulated in order to get them to embrace one's values and convictions, then the values are not of much value and the convictions not very commendable."[11] Boff has been highly critical of the compulsion used to spread Christian faith in much of South America. He deplores the wholesale disregard for human dignity that resulted in the "destruction of otherness."[12] Poignantly he asks, "Can we say that there was an evangelism here?"[13] In short, unethical methods subvert rather than promote the gospel.

This background leads to a critically important question. If proselytism of any kind is to be avoided, how can faith-based development agencies share in the work of spreading the gospel? I believe it is possible. The godly character, presence, and relationships of their personnel can be a powerful witness. It has been stated that "generous love is the best witness to the God in whom we believe."[14] In this regard, a humble, serving posture requires that humans resist the temptation to judge the salvation of others. It would be arrogant to presume that we have the insights of God. Faith is a gift of God, and spiritual regeneration is cloaked in the mysteries of the Holy Spirit. It is folly to make judgments about the salvation of others. We are explicitly warned against it. Needless to say, I'm sure it is a highly unreliable exercise. Those convinced of their own righteousness may be at greatest risk. Scripture hints that there will be surprises when it comes to those seated around the banquet table in the kingdom of God. We can be confident that God is already at work among all his peoples, although how this happens is often unclear.[15]

Those working in international development are urged to pray for the communities in which they work. Mature Christians will have an acute understanding that their faith is an embodied faith and their personal actions speak most clearly about what they truly believe. They will hope that the communities where they work will experience profound love in Jesus Christ and not some shallow caricature of it. Christians, ideally, will always be willing to give an account of the hope they cherish within them, in a spirit of respect and love, and may pray for opportunities to share what they believe. An important scripture in this regard is 1 Peter 3:15: "but in your hearts sanctify Christ as Lord. Always be ready to make your defense to anyone who demands from you an account of the hope that is in you; yet do it with gentleness and reverence..."

It is always appropriate to give a clear account of what motivates faith-based development work when called upon to do so. Apart from the biblical imperative, this kind of explanation is required if we are to be transparent and open with one another. Notions of free speech and freedom of conscience are also relevant here. When a full explanation is given the injunction of Australian church leader Peter Adam is satisfied:

Incarnation without verbal revelation means a dumb incarnation of uninterpreted presence . . . There is no reason to be content with a notion of incarnation which is only personal or
sacramental, and which does not value verbal revelation in
Christ's ministry . . . verbal revelation is part of Christ's incarnate
ministry, and . . . incarnated ministry should also include incarnated words, the message of the Gospel.[16]

The position reached is a nuanced but faithful one. Christians working in international development can give an account of the hope within
them without making judgments that are not theirs to make or confusing the agenda that underpins their work. At the same time, they may be
assured that the work they are engaged in is inspired by the coming
kingdom, and in that sense *is* an important work of salvation.

Organizational focus and access to communities

Faith-based development organizations can know that they are engaged
in a biblically based ministry of salvation. This should be a source of
organizational and personal encouragement. Personnel can also be involved in the work of sharing the love of God by verbal explanation in
response to community-initiated inquiry. Having clarity about roles and
responsibilities will help ensure ethical and well-focused behavior.

Religious sensibilities within communities can run deep. These
convictions can go to the heart of a person and can have a defining
role for that person within a community. The broader vision of salvation that has been outlined above enables common ground to be established with communities from other faith traditions. The vision of
health, restoration, prosperity and peace—presented as community-
based development—is one that transcends religious difference. It is
also a vision that can speak authentically to an organization's purpose
and theological foundation.

Where verbal proclamation of the gospel is made a programmatic
activity, this can place an FBO's presence within many communities at
risk. Overt evangelism may be alienating and threatening in some contexts. A commitment to biblical holism, on the other hand, means an
organization can do a great deal of good while responding transparently to community-initiated inquiry about its beliefs. The concern
about winning converts also extends to Christian Orthodox communities, where evangelical denominations may be seen as "sects." In this
regard, the evangelical heritage of an organization can raise significant
concerns that are best assuaged by building long-term relationships
based on trust.

Building church capacity vs. evangelism by proxy

For reasons discussed in detail later, faith-based development organizations see their work standing in continuity with that of the local church. Agencies may desire to build the capacity of the church, especially in its understanding of development issues, so that its impact within civil society is both sustained and magnified. This is entirely appropriate. The church has, however, a general commission to evangelize, and this will require development organizations to reflect carefully on those areas in which they choose to engage. The line between capacity building and evangelism by proxy can be thin.

From this point, and in the chapters that follow, I will begin to draw on "the data" to illustrate certain points. By this I mean a series of World Vision studies listed in Appendix 1, research based on interviews and focus groups. Broadly, these materials examine the role of Christian faith in its development work. Referencing these materials will help shift the discussion to a more concrete level.

Study results sounded clear warnings about mixing evangelism and development, cautioning that "some activities proselytise, Muslim kids are encouraged to convert, and the distribution of Bibles in mixed communities can send the wrong message."[17] This can rebound on the faith-based organization in a negative way. In particular, when development organizations deal with churches that have a revivalistic ethos there is a heightened risk. This is the case in many parts of East Africa. There, "development" activities can be a short step away from direct evangelism. Problematic activities can include distributing Bibles and hymn books, training Sunday School teachers, sponsoring church committees with evangelical agendas, and supplying equipment or facilities for evangelistic events, such as screenings of the *Jesus* film.[18] By sponsoring activities of this kind, the development agency itself may be co-opted into socially divisive agendas and may confuse or compromise its own position within the general community.

When the agency for evangelism programs sits clearly with the local church, most of these difficulties are avoided.

"Voluntary" activities, power, and culture

Careful attention must also be paid by the development organization when choosing to conduct or sponsor activities even when they are ostensibly voluntary, such as running educational programs to learn more about the Christian faith. In theory, there is nothing objectionable about voluntary programs. It will be the desire of all Christians that others will come to know and name their hope in Jesus Christ.

The problem is that the power dynamics within a community can sometimes make a "voluntary" activity very difficult to resist at the level of practice. Communities may feel tacit pressure to accept an invitation in view of the good that development organizations do, and the importance of their programs within local communities. Cultural expectations may also dictate that invitations should be accepted. Notions about good hospitality or the desire not to offend can also mean that "voluntary" attendance becomes a matter of form rather than substance. Caution should be exercised to ensure that "voluntary" really is voluntary.

Again, when evangelism programs are left to the agency of the local church, ethical dilemmas are more easily overcome.

Transparency always

International development organizations should operate transparently. Occasionally, stories circulate about organizations that use development work or programs as cover for a hidden agenda of evangelism. In other words, the development work is really about gaining access to communities under a false pretense. This is reprehensible and plainly dishonest. There is nothing virtuous about lying. The presumed greater good underlying such instances is ill conceived. It will inevitably deepen mistrust and damage the efforts of fellow Christians committed to serious development work. Honest consultation with community leaders upfront is essential in every case to start out in the right way.

Thy kingdom come! The not yet

An important understanding for development agencies is that God's kingdom will be established on earth, not in heaven above. The New Testament does *not* teach that ultimate hope is found in the immortal soul of the redeemed ascending to God in heaven for an afterlife commencing upon death. That popular but mistaken view is gnosticism. The Christian teaching is that the redeemed inherit a renewed, transformed earth at the time of a general bodily resurrection. Walter Wink emphasizes that "the gospel is not a message of personal salvation *from the world, but a message of a world transfigured, right down to its basic structures.*"[19] God's eternal kingdom will reign *on earth* forever. The many profound implications of this teaching are explored in N. T. Wright's book, *Surprised by Hope*.[20] It is clear that Christians need to care for this world which is loved by God and which is the ultimate home for both God and humans.

Jesus taught his disciples to pray about the kingdom in the Lord's Prayer. This is very telling. As has already been noted, the prayer's first intercession confirms that the home of the Christian's calling and sanctification is in the present time and place.[21] Christians constantly enlist themselves in the service of God's kingdom whenever they pray this prayer. They commit themselves "to initiate, here and now, approximations of God's reign."[22] The biblical picture we are given is of a God who graciously invites his people to have an active, participatory role as he builds the promised kingdom. When faith-based development organizations urge their staff to live for the kingdom of God, they commend "a process of change that affirms the joint roles of God and humans."[23] The fullness of Christian salvation consists in the reversal of the consequences of human sin, which will be demonstrated in acts of co-creation at the prompting of God. And that process of change involves working toward the comprehensive vision of *shalom* in all its dimensions.

The Hebrew word *shalom* refers to the transcendent peace of God, which is achieved when the whole created order takes its proper place and relationship before God. Leonardo Boff captures this well by saying: "Biblically it signifies the totality of God's creation redeemed and organized on the criteria of God's loving design. The reign represents the comprehensive politics of God, to be implemented in the history of the cosmos, of nations, of the chosen people, and in the depths of each human heart."[24]

Implicit in this understanding are two features that together should form the theological bedrock for faith-based approaches to development. The first is the conviction that God is the ultimate change agent in the world and that development practitioners are working cooperatively in this God-inspired agenda. The second is that development work takes place within God's overarching redemptive metanarrative for all creation. This provides powerful theological assurance.

N. T. Wright identifies 1 Corinthians 15:58 as an important biblical text in this regard.[25] This verse is at the end of a dense passage about the fullness of resurrection life. Development workers know how frustrating and complex their work can be. The very best efforts of development organizations can seem weak and inadequate. The passage boldly assures that workers in God's service should stand firm: "Be steadfast, immovable, always excelling in the work of the Lord, because you know that in the Lord your labor is not in vain." Somehow, God takes those efforts offered in the service of his kingdom, no matter how inadequate they may seem, and transforms them for his eternal purposes.[26] The final outworking of God's kingdom will be when he comes and makes his home among his people in the renewed earth, which is his eternal home.[27] This promise enables development workers to live in anticipation of the renewal of creation whereupon every manifestation of suffering and evil will be overcome.

In the meantime, many Christians draw inspiration from a gospel that is transformative, involving important questions about life before death and the search for justice.[28] They take to heart the call to actively seek that God's will be done on earth as it is in heaven.[29] Jesus speaks of a new way of living because the kingdom of God at hand.[30] God is understood to be immanent, active, and present. Theologians like Jürgen Moltmann argue that transcendent living means working with God to bring the future forward in hope and power.[31] The gospel must not be allowed to become insipid and detached: "If faith does not lead to real impact and influence in the real world then it is a mere shadow of its own meaning and a betrayal of the poor. If it is restricted to pious personal spirituality only, it is a fundamental denial of itself."[32] When this happens the goodness of the Good News is found wanting.

Faith-based development located in the grander plan

Only God can renew God's world. This is his sovereign work. And yet it is humbling that God includes us in his plans for its renewal. International development work is one way Christians can live out their prayerful aspiration for the kingdom to come. The work of faith-based development agencies is located in a broader God-inspired narrative of change.

The narratives of other types of development organizations will be different. They will place their confidence variously in economic theories, scientific interventions, the attainment of human rights, or political processes. Christian faith-based development organizations anchor their hope for a renewed world in the promise of God. In this way they can know with certainty that justice for the oppressed will come and that the poor will finally receive their inheritance. This reassurance is important because engagement in development work, with all its complexity and tenuous gains, might otherwise be profoundly demoralizing. While we live in anticipation of what God is doing, present realities can easily overwhelm or dishearten. For this reason, Christian development is anchored in the promise of God.

God's promise builds resilience

For development workers an important practical point flows from this certainty. It provides a firm basis for resilience in the present. In some contexts, Christian communities may also share the ultimate vision of God's kingdom and the confidence it brings. God is at work in his world, and in the end all things will be renewed and put right. Scripture presents a magnificent vision of things to come in these beautiful and expressive verses:

And I heard a loud voice from the throne saying, "See, the home of God is among mortals. He will dwell with them; they will be his people, and God himself will be with them; he will wipe every tear from their eyes. Death will be no more; mourning and crying and pain will be no more, for the first things have passed away."[33]

The power of this vision is one that speaks into the present.

For most people living in this world, the present requires engagement in spiritual life. For them, this is an important part of what it means to be human, and it is to this theme that we now turn.

CHAPTER 5

A Spiritual Worldview—
Meeting Communities Where They're At

Every organization has a worldview that underpins its work, whether explicitly acknowledged or not. That worldview may help or hinder the attainment of development goals in a given context. Organizations with a scientific focus may see development as a series of mechanistic or technical fixes. Economic approaches may reduce development work with communities to a series of crude financial measures. Human-rights approaches may promote an individualistic agenda in non-Western settings where rights are mediated through community-based structures. It has been pointed out that the moment a development worker steps out of his or her air-conditioned four-wheel-drive vehicle in an African village a statement is made about technology, wealth, and power.[1]

The widespread and intensifying theistic belief in much of the Majority World raises an important question about the "connectedness" of worldviews. On the topic of proselytism, Anna Wrigley has pointed out that it should not be regarded as a problem confined to FBOs. She cautions that some organizations remain unaware that they have "disregarded culture themselves, tramped on belief, undermined traditional social networks and imposed a secular mindset, engaging in dangerous, subtle proselytizing of a material gospel."[2] Rationalistic approaches sometimes preach a gospel of market-based prosperity so that development cooperation involves a community in a kind of quasi-religious conversion.[3] I have formed the view that the question of the compatibility of beliefs and methodologies receives insufficient attention in development circles. The problem may be a lack of organizational self-awareness or the capacity to be genuinely self-critical.

Methodologically, holding to a "scientific gospel" or arguments against the Divine is not a neutral position.[4] No worldview can ever be impartial on matters of ultimate concern. The persistent bias in academic circles against religious viewpoints must be acknowledged as *itself a viewpoint.* In short, the argument for "methodological atheism" serves to advance one culturally loaded belief as dispassionate neutrality while unfairly critiquing religious viewpoints as inherently biased.[5] Every organization should recognize that it has a worldview, and then reflect on how its core positioning affects both its definition of "development" and its ability to achieve it.

Leveraging community goodwill toward an organization's faith basis

Many development organizations have their head offices in Western countries. The question arises whether the views prevalent in these countries, which have become increasingly secularized, are sometimes "exported." Some commentators have pointedly blamed the failure of previous development efforts on their narrow rationalistic and economic focus.

A key to the success of development organizations will be the level of trust and engagement afforded to them by the local community. Where developing communities are positively disposed toward an organization's religious underpinnings, this may improve the success of their development undertakings. Faith-based development organizations will not be readily accepted in every setting, but in many they will be. Christianity remains the world's largest religious grouping (32 percent), with Islam a close second (23 percent).[6]

In Christian nations/regions there may be a natural sympathy for the work of FBOs. The data, while at risk of being self-serving, has supported this. It has been reported that: "because we are Christians it is easier for the community to accept us compared to others. As Christians we know what to do and how to approach the community."[7] In Rwanda and Tanzania, the leverage of FBOs was based on the perceived authority of the Christian faith in the general community. As was noted in a World Vision Evaluation Report on Rwanda, "the Christian faith is accorded a high degree of moral authority and the general populace is positively disposed towards Christian teaching. Christian faith therefore has the potential to be harnessed in development activity at a grassroots community level."[8]

More surprising was data from some Muslim and mixed areas which suggested that having a theistic worldview was a definite advantage. Women from one program stated that in doing development, it is "important to have faith. Christian or Muslim doesn't matter."[9] In Senegal, a Muslim staff member explained that when going into a strongly Muslim community the Christian organization can assert with integrity: "We have ways to follow what God wants."[10] As explained below, the assumed "neutrality" of non-faith based agencies can be undercut by their inability to frame development messages in a way that is meaningful to local communities.

Secular "neutrality" versus theistic worldview

The data from Senegal was especially interesting on the question of neutrality. Senegal is an open theistic society that has no cultural history of the Enlightenment or modernity. In such a society, the evidence indicated that development messages needed to be framed theistically to be received and understood. For example, one imam, when questioned whether belief in God is important to development, replied: "Not important [but], very important. God created us to live in good conditions. We are not in a good condition, so we cannot separate God from development. God is the origin of development. Without faith I cannot believe in development because God shows the way that faith is in the heart of development."[11] Some personnel expressed the view that when an organization has no faith position it is more difficult for it to communicate its work. It is "easier to speak to people of faith if you have a faith, even if it is different."[12]

An important qualification is that the organization's underpinning faith must be taken seriously. The data indicated that serious Christians are readily respected in moderate Sunni contexts as people who pray and as "People of the Book." In Senegal there is a tendency to equate Christian faith with the lifestyle of former French colonialists, which was often far from devout. However, once a Muslim sees that the organization is about prayer and spirituality, then a Muslim will say, "Now we can do business together."[13]

It is unremarkable that Christian communities should have a degree of affinity toward the work of Christian faith-based agencies. What is remarkable is that communities within theistic societies may have stronger resonance with an organization from another faith when compared with secular agencies. This contradicts the standard argument that religion is a source of division between people and that secular agencies have the advantage of being more "neutral." "Neutrality" may be a myth. An inability to frame development messages in an authentic way, in theistic terms, may lead agencies to be less effective. In particular, the data showed that in several mixed faith settings Christian organizations can be very well accepted. This is because there is a sense of place for Christians within Muslim belief, with some common theological premises and a mutual respect for devout adherents. It goes without saying that in more fundamentalist settings, where religious difference is sometimes exploited, a faith-based development organization could be viewed with greater suspicion or even hostility. The critical point is that "secular" does not automatically equate to "neutral" or "more effective."

Spirituality and program integration

A commitment to a spiritual worldview may enhance the perceived value of physical interventions. This is because physical interventions occur within a broader narrative of change that engages community relationships, ways of living, and religious convictions. The underpinning faith commitment of the faith-based development organization may supply an overarching narrative for its suite of activities. Physical interventions are not then "disembodied" from the religious convictions of staff or the communities they serve. The World Vision data reports that this programmatic holism amplifies the value of development work. In Tanzania it was observed that "all community members reflected on the value of development interventions; they cannot be understated as they address real needs and bring much hope. Attention to the spiritual doesn't replace or supplant the physical requirements of food, water, and shelter, *but greatly amplifies the value of them.*"[14] The basis of that amplification was the congruence between action and existing spiritual belief.

For some, a holistic worldview informed their entire approach to development: "Development is not a matter of assets, rather of relationships. Food security and education are not enough—the essence of life is more than this ... A person needs pure conscience, peace with self and others, and relationship with God. This [will be] reflected in a sharing [of] resources so that all the community prospers."[15]

It can be expected that the strongest resonances will occur when the community shares, or at least respects, the development organization's underlying beliefs. The community will do its own theologizing, drawing connections between development initiatives, the organization's beliefs, and its own faith narrative.

Normalizing spiritual life in communities

Many FBOs will pursue a vision of development that seeks to normalize spiritual activities within communities. By doing so, they can help build social meaning and identity. This is an important development issue, especially in contexts where there has been major social dislocation or change. In the increasingly secularized West, this concept can be hard to understand. In many contexts it is clear that "Faith is hugely important. Your identity is your faith ..."[16] For this reason, agencies may place an emphasis on organizing activities, including interfaith activities, that seek to normalize the role of religious faith in community life.

In ex-Communist countries such an approach has been very important in community rebuilding. Common issues in these contexts can include disillusionment, corruption, passivity, cynicism, economic malaise, loss of industrial production, growing unemployment, and mass emigration. Rekindling a sense of community is critical. A senior leader from the Armenian Apostolic Church drew this contrast:

> In the West Christianity is seen as a private faith but in the East it is a community way of life. Westerners have to understand the East. Faith helps to make a community. The destruction of Armenia is the destruction of faith. Development programs to promote community life have failed because they have ignored the church and the role of faith as the centre of the community.[17]

In some contexts a person's faith identity and national identity can be largely coterminous. To build up one is to build up the other. In places like Armenia and Georgia, there are established national churches of very ancient origin representing the vast bulk of their populations. The Armenian Apostolic Church and the Georgian Orthodox Church date back to 301 CE and 327 CE respectively. The data reported: "During communism the people were not allowed to express their faith, but now there is a distinct sense of recovering their identity and a societal returning to the church."[18] Elsewhere it was remarked: "Once we have change in the church we will have change in society; the two are inseparable. To separate is a Western way of thinking. If we see change in the church we will see change in society."[19]

While FBOs may be happy to facilitate processes that normalize spiritual activity within communities, they will not allocate resources to promote another religion or faith. They will also stand against some spiritual activities that they see as damaging to personal or community wellbeing. For example, some aspects of African Traditional Religion (ATR) have been actively targeted, as discussed in chapter 9. Therefore it should not be assumed that faith-based development organizations are invariably accepting of all manner of spiritual beliefs.

It seems unlikely that development organizations operating from a non-faith basis would invest time or money in building up churches or faith institutions as a development priority. While they may engage with them for tactical purposes, to seek to build them up for their own sake, or for the community's sake, would be incompatible with the underlying ethos of non-faith-based organizations. In this regard, it is suggested that there is a gap between strongly secular models and their ability to meet a full range of development needs. In short, not every organization will embrace the idea that spirituality is a legitimate part of personhood or of community life. This simply reinforces the notion that ideas about what "development" is are heavily contested.

The data showed that in some contexts the church was intertwined with society and not a separate component. In Africa especially, the expression of faith is significantly different from that in Western cultures. One important aspect is that in the African psyche it is completely alien to make a separation between religious faith and daily life.[20] A related aspect is the open, visible expression of faith within African communities. This represents a contrast with Western countries, which tend to treat faith as a personal choice belonging to the private sphere. Among the important implications that flow from this, and that are discussed later in this book, is the ability of the development organization to engage in prayer or other faith-based activities, which may help legitimize and embed development work within communities.

Implications for the recognition of spiritual capital in development

One of the great social researchers of recent decades, Robert Putnam, has focused on the horizontal links that are necessary for a coherent and productive society in the context of North American democracy.[21] His research identifies *social capital*—the voluntary links between people and different groups—as critical for civic development.[22] Putnam has pointed out that with the decline in traditional organizational structures, such as churches, society has become more disassociated and atomized. There is an important corollary here in developing countries.

Social capital and spiritual capital are closely related. Peter L. Berger and Robert W. Hefner suggest that "spiritual capital might be thought of as a sub-species of social capital, referring to the power, influence, knowledge, and dispositions created by participation in a particular religious tradition."[23] Others see spiritual capital as simply another term for the power and influence generated by religious belief and practice.[24]

It is argued that religious belief and institutions can play a strong role in achieving development outcomes. Religious faith helps to build long-term hope and reliance within developing communities, and it can strengthen social identity and meaning. The data revealed the role of the church in providing strong participatory networks, highlighting its locus as source of teaching, social care, inspiration, and belonging. These findings were consistent with the emerging literature on "spiritual capital" as a valuable resource within communities.

One commentator has pointed out that there are important links between spiritual capital and health, observance of the rule of law, volunteerism, and education.[25] While it can be difficult to reliably measure, spiritual capital can be especially significant in developing communities. The poor may not have access to more traditional types of capital, such as financial capital. Stocks of human capital and intellectual capital can be depleted by poverty, making other forms of capital relatively more important.

Spiritual capital exists as a reflection of the social strength of a community, arising out of its religious convictions, networks, and practices. The importance of spiritual capital in carrying out development work is only beginning to be appreciated. It also leads to an important question: Given that spiritual capital is so important to developing communities, could its value be exponentially enhanced by providing faith communities and their leaders with specific knowledge of development principles? Intuitively, it seems likely that if development knowledge were more widely disseminated within religious networks, then spiritual capital could be more easily deployed in socially transformative ways.

Some researchers have focused specifically on the economic impacts of spiritual capital. In this sense, spiritual capital may not be such a new idea. As noted earlier, it was Max Weber who proposed that Christian enculturation created the conditions necessary for the capitalist system to flourish, especially the so-called "Protestant work ethic." However, spiritual capital is now being examined in a fresh light. For example, Rebecca and Timothy Shah assert that "a comparative research program investigating spiritual capital in different civilizations remains a matter of central intellectual and policy importance. The urgency is all the greater in the light of the fact that, contrary to the forecasts of modernization theorists a generation ago, the past 20 years have seen an unprecedented religious revival in much of the world."[26]

The global trend toward increasing religiosity in developing countries is commented on elsewhere in this book, and it shows no sign of abating. It follows that "if religion aids economic betterment by serving as spiritual capital, then it is urgently important that the faith of the poor be tapped as a resource for economic development, and faith-based anti-poverty policies and strategies may be one way to do this."[27] I completely agree that spiritual capital has an important role in combating economic poverty and deserves far more attention than it has received. I would add, however, that it also points to broader conceptions of what true development looks like—including the creation and enhancement of real community and the social support it offers.

A broader vision of development will involve the nurturing of community relationships, social participation, and appreciation of the many positive aspects of local culture and tradition. While in the West the rise of material affluence has coincided with a historical decline in religious structures, it is important to remember that correlation is not the same thing as causation. It is not necessarily the case that a rise in material standards of living will lead to the abandonment of God. For this reason I do not accept that utilizing spiritual capital to achieve development goals is ultimately self-defeating on the part of religion. This is because when it is authentically deployed spiritual capital will always entail a broader non-material vision of "development" consistent with its underlying ethos.

The next chapter looks at another aspect of spiritual life for Christian development workers, the living out of kingdom values in the present.

CHAPTER 6

Living for the Kingdom: The Now!

The kingdom was at the center of Jesus' life and ministry. It is some-times forgotten that his call to repentance, which tends to have a more familiar ring, did not occur in a vacuum; it was made squarely in the context of the coming reign of God.[1] The kingdom of God was the most consistent and pronounced theme of his teaching.[2] In the synoptic gospels (Mark, Luke, and Matthew), more attention is given to this topic than any other.[3] The kingdom motif was present in Jesus' procla-mations, in his parable teachings, in the Beatitudes, in his expositive discourses, in the apocalyptic material, as well as in other sources.

Jesus' life of actions also speaks about this anticipated reign of God. There is eloquent testimony about the kingdom in his miracles, his relationships with the poor and the outcast, and his indignation and anger at injustice. Most profoundly, the promised hope of this kingdom is vindicated in the person of the resurrected Christ. If the idea of the kingdom was so pervasive in Jesus' life and teaching, then it must also provide constant inspiration for faith-based development organizations as they seek to follow Jesus in their own ministries.

The Christian teaching about the kingdom of God is that God was unhappy to leave the world in its fallen, broken state. He sent Jesus to redeem all of creation and inaugurate a new and completely righteous reign over all things. While God's reign or kingdom has broken into the world, it will not be fully consummated until some point in the future, often believed to coincide with the return of Christ. Christians are called to live as signs and incarnated expressions of the kingdom, rec-ognizing that God's reign has begun while also anticipating the fullness of what is yet to come.[4]

People of faith who have accepted a call to work in international development will try and live for Christ in their daily interactions. Faith-based development organizations will seek to reflect the eternal values of the kingdom of God—such as peace, justice, and love—as a present expression of an unfolding reality. This means following Jesus Christ in working with the poor and oppressed, seeking abundant life for all, and striving for justice. It involves expressing solidarity and friendship, displaying a lived empathy for others, and leading a Spirit-led life that infuses a real compassion and faithfulness. While some would regard values like peace, justice, love, responsibility, respect, and reciprocity as indistinguishable from universal human values, faith-based development organizations will see them as expressions of the kingdom of God.

Living for the kingdom of God is a *present calling* that shows the reality of God's reign. God creates, loves, and gifts all people and continues to suffer along with the poor and oppressed. Because God has scandalously poured out his limitless grace on all people in the person of his Son, faith-based development programs will not intentionally exclude, discriminate against, or devalue any human. And because God-in-Christ has willingly entered into the suffering and brokenness of this world on our behalf, our challenge is to do the same for others. Faith-based development work actively lives for the kingdom of God, and proof of his coming reign is found in the daily instances where compassion blossoms, relationships are healed, and justice and dignity are upheld.

In this chapter we look at some ways faith-based development organizations attempt to live out these kingdom values.

Kingdom values earning trust and acceptance

Most organizations publish a set of corporate values of one kind or another. These "menus" tend to look very much alike, and producing them is a relatively easy task. That said, not all development organizations display the same values or level of commitment to them.

Christian personnel of faith-based development organizations have a prior obligation. They are committed to live out kingdom values in their daily activities and the demonstration of these values will underpin the acceptance of their work within developing communities. These kingdom values will be enlivened by a personal faith commitment. God-given values are patiently nurtured by the Spirit as an expression of the living Christ.

The idea that organizational values exist as some kind of floating abstraction should be firmly disabused. Values are only ever realized by a consistent pattern of personal interaction that gives them a real substance and meaning. Where demonstrated values positively resonate within a community, then the development organization's work is more likely to be embraced. "Words don't count as much as living kingdom-of-God values."[5]

In the data, the values mentioned included empowerment and working for justice,[6] respect and acting in good faith,[7] and exercising love and care.[8] A Muslim leader observed that "Christianity is a religion of forgiveness and love."[9] The proactive style of practical engagement evidenced by some faith-based agencies may itself be described as a value. To this could be added an embedded, relational, hands-on ethos. While development workers will not preach, their work will speak clearly about their character and commitment.

This may sound aspirational, and it probably is. There is no shortage of Christians who are judgmental, triumphal, and graceless. A little enthusiasm can be a dangerous thing, especially when zeal outstrips maturity. The basic point, however, remains true. Where kingdom values are consistently embodied in the work of faith-based personnel this will be respected by communities. It will move the organization beyond transaction or service delivery into a shared, relational journey. These themes will be explored more deeply in the next chapter.

Briefly, the data highlighted the importance of *modeling* behaviors in several places, especially "the Christian values of peace, reconciliation, forgiveness, and trust."[10] In Georgia, the inculcation of Christian values such as love, caring for one another, and encouragement were seen as essential to move beyond the Soviet legacy of dependency. Likewise, in Lebanon it was stated that the difference between a faith-based development organization and other organizations is that the lived values of faith made a difference within that culture.[11] In Georgia it was claimed that "we have some values which increase our leverage over other agencies when working with the community and collaborating with the church. [This] gives us 'extra salt'..."[12] These types of comments may be discounted as self-serving, but collectively they do point to an important underlying truth about what an agency stands for. If kingdom values are truly universal, then living them out will resonate in developing communities everywhere. The difference between kingdom values and universal values is the Spirit who brings them to life.

Distinctive emphasis on working for harmonious interfaith relationships

A particular kingdom value that must receive constant attention in the work of faith-based development organizations is respect, especially respect for other faith traditions. Building trust and understanding between different religious groupings is a prerequisite to achieving sustainable development in almost every context.

The theological imperative behind this value is its commitment to live in anticipation of the kingdom of God. God's reign on earth will not be achieved by disparagement, violence, mistrust, or suspicion. Nor will

God be glorified by these kinds of attitudes. Faith-based agencies need to adopt a careful and nuanced position. They will discourage staff from judging the salvation of another, while acknowledging Jesus Christ as the revelation of what God is like. This positioning provides a firm basis to uphold the integrity of key Christian beliefs while providing space to constructively engage with people from other faiths or traditions.

A positive relational posture toward groups from other faiths is consistent with the understanding that all people in some way reflect the image of God. An emphasis on orthopraxy, that is, godly practice, rather than contentious matters of doctrine allows people to work together in practical ways and build closer relationships. For some, the commitment to interfaith understanding arises out of an appreciation of our shared humanity. Christianity "is about Christian values—Jesus values. Getting the wider picture about the world. All creatures are children of God, all brothers and sisters."[13] Others will see it as an outworking of the Christian commitment to unconditional love, friendship, and hospitality. The data provided evidence of meetings of Christian and Muslim leaders convened "not only for teaching, but just to be together."[14] Getting to know others is always a helpful first step in removing suspicion and barriers.

Community goodwill can be built by seeking common ground. A theistic worldview that emphasizes altruism and empathy for the poor is a solid foundation. It goes without saying that the personnel of faith-based development agencies should behave with due sensitivity to local culture. Programmatic evangelism may be seen as triumphal, threatening, and imperialistic in many contexts. In contrast, an emphasis on peace building, reconciliation, and transfiguring of inter-ethnic and interfaith relationships will be a steady feature of the work of many faith-based agencies. The internal devotional life of an organization may provide an opportunity to model what it believes, setting an example to staff and the broader community. Finally, relationships with churches will reflect a practical ecumenism. Taken as a whole, faith-based development organizations will see respectful interfaith relationships as a kingdom-inspired theological imperative, one with enormous practical implications in terms of achieving sustainable development in the present.

Approaching interfaith relationships from a position of vested interest

FBOs have a theological imperative to advance interfaith harmony. Accordingly, they should approach interfaith relationships from the position of a participant/actor, and this should positively affect the qualitative nature of their engagements.

Secularism has tended to regard religious belief as a source of conflict that needs to be moderated or controlled. Some agencies therefore approach this topic from a distance. They may regard religion as a private matter or something to be repudiated, or they may feel that their own secular underpinning does not enable them to engage religious institutions in the same way.

Faith-based development organizations, on the other hand, are presented with a valuable opportunity. They are able to address interfaith relationships in a positive way, with the conviction of a vested interest. Despite a sorry history of sectarian conflict, "religious faiths typically encourage members to work towards resolving conflicts and develop peace."[15] It is argued that ultimately harmonious interfaith relationships can be addressed only *from within*. Christian FBOs are able to pursue interfaith initiatives in an authentic way by appealing to a rich theology and sacred sources.

Implications for development cooperation between Muslim and Christian faiths

The data contradicted the commonly held view that religion is inevitably a source of divisiveness and conflict. The evaluation reports illustrated a remarkable degree of cooperation between representatives of the Christian and the Islamic faiths. In all mixed-faith environments, there were strong examples of interfaith cooperation.

This issue was tested most closely in Senegal. There were examples of joint programs, cooperation between faith leaders, and strong goodwill exercised by staff of different backgrounds. Most surprising was the desire of Muslim staff to work for World Vision precisely because it was a Christian organization.

There were several factors at play here. Christianity was a known faith, because Christians are regarded as People of the Book.[16] There is a sense of place for Christians within the Islamic worldview, and the common Abrahamic heritage is helpful for both Christians and Muslims in their shared understanding of the identity of God. In particular, the recognition of Jesus respectively as Savior or Prophet was sufficient common ground for staff to render faithful service. The data indicated that Muslim staff saw working for a Christian faith-based agency as a way of serving the Prophet and living out Koranic values.

It helped that World Vision took its faith seriously and Christian staff were identified as having lives that demonstrated piety. Most important, however, was the organization's commitment to faith, a commitment that was respected by staff and the communities where the organization worked. Its strong faith perspective enhanced its reputation in communities that viewed development challenges from a theistic frame of reference. It was also significant that the organization had a proven track record of non-proselytizing behavior, although some staff had become Christians. Interestingly, some staff also reported becoming better Muslims because of their exposure to the organization.

Like most of sub-Saharan Africa, the strand of Islam present in Senegal is Sunni, and it has been historically influenced by Sufi mysticism. It is doubtful whether the same level of cooperation could be achieved in fundamentalist or hardline environments. In the Balkans, Lebanon, and Tanzania, there was consistent data, including from Islamic community leaders, supporting the organization's presence, impact, and operational style.

The implications of this finding are significant. In multiple contexts, World Vision was able to enjoy very positive relationships within Muslim communities. In several of those communities, its faith perspective was identified as a positive advantage. This contradicts the view that religion is typically a source of social division. It certainly contradicts the "clash of civilizations" thesis, which has gained currency in the populist Western media. These instances serve as an example and, in some respects, a model.

There were also examples of cooperation between Muslim and Christian faith leaders in carrying out projects and training together. In Senegal, there was also evidence of World Vision enlisting the support of Muslim leaders to take a stance against harmful practices from local traditional religion. The ability to form a coalition of this type indicated a high degree of trust. Koranic teaching was used by World Vision in a specially adapted version of one of its HIV programs, with the relevant components designed and delivered by Muslims, and also in promoting children's rights among Muslim communities in Tanzania.

Second, the data contradicted the claim that secular agencies have the advantage of being more "neutral." This is meant to place them above religious conflict and beyond the dangers of proselytism. This type of claim was refuted by the data. The "neutrality" of secular agencies in Senegal and Tanzania meant that communities were sometimes confronted by an unfamiliar modernist philosophy. There were clear reports of secular organizations that presented as culturally and philosophically distant.

Hope and community resilience

Living for the kingdom inculcates hope in communities, and this is critical in building resilience. Development projects fail when communities become disengaged, cynical, or just give up. Many aspects of development work are incremental and long-term in nature. It may take more than one generation for changes to really take hold. There are often unpredictable setbacks, so there is a need for communities to have confidence about the future and believe in a process of change.

A Christian faith-based approach to development takes place within a framework emphasizing kingdom values. The first aspect is about encouragement in the present through displays of human solidarity. This part of the narrative is about people caring for one another, recognizing that everyone has an intrinsic dignity and worth, and that all people are bound together in their shared humanity. Professor Emeritus Deryke Belshaw is director of the International Institute of Development Research at Oxford. He has observed that "spiritual and relational experiences can raise the self-regard and confidence of previously excluded poor people."[17] The application of the Golden Rule—that is, important ideals of self-sacrifice and unconditional love—and the living out of kingdom values underpin this kind of encouragement. Most faith traditions will reflect some of these elements.

The second element is an appreciation that God cares. This aspect of faith often takes deeper root through adversity. Christian faith claims that not only does God care, but ultimately he is seeking to change the world so that it reflects his intentions, thus offering a transcendent hope of a better world to come.[18] This is an especially rich collation of ideas, involving elements of divine empathy, participation, re-creation, overcoming, and abiding hope. These themes may be especially resonant in developing communities where life is fragile and precarious.

As in other agencies, a wide range of development themes, such as child rights, gender empowerment, income generation, micro-finance, water and sanitation, and improved agriculture will form part of the work of FBOs. Importantly, these themes are able to be incorporated within the faith narrative accompanying the organization's work, or within the community's own religious narrative. Religion can provide a strong metanarrative of hope and belonging. This is perhaps one reason why, despite earlier predictions, religion is patently not dying out. It is speculated that communities may take comfort in knowing that their life is significant to God, that he grieves with them in the present, and that God's plans are ultimately benevolent. In this way, a religious narrative may provide a deeper, existential meaning in environments of exceptional challenge.

There is a multi-layered connection between faith-based development and the inculcation of hope. Part of this is about living out kingdom values like love, care, and encouragement, which may build trust with the development agency and its staff. The particular way in which kingdom values build hope within communities may differ according to the context.

The differences in the data were striking. In Senegal, a predominantly Muslim context, the focus on living out kingdom values challenged the prevalent idea of *insha'Allah*. The idea of *insha'Allah* is that

God wills our present circumstances, thus fatalistically precluding any action for change. This notion can be used to avoid personal responsibility and can "cause a sense of apathy..."[19]

In post-communist settings, the restoration of kingdom values was seen as vital to restoring hope. Many communities have a damaged psyche, an engrained dependency, and a sense of passive resignation. For example, the evaluation report for Bosnia and Herzegovina laments: "In the post-communist period people behave like somebody else will solve their problems."[20] A more detailed explanation came from Armenia:

> Development is not just economic; it is much more than that. We have been under communist propaganda for 70 years and the church has been severely damaged as the propaganda has changed the mindset of generations, especially subsequent generations. This propaganda has established an atheistic generation and our values have been completely changed. Right now Armenia is in a state of transformation and we see development as the process to restore values. We do this as an organization and support churches to restore values. The result will be people who will have values to serve their country and neighbours. It is easiest to start with children as they have not been affected as much.[21]

Senior clergy in Armenia expressed the view that the Soviet regime almost destroyed national and spiritual identity. A national leader stated that he saw the key to national reconstruction as re-establishing the moral authority of people. The essential task was moral formation leading to renewed hope.[22] This observation echoes the comments of one theorist:

> To survive, all societies need a minimum moral sense; acts of mercy are best done by the citizenry and not by an impersonal welfare state. Education, value formation and the use of power are approaches to changing social behaviour; but even more important than these is the ability to constructively engage structures, help communities to resource their own needs within their own context, and nurture a strategic minority that will create a presence and a voice in public space on behalf of the poor.[23]

The promulgation of kingdom values, which had dissipated within the general community during Soviet times, was seen as vital in overcoming a sense of widespread and entrenched hopelessness. In addition

to this emphasis, a focus on inner transformation and strengthening relationships within civil society, especially through the church, opened
up a window of hope. These themes are explored in later chapters.

In East Africa, hope was transmitted by staff who would work
"human to human."[24] A highly relational approach contributed to effectiveness. For example, in Tanzania it was reported that "Our loving
approach and commitment to people . . . are the main reasons that
caused impact."[25]Again, in Rwanda the link between development
work and kingdom values was explicit: "We reflect Christ in the communities . . . All activities we do, we do from a Christian perspective,
taking the example of Jesus. In living with the poor, and in not separating people, He gave them value. We take the image of Him."[26] These
quotes indicate the embodied nature of Christian faith, and the values
followers of Christ can portray.

Short-term project work versus long-term incarnation

There is a case for saying that secular agencies may be better suited to
short-term project work, typically the carrying out of discrete projects
as well as emergency and humanitarian response work, in some faith-
infused settings. The reason for this is that these agencies may not be
able to engage as meaningfully on a longer-term basis as development
partners in these contexts.

Long-term commitment is seen as one of the distinctive advantages
of faith-based development organizations: "They are likely to remain in
place through a variety of difficult circumstances."[27] Personnel operating from a faith commitment may be more willing to submit themselves
to the privations of living with impoverished communities on a long-
term basis than those operating out of "career" rather than "vocation."
The data affirmed this conclusion.

A long-term community relationship is necessary to build trust and
achieve true participation. There is a vast difference between the translation of projects so they can be acceptable and useful in a religious
context and the generation of development projects as the fruits of lasting partnership. This observation is not meant to disparage short-term
project-based initiatives, which can do much good. It is, however, important to be clear. The most effective development will be community-
led, strength-based, and highly participatory.

This requires much more than brief association or *ad hoc* visita-
tion. The data indicated a level of cynicism and resentment toward organizations that operated in such a manner. This phenomenon was
reported in several communities and serves as a caution.

Where values include incarnational living, longer-term engagement
is possible. There are some resonances here with data gathered from the

World Bank's *Voices of the Poor* research.[28] One finding was the higher confidence in religious organizations and leaders than in most others (including government and many narrowly focused NGOs). One clear contributing factor was their ongoing presence within communities. A lived solidarity can build the kind of trust needed for the most effective development. A second finding concerned the very holistic understanding among the poor of the phenomena of poverty.[29] These findings are both relevant to this topic.

It is unrealistic to expect all development NGOs to localize their operations within remote, impoverished communities, even if there are sound theoretical reasons for doing so. This reality, however, reinforces an important conclusion expressed elsewhere, namely, that there may be a substantial benefit in training local religious leaders within communities in their understandings of development. These leaders will have an ongoing presence and an improved knowledge of development principles that may help them to respond to poverty within prevailing spiritual frames of reference.

Such an approach may enable trusted leaders to work more effectively with development organizations. This could improve the quality of the interactions with visiting agencies and enable a more effective intermediation to occur. However, the ideal situation is an embedded long-term incarnational presence within communities. Faith-based development organizations are well placed to engage in this manner. One of the reasons why this is the case is that many of their personnel conceive of their work as a ministry or calling, a subject that is addressed in the next chapter.

Chapter 7

Work as Ministry

The unifying feature of every Christian ministry is the knowledge that it is Christ who is served. This is what transforms work or an activity into a ministry. Jesus Christ both pioneers and calls. He leads the way. Karl Barth affirms that "the action, work, or activity of Christ unconditionally precedes that of the human called by Him..."[1] Faith-based development organizations will therefore try and inculcate a ministry understanding and offer a facilitative work environment for staff as they follow Jesus Christ in seeking justice and mercy for the poor.

There is abundant scriptural assurance about Christ's affinity with the poor. Matthew's gospel teaches that Jesus' own identification with the poor is so close that serving the poor is equated with serving Christ himself.[2] Theologian David Flett puts this elegantly by saying that "the Christian community's holy distance from the world is her active existence in solidarity with those for whom God has decided."[3] It is salutary to remember that the purpose of God's election is to enlist Christians in his service. It can be nothing else. When that service is withheld, election loses all meaning.[4] Ministry is not about parochialism or privilege or any notion of presumptive blessing. It is primarily understood as service.

Believing that it is Jesus Christ who is served through human efforts may change the outlook for workers in development organizations. Ideally, staff will not conceive what they do as simply service delivery, the application of professional skill, or even a commitment to work alongside the poor. The recruiting and induction process will help employees understand their work as a Christian *ministry*, which primarily serves and *follows* Jesus Christ. This is a daily, contextualized walk involving both joys and struggle.

Such an understanding of work as a ministry can imbue a strong sense of passion. This is because it connects a person's job with his or her deepest personal motivations. Some commentators believe that this can have a profound impact. For example, Rick James in his research on development NGOs makes reference to the "extremist commitment" of Catholic nuns. Their commitment was said to have come from a deeper place than mere humanitarian values:

> The nuns in particular were working from a sense of calling not career. They displayed extraordinary, long-term commitment. They coped with incredible difficulties in a sacrificial way. "Even when you are having an awful time in Soweto watching necklace killings you go on." They expected testing and suffering and accepted difficulties with humour. They were in a different league to career-orientated NGO workers.[5]

Many staff of faith-based development organizations will see their work in highly sacrificial terms as a kind of faith commitment. In many places organizations will hire non-Christians because there are insufficient Christians available or for other good reasons, such as compliance with local discrimination or labor laws. However, the preferencing of Christian staff in recruitment, especially for key leadership positions, remains policy for most faith-based development organizations. The fundamental reason for this is the idea that work is seen as a ministry, not simply a job, and the expectation is that leaders will act as "culture bearers" in leading by example.

Understanding work as Christian vocation may also affect notions of personal accountability. This observation is not intended to disparage the contribution of those non-Christians who work for faith-based agencies and are highly committed and skilled in their work. Christians must never indulge in feelings of superiority; they must repent of them: "Faith should not be used as a weapon for exercising control, nor to encourage judgmental, exclusive, and intolerant attitudes."[6] It is the case, however, that when an employee has an active Christian faith he or she may frame the concepts of accountability and service differently. This is because of the understanding that, ultimately, it is God who is served through one's personal efforts.

Faith-based development organizations will implement programs for the Christian formation of staff, so that they will be able to express their Christian identity and commitments in their life and work. This goal recognizes and reinforces the embodied nature of Christian faith. The remarks of Pope Benedict XVI seem especially resonant:

> With regard to the personnel who carry out the Church's charitable activity on the practical level, the essential has already been said: they must not be inspired by ideologies aimed at improving the world, but should rather be guided by the faith which works through love (cf. Gal 5:6). Consequently, more than anything, they must be persons moved by Christ's

love, persons whose hearts Christ has conquered with his love, awakening within them a love of neighbor.[7]

A different recruiting paradigm

The idea of Christian ministry contradicts standard management theory. That theory supposes that the misalignment between personal and organizational goals is bridged in the recruitment process by haggling over remuneration and conditions. People will normally take jobs in consideration of the pay and conditions, and because they need those jobs. A vocation or ministry understanding is fundamentally different. This is about taking gifts and experience and bringing them to the service of others. It is less a choice and more a personal conviction. While terms and conditions are not unimportant, the critical issue is the discerned alignment between personal goals, as an outworking of faith, and the mission of the organization. The process is likely to identify workers with a deeper level of commitment and a sustaining passion for the longer-term.

When faith-based development organizations refer to their work as "ministry," this language helps to capture the synergy. Thomas Jeavons notes that "at the heart of the Christian conception of ministry is the idea that it is intensely and essentially personal … To ask people to be involved in the ministry of a Christian service organization, then, is to ask them to bring their gifts, their personal attributes as individuals and as believers, to that work."[8] This close alignment between personal and organizational drivers can produce a dedicated and passionate workforce.

The connection can be especially significant when one considers that non-material aspects of caring for others can be undervalued or ignored in secular charity and social service.[9] Community support is about much more than material provision. The most effective support will offer a relational framework. The British Overseas NGOs for Development (BOND) is the UK peak body for the development sector. It commissioned research, which found that "the quality of an NGO's work is primarily determined by the quality of its relationships with its intended beneficiaries."[10] This has clear implications "requiring re-consideration of existing systems and the development of new ways of working."[11]

The added value of Christians understanding their work as ministry was captured powerfully in the data. It was explained that it "involves a 'felt' relational claim by God upon the development practitioner which then informs their work; at its fullest this claim will transmogrify development activity into lived worship."[12] The understanding of vocation enabled some staff to accept hardships and sacrifices with equanimity. Importantly, I am not suggesting that people from other types of development organizations do not see their work in a committed way. What I am saying is that employees with deep religious convictions may look to faith-based development organizations as a way of giving expression to their sense of vocation or calling. This involves a different process of recruiting that may end up producing real benefits for communities.

The communication of love

The secularization of Western society has coincided with the professionalization of the development sector.[13] Earlier generations of development work were associated with missionary endeavors,[14] church volunteers, or skills co-opted from other disciplines. However, international development is now recognized as a profession in its own right, with most practitioners receiving their training through degree and post-graduate level courses.

Professionalization has undoubtedly brought many advantages. There may, however, have been one especially critical loss. Amid the debates about theories of change, rights-based approaches, the nuancing of design documents, and the simplification of reporting requirements, one inspiring humanitarian ideal underpinning development—the communication of love—may have been lost. Practical expressions of love allow access to communities of different faiths. Love will underwrite a relational and incarnational style of interpersonal engagement. The personnel of faith-based development agencies may conceive of their work as an expression of love. The data reported comments like "Our staff are really committed to showing love, not just giving stuff"[15] and "We care. It is not just a job. We do something good and it feels good to do it."[16]

The implications are significant, providing a strongly positive reason for open, non-discriminatory, non-proselytizing behavior. Love provides the basis for committed and sacrificial service. Love helps explain an embedded, trusted presence within communities. Love stirs up a focus on kingdom values and incubates hope. Love is an inspiring devotional theme that foments social action. Love is a motivation for prayer and helps nurture the transformation of personal and social behaviors.

This unusual implication was consistently and pervasively present throughout the data. One of the downsides of the professionalization of development work has been an emphasis on more theoretical aspects. It is argued that professionalization should not be at the expense of the communication of love or human empathy. When development becomes a theoretical exercise, it will parody those whom it exists to serve. Human connectedness should remain at the center. When it comes to the attainment of development goals, organizations with explicit religious values may be at an advantage. These organizations may be more "permission giving" when it comes to the expression of love through work interactions compared with other types of organizations governed by standard corporate norms. As one worker reported, "[There is] love and compassion within us and we are sending this message along [with] our work within the communities we serve."[17]

The nurturing of love as a characteristic of work life requires spiritual formation, and a reflective, devotional culture. This is a fundamental difference between faith-based development organizations and other types of NGOs. The intentional nurturing of interior life and connecting it with work practice will be unpacked in the next chapter.

A Christian understanding of love demands full commitment to God and others. In a development context, the commandment to love one's neighbors may require not only a solidarity with communities but also a desire to achieve the best possible ministry outcomes on their behalf. In this regard, there can be a harder edge to love. A mature understanding of love may move an organization beyond basic charitable responses into the more difficult territory of justice. Making this vitally important transition is a particular challenge for development organizations, especially when they seek to encourage churches and other faith institutions in this direction. These institutions tend to be socially passive and locked into more traditional responses to need. A deep and patient love may be required to pursue shifts in thinking.

Love is a powerful and universal driver. Any act of love can be an encouragement and a source of hope, and the value of human empathy in undertaking development work should not be underestimated. The Christian faith asserts that God is love, and to show love is to point to God. In this way, development staff may understand their work as a kind of living witness. It is posited that engaging with communities in a loving way aids the development process. When the approach is loving, this is conducive to learning. Such an environment is more likely to be marked by listening, respect, trust, and a true sense of reciprocity.

An FBO should be able to say, without any trace of embarrassment, that its work involves not only professional and practical engagements but also the provision of moral support, human empathy, and the communication of love. This distinction may stand as a corrective to rationalistic approaches, which may be more concerned with the theoretical aspects of project design or the clinical efficiency of an intervention. Even the language of "intervention" can be jarring. A relational, incarnational approach will focus on changes organically from within, involving a full participation. An "intervention" in this light may mean something very different.

A relational/incarnational style of engagement

In a similar way, it is easy to have a commitment to community participation and local empowerment at a rhetorical level. For that to be meaningful requires a long-term presence and deeper relationships. Where development agencies are city-based visitors, a level of mistrust can arise. Living with communities brings first-hand insights, a lived empathy, and greater reciprocity. The data reflected a level of cynicism by communities and faith-based development practitioners toward other models involving reduced or episodic community contact.

It drew a sharp comparison between development organizations that would visit communities for short-term projects and those with an enduring presence. Skepticism was expressed in the community about some secular NGOs that "exist in words only," whose "money often does not get to the most vulnerable" and which maintain only a head office far away in the capital city. A clear contrast was drawn with agencies that were geographically and relationally closer to communities and walked the talk.[18]

Developing communities are sometimes located in remote, impoverished, and fragile settings. To be willing and able to meet this challenge means that work must be seen as more than a job. By understanding work as ministry, the personnel of an organization may have a better chance of sustaining their presence and having an impact. For many staff, the acceptance of hardship was one aspect of the high coefficient between religious motivation and work commitment.

The effect of a highly incarnational and relational style of engagement is to build respect and trust in communities. The data reported: "Other NGOs, where there are any, will come and go, whereas [our] staff are seen as more 'loving and caring,' especially those who live in the communities and suffer the same conditions and challenges."[19] The claim was made: "We are different because we live with the community, these other organizations visit only and go back to their offices or hotels. We are very close to the community; we share plans, budgets, collaborate in the implementation and realize results together."[20] Sacrifice was also sometimes expressed in terms of staff refusing higher-paid jobs and choosing to remain in the communities where they lived and worked. One UN official reported: "The difference between FBOs [and other development organizations] is in the attitude and seriousness in which they do what they do."[21]

A sense of God's presence, and the ability to invoke spiritual strength in a temporal way through prayer, is vital in managing the challenges of community life. While this is relevant to "hardship" settings, it is also important for other contexts. The active spiritual nurture of staff will help maintain prayerful and discerning lives, and will help instill the kind of spiritual resilience and sensitivity needed for an effective development program.

There are important theological emphases here. It can be confidently affirmed that God is the ultimate change agent in the world. He is already active in every community. A faith-based model of development therefore inevitably involves connecting with God's broader redemptive purposes and his existing presence. An active spiritual life is necessary to live out that understanding. Discerning God's presence and seeking his guidance through the Spirit is the heart of the interface between faith and work.

Becoming part of the daily life of a community will be important in building an authentic rapport. In addition, it has some very particular practical advantages. One of the clear advantages is the opportunity to observe up close less obvious needs within communities—for example, the treatment of the disabled.[22] Another example is being able to recognize and appreciate the community's own initiatives and priorities for change, and seeking to incorporate those within development programs.

Incarnation and subsidiarity

An embedded community presence is consistent with the idea of communities participating as fully as possible in the decision-making that affects them. This is an important development principle that helps communities to accept responsibility and be empowered to influence their own future. Development should be a community-led and participatory process. It is disempowering and condescending to assume that communities do not know how to act in their own best interests. The principle of subsidiarity asserts that decisions should be made at the lowest possible level in a decision-making hierarchy. In this way, responsibility can be devolved to those who are most directly impacted. "The characteristic implication of subsidiarity is participation..."[23]

The exercise of agency by the community itself will help build its own capacity in the longer run. The corporate expression of work as ministry is participatory, inclusive, community-based decision-making. Theologically, it involves respecting the value of the other under God, and resisting the asymmetric exercise of power that has been typical of so many development programs. Faith-based organizations should be especially sensitive to issues concerning the exercise of power. A humble, learning, and serving posture—one that promotes the dignity of the other and seeks the common good—is advised.

The values that are accented within organizational life really do matter. History is replete with instances of "development" work that is imposed, disempowering, and socially divisive. An accountability to God, and a downward accountability to the poor, will be willingly embraced by serious faith-based development organizations. This is discussed in more detail in chapter 14.

Risks from being too exclusive in employment

The understanding of work as ministry creates and exposes a tension. On the one hand, Christian faith is an embodied faith. It is therefore appropriate and necessary for FBOs to recruit staff who are able to fully embrace and live out the organization's mandates. Staff with a lively personal Christian faith are essential to do this. The contribution of faith to faith-based development is not a negotiable extra but a defining feature.

On the other hand, the Christian faith is one that welcomes fellow travelers. It is inclusive and gracious religion that recognizes that all people are gifted by God. Working at an FBO may stimulate a person in his or her own spiritual journey. It is abundantly clear that God can use anyone to fulfill his purposes, and this is evidenced by many unlikely candidates in scripture used in important ways.[24] That said, it is going too far to turn the inscrutability of God into some kind of normative assumption that personal faith is unimportant in recruitment. The position arrived at is a tension that needs to be negotiated.

The data indicated that there were some clear advantages to be gained from the hiring of non-Christian staff in some contexts. Hiring more non-Christian staff could leverage development advantages in mixed religious communities by fostering greater understanding, demonstrating goodwill, and modeling positive working relationships. In Lebanon, for example, the data indicated that 60 percent of the community was Muslim, but 99 percent of staff were Christian.[25] For some, this was difficult to reconcile when the organization emphasized inclusion and tolerance as important development goals. Similarly, there can be a dissonance between the organization's policy of not discriminating on the basis of faith in its field work while doing exactly the opposite in its own employment.[26] In many contexts non-Christians will better represent community perspectives and be able to offer alternative ways of thinking.

The problem of abandoning or softening faith criteria in hiring is the dilution of the organization's Christian identity. This can easily happen by including too many people who do not specifically proclaim

Christian faith in leadership positions. It may lead to overly permissive or subjective interpretation of what it means to be a Christian organization, ultimately diluting or eroding any distinctive development praxis.[27] This book attempts to demonstrate that Christian faith infuses the work of faith-based development organizations in a variety of fundamental ways. There are no easy answers.

Understanding work as a ministry has very significant implications for individuals and for the faith-based development agencies for which they work. Sustaining a vibrant understanding of work as ministry is partly a function of organizational culture. It requires a level of intentionality and investment, as discussed in the next chapter.

CHAPTER 8

A Devotional, Reflective Culture

The ultimate locus of truth for faith-based development organizations is the revelation of God. Recognizing the vital role of science and technology in their work, they will take "light from the Enlightenment" but without becoming captive to modernity. A devotional practice will be cultivated that overarches all the organization's activities. This is necessary to help center the organization on its foundations and to build a distinctive practice. Spiritual life will be recognized as a powerful asset alongside human and economic resources. It will be given an openness and legitimacy in organizational life. This will affect work patterns, the conceptualization of development programs, and staff and community relationships.

To help staff fulfill their ministry requires teaching, encouragement, and spiritual replenishment. Scheduled corporate devotional times are a defining cultural feature of many faith-based development organizations and may be considered the *sine qua non* of spiritual nurture of staff. In restrictive contexts, such as strict Islamic contexts where freedom of religion is sometimes curtailed, a special accommodation may be required to support personnel in Christian worship, spiritual nurture, Bible study, prayer, fellowship, and pastoral support.[1]

Devotional practice will vary in length and frequency between organizations. Typical ingredients include worship or worshipful reflection, a time for corporate prayer, and a teaching or motivational address usually in the form of a short homily or sermon. Importantly, corporate devotions will be highly contextualized. For example the data showed that in East African settings, devotions are usually at least one hour in length, and are held three to four times a week. These are very vibrant gatherings, with singing and praise-filled worship in keeping with local culture. By contrast, in Georgia, where most of the staff were affiliated with the Georgian Orthodox Church, fortnightly devotions were more liturgical and were led by an invited Orthodox priest. This is because the Orthodox tradition requires that public prayer be offered through a priest.

External speakers, such as local pastors or clergy, may be invited to take part in the devotional life of some organizations, addressing staff on a topical issue or Bible passage. Most often internal staff will lead the proceedings. Where the organization is ecumenical, sacraments are not generally offered at devotional times. This is because it would create confusion regarding the role of the churches and may offend some denominational understandings. Devotions may also take place at a local project level, with the responsibility for preparing and leading these devotions shared among staff. In my own visits to projects I have been asked to fulfill this role.

In mixed-faith settings, the conduct of corporate devotions can have particular challenges. Here there may be a tension between seeking to affirm the Christian identity of the organization and supporting its Christian staff while not wishing to exclude or make non-Christian staff feel judged. An interesting range of local compromises and innovations can apply. The voluntary nature of devotional times means that staff from other faiths may occasionally attend as an expression of collegial goodwill or to sometimes learn more about the Christian beliefs underpinning the organization. While the fundamental purpose of corporate devotions remains Christian spiritual reflection, there are also opportunities for teaching, especially on topical themes related to development work.

Understanding the internal dimension of development work

The hardest development challenges are those that lie within. It is important for development work to be personally transformative. For development practitioners, going through a process of reflection is a necessary step in order for them to model the kind of changes they aspire to see.

A consistent spiritually based interiority is a distinguishing feature of many faith-based development organizations. This is because devotional times are concerned with integration and change at a personal level. In this regard, some organizations have pre-empted suggestions from some of the world's most eminent development theorists. For example, Michael Edwards and Gita Sen have written about the need for personal integration by development practitioners.[2] They argue that "even the socially committed will be unsuccessful if they ignore the inner basis of change,"[3] and declare that "if people are not caring and compassionate in their personal behavior, they are unlikely to work effectively for a caring and compassionate society."[4] In their analysis, rarely do empowerment strategies generate the shifts in inner values that are needed to be truly effective.[5] Robert Chambers has similarly decried the hypocrisy of some development practitioners, noting that personal behaviors and attitudes are a peculiar blind spot.[6] He comments that practitioners find it extremely difficult to cede any responsibility or power, contradicting their own rhetoric.[7]

Faith-based development organizations certainly know that development cannot be disconnected from the interior world. Beliefs, attitudes, and critical self-awareness are just as important as those interventions that alter the physical world. This statement intuitively rings true. It also helps to explain the failure of countless development projects that have paid too little attention to the quality of ongoing human relationships within communities. I recall that in Rwanda I once made an innocent comment that provoked a salutary response from the driver of the car in which I was traveling. I remarked on a shiny new school building that I observed as we passed by. The driver, a Tutsi, quickly reminded me that the building in question could be torn down tomorrow in civil unrest. He asserted that the greater development challenge in Rwanda was not education, but people learning how to live with each other.

An appropriate emphasis needs to be given to the topic of inner change. In many organizations this is a highly sensitive area; it touches upon personal values and therefore is kept at arm's length. Faith-based organizations are not so reticent. They know that while education and training are undoubtedly helpful in challenging personal values, spiritual engagement can anchor the process. An active religious faith involves the relational claims of God and neighbor. These relational claims may help bring good values to life in a more concrete way. This is part of the rationale for having a devotional program.

The intensification of religious faith in the Global South has the potential to be of significant benefit to developing communities, because it offers a platform to help change social attitudes and behaviors. Transformative change can happen when people purposefully connect with their deepest source of meaning. Devotional programs run by faith-based development organizations are one important element in bringing about personal change.

Distinctiveness based on structured, internal, reflective practice

Secular development organizations may also encourage critical reflection based on universal values, human rights, and the attainment of justice. The key difference, however, is that they do not see these emphases as deriving from, or responding to, the call of God. It follows that there are no officially sanctioned devotional or other spiritually based rituals or practices in their workplaces to positively reinforce values. Secular organizations do not explicitly link internal formation and exterior change in the same way, and they tend to adopt standard corporate rather than religious norms within organizational life. Religious positions tend to be seen as a private matter, with no legitimate place in a work environment.

By contrast, there are many aspects to the overarching spiritual narrative of FBOs that are reflected in work life. Staff are recruited, inducted, mobilized, and encouraged on the basis of their faith or acceptance of its specific faith-based values. It is a huge advantage to explicitly and openly link private motivations with the organization's development practice. In this way, a distinctive community of practice can be established and maintained.

Critically, the integration of faith and development will be articulated and reinforced through structured devotional practices. There will be a consistent emphasis on personal and civic formation based on religious values and ethics. Inner regeneration will be emphasized as vital for sustainable change. Discernment will have a role to play in the organization's work.

It will not be unusual for meetings to open and close in prayer. There may be a shared understanding about working for the kingdom of God and living out its values. Christian staff will be encouraged to serve the local church and to celebrate with the community the many blessings of God. There will also be the constant inspiration of sacred scripture, which will inform work practice in all sorts of ways as detailed below.

The resonances between scripture and development practice

In framing development work, the general ethic of altruism found in most of the world's major religions[8] together with other foundational values such as solidarity, love, justice, trust, and hope are important. The existence of such values within religious teaching may represent a significant asset that can be deployed. A strength-based approach to development will look for those assets that exist within a community and can be harnessed to help achieve development goals. Although a community's faith and theology are not normally thought of in this light, they may provide impetus and direction for development initiatives. Sustainable development can happen only if people build on and from their own resources. For the Majority World, these include spiritual resources.[9] Specifically, Christian theology has the potential to be the basis of many programmatic tools.

Bible study and reflection will be an important feature of the internal devotional life of faith-based development organizations. The Christian faith is a revealed faith. In epistemological terms, sacred scripture is seen as revealing the character and redemptive purposes of God and providing a window into the life of Jesus Christ. For many staff who seek to follow Jesus, biblical reflection is therefore an essential source of truth and meaning. The New Testament contains the earliest authoritative written depiction of the emergence of the Christian faith. While there are critical hermeneutical issues in interpreting the life of Jesus,[10] there are in scripture many general themes that may have strong resonances within development contexts. Some instances worthy of consideration are briefly listed:

- The way Jesus is depicted as welcoming and valuing children arguably speaks to the rights of children.[11]

- Jesus' defiance of patriarchal cultural norms indicates a different understanding of gender relationships.[12]

- Interdependence and inclusion appear to be modeled in the strong communitarian values of the earliest faith communities.[13]

- Organized, non-discriminatory food distributions, such as those described in the Book of Acts, may anticipate later humanitarian principles.[14]

- When Jesus speaks and acts prophetically, this focuses attention on advocacy as a potential way of overcoming injustice.[15]

- By touching the lepers, Jesus resists the stigmatization of a disadvantaged minority.[16]

- The injunction to care for widows and orphans provides a reminder about human obligation towards the most vulnerable.[17]

Scripture also contains accounts of Jesus affirming the humanity of the disabled[18] and welcoming the outcast.[19] He appears to heal in multiple ways and on multiple levels.[20] There are repeated challenges to the wealthy and the powerful, challenges that have been championed by the social justice traditions in the church.[21] Especially topical are broad biblical motifs that speak about stewardship of resources and care for the environment.[22] Similarly, in a world of transmigration, we recall that Jesus' own story includes the experience of being in a refugee family, and we note his radical teaching about who is our neighbor.[23] His disciples are commanded to live simply and are mobilized as a kind of agile social movement.[24] While Jesus is sometimes depicted as engaging in acts of symbolic protest, he does not indulge in retaliatory actions.[25] Peace-building is praised,[26] forgiveness is commanded,[27] and Jesus (arguably) supremely models reconciliation in his death and resurrection.[28] There is also a rich body of teachings about justice,[29] inclusion,[30] honesty,[31] and hard work.[32]

Overarching all of this is the constant refrain about the coming kingdom of God in which all things will be put right. This is a powerful vision of an alternative future, providing encouragement to the persecuted, the oppressed, and the disenfranchised.[33] And the image of Jesus, lived in firm solidarity with those on the margins,[34] may model what it means to incarnate hope among the vulnerable.

What do these resonances imply? It is suggested that where a community has an affiliation with the Christian faith, this may itself be a latent asset in pursing development goals. Civic participation in the form of regular church attendance can also present opportunities for learning and mobilization. It follows that an applied Christian faith has the potential to be a strategic asset in undertaking development work in such contexts. Having said that, the hermeneutical challenges must not be downplayed, because there are egregious examples where scripture has been misused to support patriarchal, discriminatory, or triumphalist agendas.

Researchers have identified four key areas where religious beliefs may intersect, sympathetically or otherwise, with development goals: conflict prevention and peace-building, governance, wealth creation and production, and health and education. One example that draws on Christian faith principles is the work of the South African Truth and Reconciliation Commission, which is "based on the idea that long term reconciliation depends crucially on religious notions of reconciliation and healing, even in the absence of formal justice."[35] Another is the reintegration of child soldiers into society in Sierra Leone by rituals associated with charismatic Christianity that are evocative of traditional initiation ceremonies. The teachings of other faiths may also support key development themes; it seems neglectful to not explore those points of intersection that may be conducive to the attainment of development goals within communities.

Devotional life—an indulgence for the pious?

An organization's devotional life can contribute to the quality of its work in multiple ways. Development workers can work in tough environments with all kinds of challenges. Devotional activities may be a source of inner strength and inspiration. This kind of spiritual nurture may be essential in carrying out development tasks. Devotional activities "contribute to increased staff awareness and consciousness of God's presence"[36] and provide "access to information which helps your inner self."[37]

A devotional program will also help in enculturating the kind of values that an organization aspires to. These are usually values associated with the kingdom of God. A key output from devotional activities is to build personal attributes that are helpful when serving within communities. A final aspect is the purposeful integration of devotional teaching into daily work-life. Devotional teaching can engage staff in critical thinking about the best way to do things. Over time, this type of sharing provides approaches and exmples to draw on in daily work.[38] This can lead to excellence in field outcomes.

Taking this suite of advantages as a whole means that a devotional program should not be seen as tangential or an extracurricular option for pious staff; it can be the foundation of a distinctive and effective culture. Where this is so, faith will be seen "as more than just a religious activity or an expression of personal piety, but as something which directly informs daily life and work."[39]

Stronger teams

A devotional life also contributes to development work by building stronger teams and a shared sense of mission. Teamwork can take off when staff members begin to connect on a spiritual level.[40] It makes sense that a development organization's work will be strengthened when staff have a unified vision. This is consistent with general research into development organizations. Rick James's research into the distinctiveness of FBOs confirms that "organizations are more effective if they have a clear identity and their beliefs and values permeate throughout their organization."[41] A separate study of effective American FBOs in the aid and development sector likewise noted that the coherence of the culture, at a level of substance, was essential.[42] In other words, where an organization's identity is clear and embedded, the more effective it is likely to be.[43] Sharing a faith identity or similar faith ideals can be a potent asset. Conflicts are likely to be reduced where employees have shared cognitive premises leading to a more cohesive culture. Devotional activities help reinforce those premises.

We do not have to look far to see examples of Christian workplaces that are highly dysfunctional. They can be judgmental, excluding, legalistic, and full of sectarian tension. It is important to understand that the encouragement of devotional practice is no guarantee of worthy behavior. When approached in the right spirit, however, a devotional program may provide a way of encouraging critical self-reflection and a shared vision under God.

Modeling to the broader community

The intentional modeling of inclusion and respect within devotional life can provide a positive example for staff and the broader community. In this way, an internal devotional life can illustrate what an organization aspires to in its development work. Devotions can be a safe place to learn about others and show respect.

As one example, World Vision permits common prayer between Christians and Muslims. Due care must be taken, and sensitivity is required, especially when Christians are praying in a mixed audience. To refer to "Jesus as *Word of God* is acceptable, but not as *Son of God.*"[44] It is also acceptable to pray in the name of Jesus, and to use The Lord's Prayer and Muslim Fatiha.[45] While World Vision sees itself as a distinctly Christian organization and does not allow its resources to be used to promote other faiths, it certainly does seek to establish common theological ground in conducting its development work. Muslim staff reported that they had a way to serve the Prophet through development activity.

An important point is that the Christian faith is known and has a recognized status within Islam. The Islamic faith claims successive revelations from God, first to the Jews in the Torah, later through the Prophet Jesus, and ultimately and definitively through the Last Prophet, Mohammed. Broadly, Christians are acknowledged as an Abrahamic faith and are referred to in the Koran as a "People of the Book." The data suggested that this status helped organizations position themselves in their development work in some Muslim contexts.

An organization's devotional life can be a source of cohesion for surrounding communities. It enables staff to get to know each other better and to model respectful interfaith and interdenominational relationships. A devotional program can increase the faith-literacy of staff about other religious traditions, as recommended by some commentators.[46] The majority of staff in most field settings will be drawn from the surrounding community; their participation in the organization's devotional program enables them to take back a positive example to their family and friends.

With care, devotional activities can be undertaken in an inclusive manner in mixed-faith communities without compromising core Christian beliefs. This requires a level of intentionality, sensitivity, and careful design. It is possible to accent those shared theological motifs relevant to development work and to pray together using acceptable forms that do not offend or embarrass. A benefit of a devotional program is to show the community that it is serious about religious faith by placing an emphasis on internal devotional practices. This can gain kudos and goodwill.

An aspect of every devotional program will be to submit the organization, its staff, and its programs to the blessing and protection of God. In this way, a stand is taken against the presence and influence of evil in the world. This bring us to the topic of the next chapter.

CHAPTER 9

Standing against Evil

Living for the kingdom has its corollary in standing against evil, as anything that dehumanizes and diminishes the fullness of life must be opposed. It has been observed that "The modern idea of development may be seen...as the secular translation of a millenarian belief, once general in Europe, concerning the construction of a perfect world. Inherent in this thinking is an aspiration to eliminate evil in all its forms from the earth..."[1] For the Christian, evil signifies the absence of the reign of God. It refers to everything that opposes God's will, debases his creation, or dehumanizes people. An orthodox Christian faith recognizes the reality of evil, which impacts our world. Any development paradigm that does not take a realistic account of evil will, by definition, be inadequate. Faith-based development organizations look forward to a time when evil is finally overcome and creation is renewed as God intended.

There are different understandings about how evil influences the world. Some approaches stress "structural" evil, such as oppressive systems, others more personalized manifestations of evil, and still others highly speculative understandings. While there may sometimes be disagreements about the "*how*" of evil, there is broad agreement within every catechism of the Christian church about its present reality. This includes its broader social impacts.

Broadly speaking, the *raison d'être* of all faith-based development agencies is to overcome the evil of poverty. Faith-based development organizations will stand in the prophetic tradition denouncing all systems that hold people captive and diminish their humanity. Some of the corporate manifestations of evil that rob people of their fullness of life include developing country debt, child trafficking, slavery, child labor, institutional corruption, military aggression, ethnic "cleansings," land seizures, gender discrimination, and unfair global trade terms. The Christian faith requires the denunciation of all that destroys or takes away life; anti-gods by whatever name must be challenged.

When it comes to influencing public policy and claiming human rights, this process has been framed in the development lexicon as *advocacy*. For FBOs this will be the most common method of taking a prophetic stand against evil. A part of that process may require encouraging the church or its supporters to become more socially engaged. In recent years, faith-based agencies have become much better organized in seeking to influence public policy. Some have dedicated advocacy departments or personnel. This has marked a significant shift away from traditional charitable and compassionate roles.

While some Christian faith traditions are deeply reticent about political engagement, this seems unavoidable if the causes of poverty are to be seriously addressed. The willingness to speak prophetically against evil, especially in its structural or corporate forms, reflects a growing understanding of the biblical call to justice. Some organizations have been influenced by a political hermeneutic in seeking to characterize the life and ministry of Christ. It is certainly difficult to read the gospels and step around their many political and prophetic undercurrents. An increased commitment to justice and activism in the name of Christ can reflect an organizational maturing.[2] This involves wrestling with a less domesticated Christ who refuses to be accommodated to the world around him.

In relation to more personal understandings of evil, Bryant Myers complains that the modern story of the West has simply no answer.[3] He suggests that development practitioners need to overcome their blind spot in terms of the spiritual world.[4] It is interesting that the developing world does not share Western sensibilities around this issue: "The poor often live in fear of an unseen spiritual world of curses, gods, demons and ancestors,"[5] which may have a deep, ongoing, and destructive impact on their lives. It follows that "accepting local worldviews uncritically is sometimes a source of poverty, not an answer to it."[6]

Christian theology affirms that evil has been conquered in the death and resurrection of Jesus Christ, and that evil must, in the final analysis, yield to the reign of God. The power of prayer in responding to evil is a matter of general acceptance within the Christian faith. The famous dictum of philosopher C. S. Lewis also offers some useful guidance: "There are two equal and opposite errors into which our race can fall about the devils. One is to disbelieve in their existence. The other is to believe, and to feel an excessive and unhealthy interest in them."[7]

It is suggested that where a Christian development organization is uninformed about this topic, it will be delinquent in taking its work seriously. On the other hand, a preoccupation will mean missed opportunities for positive change. A great deal of wisdom is needed in this area.[8]

Cultural insensitivity and imperialism?

This topic, perhaps more than any other, shows that ideas about development are contested. Christians believe that personhood involves a spiritual dimension. Most of the developing world is in fervent agreement about this. An overwhelming number of people living in developing communities hold strong religious beliefs and engage in religious practices of one sort or another. It seems an extraordinary conceit to suppose that real community development can occur without engaging with the beliefs and practices that matter to the poor. As surprising as it might seem, that has been the general thrust of Western-inspired development work since its inception.

A broader concept of personhood means that spiritual and religious life will be taken seriously. Any development paradigm that denies full personhood is deficient. The social identity of a person in much of the developing world will be intertwined with his or her religious identity. Only when religious or spiritual life is fully acknowledged as a part of human existence can its impact be properly assessed and critiqued.

One pervasive assumption that has led to the sidelining of religious practice from development discourse is that all cultures and belief systems are equal. This leads to reluctance to examine particular faith practices. They tend to be seen as a "no go" area. If they are examined, it may be considered disrespectful to seek to override or challenge local views, as this may provoke accusations of arrogance, insensitivity, or imperialism.

On some occasions the cultural relativism that infects so much development theory can be a dangerous thing. It can mask or excuse real harm to people. There are aspects of all cultures, including our own, that should be challenged and critiqued. There is no good reason why religious or spiritual practices should be beyond censure. Christians believe in a God who wants to see fullness of life for all people. When a Christian is exposed to beliefs or practices that damage human wellbeing they are affronted, just as surely as their Creator is.

It is important to note that I am not talking here about religions or belief systems as a whole. I have already argued that the values of the kingdom of God require a firm commitment to respect, peace, and understanding between different religious faiths. I am saying, however, that there are specific practices that diminish human flourishing, and these should not be ignored because of some misplaced notion of anthropological or sociological neutrality. A hard dialogue that actively seeks to change damaging behaviors may be required.

The broader view of development as understood by FBOs will recognize the influence of malign or oppressive spiritual practices. These organizations may seek to challenge influences that they see as debilitating, harmful, or dehumanizing. Listed below are some very simple examples showing the connection between spiritual beliefs and their development impact.

- Not drinking from wells believed to be haunted. The development impact is an insufficiency of potable water.

- Not farming fields believed to be inhabited by woodland spirits. The development impact is less arable land and reduced food security.

- Not using an enclosed pit latrine because of the fear malign spirits may be trapped. The development impact is compromised community health.

- Not sleeping under iron sheeting out of fear of possession (associated with the loud noise when it rains). The development impact is that a cheap, strong building material is not used.

- Reliance on traditional magic healers. The development impact is children not receiving proper medical attention.

- Enslavement to secret ritual practices or fetishes. The development impact is community fear and oppression. "These people worry 'If I leave the spirits, they will kill me.'"[9]

- The labeling of people as witches. The development impact is stigmatization and discrimination, often of vulnerable older women.

- Believing albinos to be cursed. The development impact is social exclusion and personal hardship.

There are many other examples that could be offered. These few are sufficient to illustrate the kind of linkages. It would be arrogant and wrong to assume that Christian doctrine is immune from abuse. It isn't. Two common examples with profound development impacts are:

- Believing HIV/AIDS to be God's punishment. The development impact is stigmatization, judgment, and lack of community support for people living with the virus.

- Ill-informed "male headship" teaching. The development impact may be marginalization of women's voices and, in some cases, overlooking domestic violence.

In short, FBOs will not accept local culture uncritically and will find it necessary to make judgments about aspects of spiritual or religious practice that are incompatible with the vision of fullness of life that God gives us. This may be seen by some as disrespectful to local culture and a form of imperialism.

Overcoming evil from within mainstream religious traditions

A typical way FBOs stand against injustices is through localized and targeted advocacy that is often framed theologically. The data revealed an interesting example of a local Children's Committee which had been set up to hear children's voices and to promote human rights. It showed that, from early childhood, faith and rights were intimately entwined. For example, one child stated: "We are children and have rights, desires, wishes and opportunity to worship God and please God as human beings"; a second girl shared the way the story of Esther in the Bible was used to claim rights to education and protection from female genital mutilation (FGM) and early marriage; and one Muslim boy "shared a story from the Quran which encouraged other children to pursue education no matter what the cost..."[10]

In Senegal, data again illustrated practical advocacy through youth and children's clubs. The foundation for that advocacy was an appeal to the principles of either the Christian or Islamic faiths. Issues confronted in this way included children being taken out of school early, under-age girls being married off to older men, sons working the fields instead of pursing an education, and the dangers of mistreatment of children by marabouts (Koranic teachers who sometimes exploit their pupils by treating them very harshly or forcing them into street begging to raise funds.)[11]

Increasingly, faith-based development organizations see themselves standing within the prophetic tradition, naming and challenging systemic injustices evident from within their local contexts. Their role may include the creation of structures so that children's voices can be heard. In parts of Africa, it can be more effective for advocacy messages to be articulated as an appeal based on religious principles, because religious faith infuses all aspects of life. Otherwise, the human rights dialogue may be seen as an abstract Western construct with no relatable frame of reference.

Encountering the demonic

Evil is sometimes to be found in cultural practices, particularly those associated with the demonic or occult. These kinds of cultural practices are largely unfamiliar to many Western audiences, except perhaps through sensationalized or fictionalized accounts in the media or as the subject of lurid entertainment. The kinds of practices I am referring to include child sacrifice, mutilation carried out by shamans, child killing, beliefs about people with HIV or AIDs being "bewitched," demonic possession, mutilation, and "cuttings."[12]

It is difficult to know how to respond to these accounts. In the data, staff attributed some phenomena, at least in part, to the direct influence of evil: "To kill one Tutsi child in a church with a machete because of government intimidation and encouragement was certainly an act of evil. But to then go on and slaughter a whole roomful of forty children—with the blood and screaming and physical effort that would involve—can only be described as demonic."[13] It is precisely at this juncture that any rational analysis is strained.

At one level it is easy to simply report what others have said and claimed. The trouble is that this topic quickly moves beyond the empirical, entering territory that eludes rational analysis. A spiritual worldview necessarily recognizes a broader range of influences. We should not be surprised by this. All the world's major religions explicitly affirm those influences. The data attributed some behaviors and phenomena to a malign spiritual influence. Faith-based agencies may respond in terms of their own spiritual frame of reference. For example, the data reported instances of development staff being approached by community members to deal with cases of demonic oppression.

The data also indicated the active discouragement of traditional practices by cooperating with Muslim leaders and institutions. It was stated that "the issue is not Christian vs. Muslim, it is overcoming animism and syncretism."[14] As one imam put it, "most people in Senegal are Muslims or Christian, it doesn't matter which one as long as they have faith." This meant mainstream religion, not traditional beliefs. The real problem was described as overcoming fear at the community level. In terms of specific development challenges, "lack of food, rights, justice and health are seen as a direct result of evil and spirits—the root cause of all poverty in their worldview."[15]

The example of African Traditional Religion

Faith-based development organizations will share common ground with human-rights approaches in relation to a range of matters such as FGM, gender inequality, and child protection. However, their approach to development may go somewhat further by objecting to a range of religious and cultural practices considered to debilitate communities through fear and superstition. While they will uphold freedom of religion, agencies may actively discourage certain harmful practices and will form community coalitions against them. This kind of approach is intended to help people experience fullness of life.

The data indicated the impossibility of segregating faith and belief from daily development challenges. It is clear that Africans generally do not separate physical, economic, or social issues from the spiritual life. Their worldview is a highly integrated one. This poses a methodological problem for development organizations that have a secular, modern worldview as their basis of operation. Such organizations may be unable to grapple with community development in a more holistic and integrated way, addressing the linkages between all aspects of wellbeing.

The data was highly consistent with the description of African Traditional Religion (ATR) described by researchers Namawu Alolo and James Connell in their largely sympathetic account.[16] I am using the term ATR because the negative or pejorative connotations of the term "animism" may be problematic for some readers.[17] However, it is contested in the literature whether such a thing as ATR exists.[18] Some say ATR covers multiple religions, others say they are all just variants on the same basic theme.[19] A glaring deficiency is that there has been scarcely any empirical research looking at the role of ATR in development (or its related or derivative systems), especially as there are up to one hundred million adherents in Africa.[20]

Undoubtedly there is strong prejudice against ATR based on colonial, missionary, and anthropological reports from the eighteenth and nineteenth centuries. This prejudice led to a bad reputation.[21] Some argue that ATR is notable precisely because of its ordinariness as a religion rather than its bizarre or lurid aspects. It is claimed ATR performs a legitimate and proper function in the ordering of society.

However, it is not denied that ATR can be associated with witchcraft, sacrifice and *muti* killings, although media reports may be exaggerated because they play to public prejudices.[22] Nonetheless, researchers are very open in pointing out that the use of development terms like *inclusion* and *indigenous rights* "tends to suspend their often contentious meanings" and mask highly problematic activities.[23] It is clear that ATR does emphasize ancestors and spirits of the departed as exerting influence over the present world, and arcane rituals are involved to invoke these forces for good or evil.

ATR is ordinary in the sense that it seeks to explain daily life by reference to an invisible spirit world with transcendent influences. In that sense it is similar to many other religions.[24] A significant point of departure, however, is that the Christian conception of God looks to his unchanging character and revelation as a stable source of morals and ethics. "God," as conceived in ATR, is often indifferent to the mortal world and may even be seen as hostile to it. Spirits and ancestors, especially the more recently departed "living dead," are the adjudicators of ethical, legal, and moral problems. The dispersal of responsibility in this unwritten, loosely structured, and localized belief system has led to understandings of ATR as anarchic or amoral.[25]

Resisting evil is the direct corollary of seeking the reign of God. For faith-based development organizations, this involves systematic advocacy against local injustices. Such efforts may be framed as theological appeals within mainstream religious traditions, especially in African settings. Naming and challenging the demonic can be a part of the ministry of some organizations. Faith-based development organizations will position themselves against practices, including spiritually based rites or understandings, that present a risk to personal and community wellbeing. This will place them firmly at odds with the cultural relativism underlying some post-modern development theories. Those defending ATR have noted that development buzzwords can mask more grisly realities.[26]

Standing against corruption

Corruption is a major impediment to development in many countries. It exists in many forms, including misuse of influence, cronyism, nepotism, bribery, kick-backs, and the lack of merit-based decision-making in commercial dealings. Kingdom-based values contribute to development by standing firmly against corruption. Christian ethics, at a minimum, require commitment to honesty, openness, and fairness.

There is no doubt that those FBOs that eschew corrupt behavior can be a powerful witness. The consistent application of professional and ethical standards may stand in sharp contrast to the corruption rife in the surrounding community.[27] The data gave the example of people who tried to offer bribes but gave up when they eventually saw that that the organization "was different from the usual."[28] Another personal account came from Rwanda. A project manager reported, "I was tested. The local mayor tried to bribe me. He said to me, 'All this money for these projects, and you let it slip through your fingers?' He said, 'You could offer food for work, pay less, and keep a percentage for yourself.' I had to tell him this was against my beliefs... [we] didn't do this sort of thing."[29]

An unequivocal stand against corruption will almost always receive strong community support. It models good behavior and builds trust. While many community members may personally oppose corruption, it may be accepted fatalistically as an inevitable part of life. When an organization models a different approach, this unlocks community goodwill. It is hypothesized that faith-based development organizations are perceived as less corrupt (whether they are or not), consistent with the general view that they are serious and ethical in their work.

There is little empirical data to indicate whether they are more trust-worthy than secular organizations in relation to the issue of corruption.[30] Thus far, researchers have not uncovered any definitive causal relationship, either positive or negative, between religious belief and corrupt behavior.[31] While it is a reasonable (and intuitive) assumption that personal commitment to religious ideals like honesty and fairness—and a belief in divine sanctions—*ought* to militate against corruption, this is not necessarily the case. The causal factors appear to be very complex, including personal economic factors, the type of behavior in question, the way kinship loyalties are expressed, the type of religion involved, the level of social opprobrium attached to particular types of conduct, and the general prevalence of corruption within the surrounding society.

One thing is for sure. Faith-based organizations need to make every effort to counter the evil of corruption and to lead by example. There is an opportunity to earn trust and respect by unequivocal faithfulness in this area. Internal transformations may help achieve this goal, and it is to this topic that we now turn.

CHAPTER 10

The Imperative of Inner Transformation

For a development approach to be truly holistic it must also address the topic of inner change. Christians know that human sinfulness affects the way people deal with each other. Conflicts, violence, mistrust, and enmity all come from within. Sustainable change is simply not possible without changing the way power is exercised in human relationships and in the world. In this respect, the human heart can represent the most stubborn development challenge. God's Spirit is needed to teach humans how to exercise power in godly ways, to uphold the dignity of others, and to give and receive forgiveness where there is error. This kind of internal transfiguring can have a profound impact, which is possible because God gives us the capacity to live according to his ways.

When people learn to live more closely as God intended, this will blossom in the renewal of community. According to Walter Brueggemann, this lies at the heart of the gospel and represents the goodness of the Good News: "The gospel is the news that distorted patterns of power have been broken: the reception of the gospel is the embrace of radically transformed patterns of social relationships."[1] This kind of deeper transformation requires more than shallow pietism. It is a movement of God, an act of grace. For this reason it has been argued that "To restore our humanity *completely* is to restore us in the image of our Maker...To carry out 'development' which does not potentially lead to a reestablished relationship with the Ruler of all the universe is to carry out development that is sub-Christian."[2] A commentator from the Christian relief and development agency Tearfund UK put it this way: "In the last analysis, no theory of practice that ignores our relationship with God can give us a true picture of what meaningful human life is."[3] The Christian hope is for "the reign of God in the whole created order, *including ourselves*."[4]

It has been mentioned elsewhere that the idea of inner change is starting to find its way into more mainstream development discourse.

Development theorists Michael Edwards and Gita Sen argue that development practitioners must acknowledge that "personal or inner change and social or outer change are inseparably linked."[5] They argue that increased cooperation between humans underpins all sustainable development, and this requires fundamentally "something different" in the practitioner's inner experience. Support for this view can come from surprising sources. A noted atheist in a column in *The Times* has observed: "In Africa Christianity changes people's hearts. It brings a spiritual transformation. The rebirth is real. The change is good... Those who want Africa to walk tall amid 21st century global competition must not kid themselves that providing the material means will make the change. A whole belief system must be supplanted."[6]

This starts by challenging the way the poor understand themselves. Roman Catholic theologian Daniel Groody believes that "sometimes personal liberation involves helping the poor to change the way they think about themselves, especially when they see their conditions as fate, or worse, as divinely ordained."[7] In a similar vein, development theorist Paulo Freire speaks in terms of the "conscientization of the poor," by which he refers to the fact that "if the poor do not change their self-perception, they will never be free."[8] Indian theologian Jayakumar Christian frequently speaks of transcending the "marred identity" of the poor.[9] A conversion on this level means "rediscovering the original design of creation in which people are called to be free, dignified, and loving human beings."[10]

While many Christians acknowledge a general responsibility to explain their faith, proselytism[11] remains problematic. The Christian gospel is one of grace. Pope Benedict XVI has counseled: "Charity, furthermore, cannot be used as a means of engaging in what is nowadays considered proselytism. Love is free; it is not practiced as a way of achieving other ends."[12]

This leaves the faith-based development organizations with something of a dilemma. How can it go about the essential work of inner transformation without setting out with an explicit agenda to convert people? One pathway is to conduct training and other programs that inculcate strong civic values. While these may be helpful and constructive, such courses are not a substitute for faith in the living God.[13] Socializing a set of good values may not be enough, especially in relation to people who hold religious worldviews. Values need to be brought to life in changed patterns of behavior. Faith-based organizations know this can happen when the relational claims of the Creator God are taken personally and seriously.

In the end, the staff of FBOs live with the ongoing mystery of not knowing the beginning or end of the work of God's Spirit, especially with people from other faith traditions. They continue to act in faith, praying that God will enliven and embed all those things that belong to him. Faith-based organizations pursue the goal of inner transformation through all ethical means, knowing that it is God on whom they must rely to complete their task.

Morals and values formation in development work

There is a wide range of techniques available to FBOs interested in pursuing an agenda of inner transformation. These include values-based training programs, running children's and family clubs, camping programs for youth, and working with churches and religious institutions to develop their own curricula around development issues. Agencies can also work with schools and community groups interested in values formation. These activities are seen as developmental because they improve self-confidence, connect people with their heritage, inculcate ethical frameworks, bolster community spirit, provide relevant social skills, and build personal and social meanings.

A question may be raised about the difference between community development and soft evangelism. At what point does a program stray from civic formation into Christian discipleship? Does it make a difference if the community already has a religious faith that is simply being "leveraged" to achieve a development goal? "Development" may take on different meanings depending on who is undertaking it. Measured in terms of outcomes, the kinds of programs I have mentioned can be very effective in inculcating educational, ethical, and civic responsibilities.

The use of religious teaching within existing faith communities is a valid and expanding strategy in doing development work. Faith-based development organizations know that religious convictions can provide a solid foundation in securing sustained social change. Some would argue that it is delinquent to not make effective use of available assets—such as religious teaching and infrastructure—when pursuing development goals. Critics may argue that the introduction of any kind of evangelistic emphasis places the idea of "development" at risk. The result may then be to link a community benefit with specific religious adherence. While this is an appropriate caution to make, the issue can be addressed by ensuring that the implementation of any program likely to raise such a concern sits with the community itself.

Faith-based development organizations are acutely aware of the link between the inner and the outer. This connection lies at the heart of social transformation. Every personal transformation is seen as contributing to an overall societal transformation. Under this approach, sustainable development cannot be separated from personal

attitudes and behaviors. On the contrary, it must start with those attitudes and behaviors. This contradicts the standard view that development can happen as a series of external, disembodied interventions.
For this reason it is argued that the *formation of morals* is a development issue. Some would contend that it is *the* development issue impact-
ing all others.

How this challenge is met may vary by context. In the Balkans and
Eurasia, the emphasis was on values formation in a post-Soviet era.
There, corruption, cynicism, disillusionment, and fatalism were the main
impediments to community development. In contrast, in East Africa,
moral formation looked very different. There it meant the promotion of
a conservative social agenda that seemed quaintly old-fashioned and out
of step with Western ideas that elevate personal freedoms. However, the
social problems in East Africa—including substance abuse, teenage
pregnancy, and crime—were very serious, and the inculcation of conservative morals seemed conducive to addressing some of those issues.

Inner transformation and the embedding of change

As outlined, many development organizations provide training or educational programs based on universal human values. There is nothing
wrong with this, and it is to be commended. However, faith-based development organizations may go further, undertaking or supporting
moral, ethical, or civic formation based squarely on religious principles.

It is suggested that training of the latter kind may be easier to
embed within developing communities. The reason is that religious
teaching carries with it a sense of personal accountability to God and
neighbor. It also has the benefit of social reinforcement by co-religionists. Other kinds of training do not invoke these same accountabilities
and may have less traction in strongly religious settings.

A related point is that teaching may seem abstract or theoretical if
it cannot be grounded in local experience or belief. For example, few
would argue that the socializing of "universal values"—such as dignity
and respect—in community training programs is a bad thing. However,
when these concepts are taken and framed as an expression of personal
faith or religious teaching, they may take deeper root. This is because
there is a body of existing teaching in which these concepts find meaning. Even in contexts where personal faith is shallow, religious tradition
can provide a repository of persuasive authority.

While inner change is of critical importance, it can be very hard
to measure. Development is sometimes understood in terms of the reporting of industry-approved results in industry-approved language.
In a sense, the reporting has come to define what "development" is.

Christians would claim that concepts like forgiveness and reconciliation lie at the heart of ongoing peaceful community relationships.
Similarly, the values of fairness and honesty are the necessary bedrock
of community trust. How is it possible to measure changes that lie
within a person's heart? Moral regeneration, let alone renewal by
God's Spirit, is language completely alien to professional understandings of development. Ultimately, inner change is just that—an interior
kind of development challenge. It is difficult to measure, intimately
connected with religious beliefs, and yet absolutely vital to effective
long-term development.

Transfiguring interfaith and inter-ethnic relationships

Faith-based development organizations have a particular contribution
to make in communities that have experienced internal conflict. This is
because such organizations understand the importance of inner transformation to longer-term peace and stability. Programs focusing on
peace building, healing, and reconciliation are a particular focus. This
reflects their understandings about human equality and God's constant
agenda of reconciliation.

Christian theology teaches that all humans are created by God and
are precious to him. Every person has an intrinsic dignity as a child of
God. Because all humans are made in the image of God, there is a
firm basis to respect and value each other. Our shared identity as
members of a global human family should create a sense of mutual
care. In many communities, however, the lived experience has been
vastly different.

Humans have an unhappy bias toward sin and selfishness. The
God-given dignity of the other can quickly dissipate in favor of ungodly
agendas pursued at their expense. Violence, conflict, and exclusion are
the high price paid for grasping at political and social advantage. People are objectified, dehumanized, commoditized, and exploited. That
said, God is implacably committed to the reconciliation of his creation,
and has put in place a process to restore the world. Scripture affirms
that God is reconciling all things to his son Jesus.[14]

Faith-based development organizations buy into the agenda of reconciliation through their programs. In the end, the issue of sustainability is one that starts within. It concerns the way people choose to care
for each other and the world in which they live. The data from Rwanda
poignantly summarized: "Beneath the long shadow of the genocide, all
development effort must be regarded as tenuous without internal
change."[15] The outside is a reflection of what lies within. Faith-based
organizations will conceive of inter-ethnic and inter-religious conflict,

justice, and the need for reconciliation as fundamentally spiritual issues. They will seek strategies to deal with the past honestly, justly, and, where possible, by finding a way forward in forgiveness.

The staff of FBOs may feel a particular responsibility in places that have experienced wide-spread human conflict. In Rwanda the data reported "You cannot give what you don't have," meaning that personnel felt called upon to set an example by living out personally transformed lives.[16] This can be an especially difficult task for those who have been caught up in conflicts themselves. Faith-based development organizations understand that the patient grace of God is required to overcome human intransigence.

Conversion, evangelism, and faith-based development

While conversion to the Christian faith is not a planned objective of most faith-based development organizations, it sometimes happens. Community members may be curious about the motivations for undertaking development work or the personal motivations of the staff involved. This may in turn lead to open dialogue and, in some cases, conversion. Such instances are to be celebrated. It is a wonderful and joyous occasion when a person comes to a point where they can name their hope in Christ. Christian staff should always give an honest, open, and respectful account of what they believe when called upon to do so.[17] Transparency and freedom of conscience require this.

Conversion is, by definition, a profoundly transformative experience. The convert will seek to uphold the interests of others through his or her personal service with a renewed commitment. A new vision of community and purpose will take shape. In this way converts will bring their gifts, experience and resources into the service of God and neighbor.

In contrast, explicit attempts at programmatic evangelism may be entirely self-defeating. To start with, such attempts may change the fundamental relationship between the development agency and the surrounding community, engendering mistrust and suspicion. In sensitive contexts, access to the community may be denied. In some cases, an organization may also reap a harvest of insincerity motivated by perceived collateral benefits or a desire to please. Becoming a Christian is no light matter. An organic process may prove more authentic.

The data provided examples of camping and youth programs being used for values formation with spiritual content. These events raised ethical issues. Attendees would come from highly impoverished backgrounds and would therefore represent a vulnerable group. These types of programs represented a rare opportunity for social recreation and skills acquisition. The strong desire to attend could create an environment open to spiritual abuse.

However, the weight of data suggested that appropriate care and restraint was exercised. Families were properly consulted and allowed their children to attend with a clear knowledge of the program: "The program is made available to children of all faiths, the program content is explained to families, and adult community members are invited to chaperone the children to guarantee the integrity of the... briefing. Community members interviewed were universally pleased with these activities and believed that their children learned and changed as a result."[18]

Some of the strongest advocates for the camps were Muslim parents.

In Eurasia, a similar issue arose, but the question was whether the camps exposed vulnerable children to conversion by evangelical "sects." Again, the data supported appropriate care and restraint in program design and integrity in the community briefing.

Psycho-social care and faith-based development

Faith-based development work nurtures not only inner transformation but also inner strength. Religious faith can provide a realistic and readily available alternative to Western models of psycho-social care in traumatized and impoverished communities. Agencies will have close relationships with churches and other FBOs, and their own staff may help to provide this type of care through community interactions.

In many communities, Western style models of professional clinical care and follow-up are completely unrealistic. Issues such as trauma, anxiety, and conflict cannot be dealt with by demand-driven or family support models. There is no money to pay for services of this kind even if they existed. These modes of care may be less familiar to the community in any event. The community will look to local religious infrastructure to provide spiritual or pastoral support in their challenging environments. The data reported that "People don't have psychological help, so [a] relationship with God is helpful."[19] An important role of faith-based development agencies may be to refer community members, using their own networks, to churches or other persons who are able to provide responsible pastoral support. In situations of emergency or disaster, when communities are at their most vulnerable, a great deal of care must be taken to avoid spiritual abuse or exploitation.

In an ongoing development context, the data revealed many instances of prayer opportunities being provided by the staff of faith-based agencies directly to community members at their request. The offering of pastoral care on an informal basis in this way was common. The staff of faith-based development organizations will have a keen understanding of the sustaining presence of God in their own lives and a genuine commitment to serving the community in the best way they know. It may be supposed that secular organizations would be less well-placed or less willing to provide support in this manner.

The role of prayer in undertaking effective community development work cannot be underestimated. This is examined in more detail in the next chapter.

CHAPTER 11

Prayer and Spiritual Disciplines

Karl Barth claims that "Only as God justifies it, does mission continue to exist."[1] The constant seeking of God through prayer and in scripture enables a Christian development organization to renew and re-center itself upon the God who first called it into being. This is essential to instill a godly confidence about its work and direction.[2] Protocols and practices need to be designed to nurture a culture of prayer.

Prayer is reflected in the daily life of faith-based development agencies in many ways. Staff are encouraged to pray about their work, and opportunities will exist for prayer to occur within the office. It is not unusual for Christian staff to pray briefly before meetings or even during meetings as seems appropriate. Staff may be encouraged to participate in retreats or in other structured times of prayer. Churches, donors, and supporters will be informed about particular needs, especially within the communities being served. They will be invited to participate directly in the work of the organization through prayer.

Prayer is normalized in daily life by making it visible. Prayer is a foundational spiritual activity. The FBO should look to God as its source of inspiration, providence, and power. By inviting God into daily life in prayer, a relational posture of godly dependence is built.

Many different kinds of prayers will be relevant to the work of the faith-based development organization. Most importantly, *intercessory* prayers bring before God the needs of impoverished communities. Christians believe that God has disclosed himself to all of humanity and can strengthen communities through his presence. His restless Spirit imbues all creation, seeking its renewal and true purpose. Intercessory prayers also communicate more prosaic organizational needs to God, such as fundraising, recruitment, and daily operational concerns.

Prayers of *invocation* invite the Spirit of God into the organization's development work, from the most straightforward initiatives to the most complex. Prayers of *thanksgiving* acknowledge the action and responsiveness of God. These prayers are essential in building deeper faith and trust. In addition, *contemplative* prayers are conducive to building a culture that is both discerning and reflective about its work practices. Finally, *prayers of lament* will be familiar to Christians who have undertaken development work seriously in the longer run. Things will not work out as planned on occasions, often with a significant human cost. Development gains can be fragile. These prayers voice our disappointments to God with honesty and emotion.

It is important that a proper understanding of prayer be expressed in the agency's corporate life. Prayer is misunderstood when it is seen as a magic spell, a divine guarantee, or an insurance policy. It should be seen primarily as an act of obedience by God's followers. It would be wrong to demand that God act in particular ways that conform to our human will. To do so would speak not of faith but of faithlessness. A faith-based development organization will encourage prayer as a regular discipline within work-life. This emphasis follows the example of Jesus' own life. There is something very compelling about the Son of God's own need to pray.[3]

There is also a variety of spiritual disciplines that can be used in development practice, including study, theological reflection, fasting, meditation, and discernment. There is a danger of neglect or embarrassment about these kinds of practices as organizations strive, in an uncritical way, for greater professionalism. This kind of separation of sacred and secular is unwarranted and unbiblical: "Few development workers understand prayer and fasting as tools for human transformation or for working for justice."[4] God and God's revelation should be an integral feature of our social analysis.[5] A serious faith-based development organization will try to develop a culture in which the disciplines of the Christian spiritual life become an embedded part of its praxis, and not a curiosity, an afterthought, a veneer, or an exception.

Prayer will animate not only the internal life of the FBO, but will also contribute to the distinctiveness of its practice in field settings. Christians affirm that the fundamental nature of prayer involves transcendence as a communication with the Divine. However, it also impacts the effectiveness of the fieldwork of faith-based development organizations in ways that are far less mysterious.

Public prayer and the social validation of community development projects

In Africa especially, many communities are highly religious. In these settings public prayer by representatives of FBOs has a vital role in providing "legitimacy" for development projects. Quite apart from their transcendent value, such prayers have a symbolic value that provides social validation for the project or program that the organization is undertaking with the community.

It is very common for the staff of faith-based agencies to be asked to engage in public prayer together with community representatives at the launch of a project. They will also open and close public meetings about development projects with prayers. The community will participate in these prayers and usually add their own. At critical junctures in the life of a project, development staff and the community will come together and pray. Related activities such as meetings and seminars will also start with prayer. In some places, not only are public meetings started with prayer, but also meetings with the technical service branch of government.[6] The community will see participation in prayer as a marker of an organization that takes God seriously, earning greater acceptance for its work.

In Africa, prayer is seen as a way of merging and interconnecting the physical and spiritual dimensions of community life.[7] This is very much part of the African psyche, which does not attempt to privatize faith and separate it out from activities that take place within a broader community or social setting. Many communities take their religious faith with the utmost seriousness. Against this background, the expectation of public prayer is very understandable.

The data produced a very clear explanation:

> When a Development Officer goes into the community with the intention of talking about a potential new project, and starts the meeting with public prayer about the project, this gains immediate respect. You get instant credibility. It shows you're serious. The community is serious about God, and if you pray to God about the project, it shows you and your organization are serious about God too. You will be respected and listened to. They will say to themselves: "This person is one of ours."[8]

Participation in public prayer shows the local community that the organization respects God and is committed in its faith. This provides greater confidence to the community that the project is of God and will provide blessing.

The implications of these connections are serious. Effective development requires meaningful engagement with the local community. Many communities in Africa openly and publicly express their faith in God and may expect others to join in their expressions of piety. While the vast bulk of people living in the Majority World have a theistic worldview, in Africa the percentage is higher still. It is unsurprising that some communities will want to commit their development projects to God and that public prayer is the cultural means by which this happens.

That expectation may, however, embarrass some development organizations. Modernity holds that the expression of faith should remain a private and personal matter. The data noted that when a representative of a secular agency would initiate a project without public prayer, this engendered a degree of community suspicion.[9] In short, some development organizations will not be able to authentically satisfy an important community expectation about their work.

Prayer and building community trust

Faith-based development organizations are able to enhance their work by building closer links with communities through shared personal prayer. This establishes a deeper level of trust with members of the community. In some communities there is an expectation of participating in prayer when invited to do so. Persons seeking prayer open up their personal lives, exposing their needs and vulnerabilities. For the staff of faith-based development organizations to pray with community members, often in their homes, implies a high level of trust and respect. Prayer of this kind deepens personal relationships. It can unite staff with program beneficiaries in a special way. It "makes us feel we are one, brothers and sisters. We carry each other's burdens."[10]

Christian prayers may also be seen as powerful and efficacious in Muslim communities. Invitations to pray with Muslims in their homes are not unusual, and may be associated with the perceived devoutness or piety of the staff in question. This suggests that for some community members, an overarching faith in God was more important than a particular Christian or Muslim affiliation. Sometimes this kind of prayer would take place behind closed doors.

This raises important questions for organizations that do not operate from a faith basis. In Rwanda, which was an overtly Christian context, the data reported that "families in need will always ask you to pray with them. If you don't, or hesitate, that would bring a big doubt. The family will think 'If this person is not committed to God, they can't be committed to us.'"[11] Organizations that are not able to respond to prayer requests in these environments will be at a disadvantage. For example, those agencies that see a diminished role for religion in development, or see the expression of faith as a purely personal or private affair, may face community hesitancy or suspicion. Conversely, a willingness to engage in private prayer may unlock community goodwill toward the organization and its staff.

Discernment in development practice

A faith-based development organization will sensitize itself to community needs through prayer and discernment. Wherever possible, it will directly involve the community in that process, and include representatives of the local church. This is consistent with the theological understanding that God is the ultimate change agent in the world and development work is a process of aligning with his purposes. The local community is always most familiar with its own context. It will be instructive to work with the community in discerning its own development priorities. They may already have a clear idea of the areas where they believe God is at work.

There is also a perceived relationship between prayer and good stewardship. In East Africa, prayer was seen by the community as necessary to amplify impact. In this way "God blesses the limited resources so that they will have maximum effect."[12] A related issue is the prioritization in needs. It was asserted that "without prayer you cannot solve problems, we would be overwhelmed by the poverty. We need prayer to prioritize what to do."[13] In one case, a programmatic failure was attributed not to lack of experience but to a lack of prayerful discernment.

The role of prayer in decision-making unveils a perceived tension. It may be difficult to reconcile more systematic corporate processes, such as rigorous professional design methodologies, and having recourse to apparently more uncertain practices such as prayer. Christians, of course, are commanded to love God with their whole mind. Well thought-out design tools and evidence-based methodologies will be seen as a gift that can be used in God's service. Yet within those processes inputs will be required, especially from the community, to identify and refine priorities. It is in this area that prayerful discernment has a particularly valuable role.

A faith-based agency will have an active role for prayerful discernment in its decision-making and make this a strategic priority. It is suggested that reflective practice is essential both to organizational learning and to effective development. Prayerful discernment lies at the very heart of building a reflective culture.

Prayer and harmful practices

Public prayer in development work has a particular role to play in seeking to overcome spiritual practices perceived as damaging to people's wellbeing.[14] In particular, prayer is used to identify God as the source of the organization's authority.

At the heart of African Traditional Religion (ATR) is a complex system of animistic beliefs. The adherent believes that spirits inhabit the natural world in a very pervasive way.[15] Plants, animals, and even inanimate objects are believed to have a soul or spiritual essence. The spirit world is understood to have a direct impact on the daily life of humans. Most commonly, these spirits comprise the spirits of ancestors, including the "living dead," being more recently departed relatives.[16] Spirits can be offended and may be invoked through ritual to exercise influence over human affairs. For those who practice ATR, life can be a complex negotiation of competing spiritual influences. Malign spiritual influence may be seen as the explanation for misfortune, and arcane or esoteric practices are required to appease or deflect the spirits' influence.

The significance of public prayer by development staff is to indicate its own source of power. The data noted that development staff would openly pray in community settings where certain traditional practices were a problem. This amounted to a declaration: "This is where I get my strength or power from (that is, dependence on God)."[17] The locus of power is of central importance to practitioners of ATR. The development organization may be seen as powerful or impactful, and prayer is used to identify the source of its spiritual authority.

Those who believe in ATR see life as a contest of competing spiritual forces. In this context, it is especially important for faith-based development organizations to demonstrate their faithfulness to God. Public prayer identifies God as the source of ultimate hope. Moreover, constant deferral to God in prayer indicates that technology and material assets are gifts to be used within a relationship of service to God and are not a substitute for it.

Prayer may also be used in private contexts. The data reported that development staff "will pray with people in their homes, will educate about causes of illness and will ask people to remove voodoo fetishes from their homes which link the family with traditional healers."[18] The object of these kinds of prayers was to enlighten communities about the real causes of illness and other presenting issues. This was achieved by presenting a coalition of science and potent monotheism.

Prayer, authority, and bridging the gap

The underlying issue raised by this discussion is the source of authority within highly religious developing communities. For some communities, that authority is based on scripture as mediated through trusted religious leaders. For Muslim communities, that authority is based on the Koran as interpreted by imams. Appeals within strongly religious communities for behavioral change based on other sources of authority may be less compelling. Prayer has a particular public and symbolic role in identifying the source of authority claimed by faith-based development organizations within theistic societies.

Prayer is an act by which people submit themselves and their concerns to God, a higher authority. When a development organization and a local community pray together, this is an act of humility. It shows that they together seek God's providence and blessing. This can be respectful of local culture and an important way of building goodwill and a sense of shared purpose. The data consistently showed that public prayer was an advantage in establishing trust in both Christian and Muslim settings in Africa.

Prayer is not something that can be undertaken lightly or insincerely, and not every organization will be able to engage in it. The evidence showed that organizations that were not able to participate in prayer could be viewed more suspiciously in some contexts. One implication for the sector is to consider how this divide can be bridged.

An inescapable observation is the stark difference between the way religious faith is expressed in some developing country settings and the way it is expressed in the West. Western donor countries are often highly secularized and have views about the public expression of faith that have been shaped by the Enlightenment and modernity. In short, religious faith in the West is an increasingly rare personal choice that belongs strictly in the private domain. By contrast, the public expression of faith in some development settings, especially in Africa, is socially and communally expected. The failure of development organizations to recognize this and respond in a considered way may lead to resentment or disengagement.

Some faith-based development organizations will have a nuanced policy that allows public prayer with Muslims. Care must be exercised in the way the Divine is identified and addressed—for example, referring to Jesus as the Word of God but not as the Son of God.[19] Some organizations will consider it acceptable for Christians to pray the Muslim Fatiha. In everything, it is critical that prayer be undertaken respectfully and sincerely. In many cases, a higher degree of cooperation is possible because both Christianity and Islam are Abrahamic faiths.

For the faith-based development organization, prayer is a way of building authentic connection in communities. Some contexts, however, will be suspicious of, or even hostile toward, Christian faith. In these places, prayer will not have the same public role. Different strategies will be required to build community engagement. In particular, the living out of kingdom values, which have a universal resonance, will come to the fore. That said, prayer will be a powerful, welcome, and distinguishing feature of the development practice of FBOs in many settings.

The next chapter looks at another way that the authority of religious belief can be deployed in undertaking development work—by engaging with the church.

CHAPTER 12

A Special Relationship with the Church

Working with churches may mean many different things. It may involve speaking prophetically into the life of the church. It may mean leveraging its institutional structures, authoritative voice, and geographic reach. It may mean enlisting its members as agents of change. It may mean building up its collective developmental understandings, motivating and inspiring, and influencing its theological positions. It may also mean working together as project partners, co-creating within communities, nurturing staff, enhancing devotional life, and receiving critique and challenge.

Many faith-based development organizations have a tendency to partner with local churches in the fulfillment of their mission. This is because Christian theology recognizes the church as God's lasting community of hope and salvation and the primary means by which God acts locally. In all contexts, local churches will know their community better than development agencies. The church is permanent, local, embedded, and influential. In contrast, the presence of some development agencies may be best described as transitory, imposed, peripheral, or alien. While indigenous partners may be found or created to conduct development programs, there will be few with the longevity, knowledge, or voice of the church. Churches are a key part of the social infrastructure in many developing communities. An important role for faith-based development organizations is to help churches build capacity and nurture developmental and theologically related understandings.

A relationship of accountability between the church and faith-based development organizations will recognize their responsibilities to each other. The church strengthens its apostolic character when it engages with organizations that have the capacity and gifts to deliver ministries like international development.[1] Faith-based development organizations may help the church to better reflect its true identity as an inspired community of hope fulfilling God's mission in the world, especially in pursuing justice and building up the poor. They can help enliven the conscience of the church, mobilize resources, and provide practical encouragement, advice, and skills. At all times development organizations will maintain a humble posture, recognizing that what they have to offer stands in continuity with the church's existing call. This shared vision sets apart their relationship when compared to other actors within civil society.

Faith-based development organizations can benefit greatly from their engagement with the church. The church can help them to remain faithful in their mission and grow their staff in Christian discipleship. It may bring community needs to their attention, and impart vital local knowledge. Pastors and clergy typically participate in their devotional life and may act as local champions in relation to development programs. Its endorsement can unlock community goodwill. The church may help explain development work and its theological rationale to the broader community. Through relationships of trust, churches and development organizations jointly contribute to God's mission.[2]

In its ministry to the world's poor, oppressed, and marginalized, the mission of the faith-based development organization will stand in continuity with the church. Having said that, the development agency will not seek to compete with the church or replace it. It would be unusual for faith-based development organizations to administer the sacraments or other rites. Instead, their staff will be encouraged to have an active involvement with a local church, not only to contribute to its ministry and receive pastoral care and Christian formation, but also to ensure that there is no confusion of identity.

Faith-based development organizations can help the church to realize and implement its true calling. They can strengthen the church as it envisions a holistic understanding of the gospel, exercises greater diaconal responsibility, mobilizes its congregants, and speaks with a prophetic voice. The leadership and moral authority of the local church can be an invaluable asset.

When it comes to partnering with the church, however, any romanticized picture must be quickly dispelled. As faith-based agencies well know, working with churches can have a shadow side and raise very significant risks. There is a creative tension between a proper love and respect for the church, on the one hand, and the more cautionary and realistic appraisal from those who know her well, on the other. A carefully nuanced relationship is needed.

In Western countries, development organizations have a particular task in educating churches about poverty, social justice, and the challenges of international development. Many churches still fail to appreciate God's unfailing solidarity with the poor and the impact of decisions taken in the West on impoverished communities. A former archbishop of Canterbury puts it this way: "We are not trying to solve someone else's problem but to liberate *ourselves* from a toxic and unjust situation in which we, the prosperous, are less than human."[3] It is important to remind the church about Jesus' affinity with the poor and disenfranchised. Scripture teaches that Christ's identification with the poor is so close and strong that to serve the poor is to serve him.[4]

Some churches have even been seduced by a different kind of gospel. Soong-Chan Rah insists that "the Western white captivity of the church means that capitalism can be revered as the system closest to God and the consequent rampant materialism and consumerism of the capitalist system become acceptable vices."[5] And Kosuke Koyama warns: "Man is supposed to eat bread. But what if bread eats man?"[6] A challenge for faith-based development organizations is to maintain its close relationships with the church with an integrity that requires it to confront positions that are harmful to the poor.

One example of potential harm is the emergence of the so-called prosperity gospel, in which Christian faith is promoted primarily as a vehicle for material blessing.[7] The prosperity gospel has two key ideas: "The first is that God is a benevolent deity who wants believers in His son Jesus Christ to be socio-economically prosperous, as well as healthy in body and soul. Second is the idea that believers can actively claim as a kind of covenanted *right* this-worldly abundance."[8] This is often seen as a fundamental betrayal of the *theologia crucis* (theology of the cross) at the heart of Christianity by making idols of money and self. As discussed later, this type of theology can betray the poor and undermine good development.

In some places where faith-based development organizations work there are very few, if any, churches. In these contexts, there may be a responsibility to explore how an agency can strengthen nascent or struggling Christian communities for the longer term. At the same time, many faith-based development agencies will work without any hesitation with other religious communities in ways that are welcoming, respectful, and co-operative. However, their respect for other faiths, and their own, prevents faith-based development organizations from attempting to assimilate all manner of beliefs.

Leveraging organizational influence

It has been reported that "faith organizations play major roles in communities and together constitute the world's largest distribution system."[9] Faith-based development organizations will be aware of the pervasive influence of churches within some developing communities. The data provided two very different examples drawn from East Africa and Eurasia.

In Rwanda it was claimed that "there is no question that the church is the most pervasive, trusted, and well-functioning institution in Rwandan civil society" and that "it is impossible to conceive of undertaking meaningful long-term development in Rwanda without engaging with the churches."[10] In Armenia and Georgia the influence of the church was more pervasive still. It was reported there was a blurring between the church as an actor *within* civil society and the church *as* civil society. In these countries it was difficult to meaningfully disentangle the church from the broader culture or society. This is partly a function of the extraordinary history of these national churches, which date back to the fourth century. For example: "To be Georgian, you need to speak Georgian and be Georgian Orthodox."[11] And in Armenia it is claimed that "the church is the place of national identity."[12]

Networks of participation are required to get people involved in building their community. It has been bluntly observed that "it is simply a fact that religion generates networks of participation that are far stronger, more lasting, and more committed than secular civic organizations are capable of."[13] Social capital is disproportionately important to the poor since they lack any other forms of capital, such as financial capital or human capital in the form of educational opportunities. For this reason, religious institutions have a special role to play. They can provide material support and act as an engine for both civic and political participation, which in turn generates other forms of capital.

In qualitative terms, it can be expected that the relationships between faith-based development organizations and churches will be less episodic or instrumental, in contrast to those non-governmental development organizations that see the churches merely as a convenient delivery channel for the roll-out of their programs. The emphasis will be on ongoing relationship and cooperation, recognizing that development is something that does not happen apart from religion but goes hand-in-hand with it.

A less obvious type of influence of faith-based development organizations on churches comes from staff participation in local churches. This is especially relevant in small communities. Staff members' presence can do far more than simply swell the numbers. Where congregants are in place for an extended period, important cross-fertilization can take place, particularly in terms influencing the church's thinking on development issues and on understanding other cultures.

Finally, a very practical reason for faith-based development organizations to engage with churches and other religious institutions is to try and reach remote communities. Churches or faith institutions can represent a rare permanent presence in outlying or widely dispersed areas. The use of wider church and pastoral networks to access remote communities with development messages may represent a unique opportunity. One of the reasons people congregate at places of worship in these locations is specifically for the purpose of receiving teaching. Faith-based development organizations may be better placed than non-faith-based organizations to identify and access these broader church networks.

Engaging individual church leadership

As mentioned previously, religious beliefs are the primary frame of reference for the vast majority of people living in developing communities. Religious leaders are in a privileged position of trust within those communities. They serve as teachers, custodians of tradition, pastoral carers, and persons exercising important cultic responsibilities. The influence of religious leaders within developing communities should not be underestimated. Faith-based development organizations pursue their development agenda by engaging with religious leaders in a variety of ways. These include accessing target communities where religious leaders act as gatekeepers, seeking their explicit endorsement for programs and development messages, and improving their own pastoral awareness and responses.

Engaging with religious leaders can have a kind of multiplier effect. When religious leaders grow in their understanding about particular developmental issues, they may then choose to spread key messages across their broader congregational networks. This enables access to an important and unique communication channel.

Personal endorsement of programs or projects from authoritative religious figures can give a development message added credibility. Pastors are sometimes considered the "voice of God" in their local context.[14] The manner of endorsement is not always verbal, but may come in the form of symbolic action.[15] For example, where imams or priests are inclusive of people living with HIV and AIDS in their worship, this can reduce stigma and judgment. In a similar vein, the data referred to the action of "the Patriarch who blessed a new AIDS centre to promote condom use for AIDS sufferers, for people's protection, even though this isn't something [the Patriarch] would normally do."[16] This has a major impact on community acceptance.

Similarly, it can be important to train religious leaders to be more pastoral in their response to development issues. In some contexts, church leaders are an important source of information for the general public and heavily influence public opinion. For example, a prevalent attitude in Georgia is "If I have a question, I go to the priest."[17] Against this background, it is important to educate the clergy in terms of their understanding of both development and theology. For example, the data from Georgia noted that "many [priests] still believe HIV and AIDs is punishment from God."[18] In contrast, reports from Tanzania indicated that priests and pastors had changed their attitudes from judgment and stigmatization of people with HIV and AIDS to a much more compassionate understanding.

The messages of churches will at times be presented with a moralism that would be regarded as offensive or condescending in the West. Nonetheless, this tone is resonant with a large part of the world's population. Faith-based development organizations can engage with Christian leaders as credible friends and on the basis of shared values and can moderate opinions and understandings. This can have a powerful influence.[19]

Formation of clergy—influencing understandings of development

Faith-based development organizations have an important responsibility for holding the church to account in effectively caring for the poor. This may involve encouraging churches to think critically about development issues and working with clergy in their understanding of diaconal responsibility.

There is scope to train professional religious leaders in development issues as part of their formation by relying on theological and sacred sources from within their faith traditions. Deryke Belshaw has noted that "the training of religious leaders usually emphasizes spiritual and ethical issues to the exclusion of applied social and environmental studies."[20] Providing training in development issues could also be a highly strategic move, potentially leading to a lifetime of informed and more sympathetic teaching within congregational life. A developmentally literate cohort of clergy may help churches to reshape themselves into more socially active and transformative institutions.

For example, the acquisition of development skills could enable the church to proactively contribute to the design of specific programs. It may lead to the voice of the faith community being represented more directly, sensitively, and effectively. Training in development could enable faith institutions to better understand how social movements work and the role of advocacy in influencing public policy. It could also lead to churches becoming more self-critical, vibrant, active, and socially engaged.

Improved knowledge may also help religious institutions to interact with development as a profession. That profession is close to it in heart but very distant from it in terms of language and process. For example, improved skills may assist grassroots faith communities to submit grant applications, access funds, and employ helpful evaluation and monitoring techniques. Ultimately this may lead to faith institutions gaining confidence to pursue their own development initiatives. In Christian churches it may also help make the idea of working for the kingdom of God a more immanent reality.

It has also been suggested that long-term partnerships with faith-based development organizations can alter basic theological understandings. In particular, the evidence from Rwanda pointed to fundamental shifts in the content of the gospel since the genocide, which was attributable in part to work with faith-based development organizations. For example,

> it was reported that formerly people with HIV and AIDS would be stigmatized and excluded within community. There was a strong tendency to judgment which reflected a narrow pietism based on conservative sexual ethics. This had changed substantially as the community gained a greater understanding of broader elements of the gospel such as compassion, reciprocal love and social inclusion.[21]

This data is of significance, because there has been little discussion within the resurgent academic interest in faith and development about how development has affected religious institutions.[22] It is posited that theological shifts within churches can occur organically as the result of longer-term interactions with faith-based development organizations. This leads to a broader and more strategic question about the use of theology as a development tool: how can theology serve the interests of the poor by supporting good development, and what can be done respectfully to accelerate critical shifts in understanding within churches and religious institutions?

Interactions with faith-based development organizations can encourage a practical and community-oriented vision of mission for the church, and in some places help to balance out a more pietistic or ritualistic ecclesiology. The trajectory is "to suggest that the work of social diakonia is part of the everyday work of the priest."[23]

Theological understandings and development themes can be mutually reinforcing. An important strategic issue for faith-based development organizations is how they may pursue their development aims by participating in theological education at various levels. This is an important way to gain long-term influence. One way of building development capacity is to provide in-service training around topical development issues for pastors and clergy. The data illustrated this in a variety of settings, and such an approach has helped to influence target communities on important issues. A particularly helpful methodology may be to prepare theologically informed development materials, such as Bible studies and sermons, for use within congregations. This is beyond the usual repertoire of development interventions, but it has the potential to be highly influential.

The risk of church relationships

Partnering with churches is not easy. Undoubtedly, there are some real advantages that can be very powerful. But there can also be many disappointments and a shadow side. Some of the main types of risks are outlined below.

Risks concerning the passivity of the church

Some churches are too socially passive to be effective development partners. They may resist becoming a critical prophetic voice within their society and are largely ineffectual in responding to issues of systemic injustice. For example, the data noted with regret that "Rwanda's history reveals that many people were killed in the churches, that church leaders were involved in state matters, and that a significant number of church leaders colluded with the militias to murder their congregations."[24] Because of this terrible history, there was even more reluctance on the part of the church to embrace its call as a prophetic voice.[25]

The report for Senegal also indicated that the local church was very passive, noting that it was "not part of solution yet."[26] Some complained that "the church doesn't come out of its corner."[27] A UN advisor added this sharp criticism: "The Church dives into 'safe zone' only, which is infant behaviour instead of [addressing] hard core issues. Many issues of justice are not on the church table."[28] Likewise, in Lebanon it was noted that "the Church doesn't respond to advocacy, if they do, it's only in terms of charity."[29]

Another risk is *partnering with churches that are stuck in a charitable mindset*. The challenge is to overcome the dead weight of a history that has cast the church as instinctively charitable rather than transformational.[30] This creates a real dilemma for agencies that promote a strength-based community development model in which communities are encouraged to more be self-reliant.[31]

Churches operating in a charitable mode are prone to handout programs. It was noted that "We don't do them [church partnerships] well. We tend to make it a give-away program."[32] This approach can fuel demand, produces little long-term benefit, and often exacerbates an entrenched dependency. It can also leave the church open to exploitation. It was cynically observed that "for as long as the church supports the people with clothes and things, the church grows, if not, it decreases."[33] The struggle for the church is to learn another way.

Part of the problem appears to be that many churches have only ever known charitable models and have depended on charity themselves for survival. It was stated that "the first missionaries taught us [the churches] to receive but not to give. They did not teach the African church."[34] Some churches in minority contexts resembled a chaplaincy for their membership rather than a light to society. The challenge was to help these churches become more socially engaged.[35]

A particularly risky practice is *entering into church relationships in the form of passive funding arrangements*. These types of arrangements provide minimal influence and are rarely conducive to good development outcomes. Cash grants to churches to conduct small projects are problematic. They fuel a perception of the faith-based development organization as a funding source rather than a true development partner.[36] Where church partnerships are not based on clearly articulated developmental goals, this may suggest some kind of an ulterior motive. These types of relationships can end up confusing the development organization's identity and purpose.

Risks relating to ecumenism

Faith-based development organizations, including those that are denominationally affiliated, need to operate with a generous ecumenism. Effective development work depends on ensuring that there is no discrimination within communities, there is no hint of sectarian bias, and minorities are respected.

In some places "there is evidence of violence, hatred, and ridicule perpetuated by church leaders towards minority religious groupings."[37] In particular, in some contexts faith-based development organizations need to be alert to the heresy of *philetism*, that is, the identification of Christianity with a particular nationalistic outlook.[38]

An added complication is that in some countries only the Orthodox and the Roman Catholic churches may be regarded as truly Christian, while evangelical churches can be regarded as "sects" with an agenda of conversion.[39] The implications can be serious. The incidence of poverty in places like Lebanon is tightly correlated to various religious groupings, and perceived favoritism has the potential to undermine credibility, organizational integrity, and program acceptance.

At times, *trying to maintain harmonious ecumenical relationships can be intense*. It is critical that faith-based development organizations see themselves as honest brokers, acting in an even-handed way, and not as a source of patronage.

Risk of partnering with churches
that are politically or nationalistically aligned

Every faith-based development organization must approach its engagement with churches critically and with discernment. Alignments with organizations using religion for nationalistic or political purposes may be damaging to community cohesion and discredit the development partner organization and its work. Some societies are divided on religious lines and "in some cases religion is used as an expression and tool of nationalism."[40] The data from Georgia was blunt: "politicians use churches for self-promotion and their own agendas..."[41] In Rwanda, with its troubled history of genocide, there was also a sober warning. The report noted that "the church has not fully embraced its prophetic calling, and risks being co-opted by government if it fails to maintain a healthy, critical distance."[42] In these contexts, partnering with churches may require very careful consideration.

Risks relating to doctrine

Another category of risk is found where a church partnership aligns the faith-based development organization unhelpfully with certain church doctrines. A case in point is *the risk of so-called prosperity doctrine*, which is growing in popularity in Africa. In East Africa it was reported that this prosperity teaching "appears to undermine the positive role of Christian faith in doing effective development. The individualistic, materialistic, and pietistic thrust of prosperity teaching appeared to present a serious threat to the communitarian ethos underpinning much development work."[43] Similar sentiments were expressed in West Africa: "While prosperity teaching has an obvious attraction to people who wish to escape from the grind of poverty, it may equally lead to frustration and disillusionment if material aspirations are not quickly satisfied."[44]

One of the main criticisms of prosperity gospel teaching is that "[it] exploits growing numbers amongst the world's most vulnerable populations, taking in tithes from the poorest and offering in exchange only false hope and inflated promises of miracle healings and untold economic abundance."[45] Prosperity teaching is also charged with promoting selfishness and diverting attention from the lasting and structural causes of deprivation as well as community-based responses. On the other hand, there may be some benefit to be gained in that prosperity teaching may be conducive to individual empowerment and hope, the promotion of self-worth, entrepreneurship, financial management, and certain associated virtues.[46]

An obvious risk is *being too closely associated with churches that are stridently evangelistic* in their positioning. This has the potential to associate the development organization with socially divisive activities in sensitive contexts. For example, involvement with "crusading" churches is regarded as "highly contentious in multi-faith (especially Muslim) contexts."[47] Associated risks included confusion about the organization's identity and purpose, a lack of transparency, and tacit pressure being applied in vulnerable communities. It was noted that "if we are too closely aligned to pushy practice [we] might be subject to negative feedback and even violence."[48]

Risk of engaging with churches with no real capacity to be self-critical
This risk is influenced by the ecclesiology of certain churches. For example, some churches believe they have always been guided by the Holy Spirit, and that they are therefore, in a sense, perfect. Such institutions may be innately conservative, always conscious of their historic, even defining, importance within society. These factors militate against any agenda for change. There is a risk of partnering with the church when its strongly pietistic, priest-centric, and mystical beliefs give it a largely inward focus. In Armenia, change was understood by some priests in terms of liturgical practice or personal pietism rather than broader notions of community development.[49] When pressed, some priests struggled to identify any substantive evidence of church-based change in the broader society.

Risks of partnering with churches with anti-development views
There is also risk in being aligned with anti-development attitudes and patriarchal ideas regarding the role of women. I am not referring here to the topic of ordination of women in the church but social attitudes toward women more generally. There is abundant empirical evidence that empowering women is one of the most effective development strategies available in many communities. Some churches, however, explicitly or implicitly promote a diminished role for women in society. Partnerships with these churches may be highly problematic.

Similarly, churches can have strident views against minority groups, and many are renowned for conservatism in relation to issues of sexual and reproductive health.

Risk of partnering with churches with disreputable leaders
Finally, there is sometimes a risk of becoming involved with religious leaders who are disreputable. Leaders can misuse their position or polarize communities because of personal conduct or checkered personal histories. For example, the data from Armenia reported: "Many of the leaders of church are former KGB or party officials. It will take time for these people to digest what they have learned from seminary training and promised to do...It will take three generations to bring real change."[50] Due diligence is essential right down to the local level.

Overview and future directions

Churches, and comparable religious institutions from other faiths, can have a dominant influence within civil society in developing countries. Whole communities may be strengthened by supporting those institutions, including faith-based institutions, that have a pivotal role in their life. This poses a public policy dilemma for governments, secular orga-

nizations, and multilateral organizations in knowing how to engage—
and the appropriate limits of their engagement.

Religious faith can be a source of immense pride. It can build community and provide a sense of cohesion and belonging. In some contexts, religious identity may be considered coterminous with community
identity or even national identity. Wendy Tyndale has observed that:

> Places of worship: the temple, the gurdwara, the mosque or the
> local church have always been the centre of community life, the
> place where the vulnerable seek help and those who have suffi-
> cient are expected to share. The life of all religious people is, in
> some sense, necessarily about building communities, caring for
> one's neighbour, feeding the hungry and teaching people about
> the meaning of their relationship with one another. Since the
> horizons of faith-based communities stretch far beyond the
> family, the clan or the village, they can help to broaden peo-
> ple's perspective and enable them to feel they belong to a wider
> community as well as a smaller one.[51]

As local customs and cultural events are frequently informed by
local religious beliefs,[52] a case can be made for strengthening those organizations, including religious institutions, that nurture the local community where this serves some transparent development purpose.

Faith-based institutions are the kinds of institutions that hold a
community together, reflect local preferences, and provide hope in
times of crisis. Gerard Clarke and Michael Jennings report that "the
language of faith, the religious idiom, frequently better reflects the cultural norms in which the poor and marginalized operate. They are better able to draw such individuals and communities into global discourse
of social justice, rights and development, without recourse to the often
distancing language of secular development discourse."[53] It seems there
is a strong case for enlisting the support of faith-institutions in carrying
out development activity.

Nonetheless, there has been an understandable reluctance by governments and multilateral institutions to directly support religious institutions through development work, because this may be seen to be
promoting a particular religious standpoint. It is suggested that a more
flexible position is warranted. To not engage with religious institutions
on ideological grounds risks devaluing the role of faith within community life and, by default, makes a statement that diminishes the importance of religion within human affairs.

A distinctive aspect of many Christian faith-based development organizations is that they see themselves as inextricably bound to the
church. This reflects a theological understanding that their work is an

expression of the church, in the broadest sense, or a ministry standing in continuity with the church's mission. A relationship with the church can represent a great strength. There is a growing body of literature that recognizes the influence of religious institutions and faith leaders within developing communities. The leveraging of the organizational influence of the church can be a potent asset, as can the authoritative voice of individual church leaders. Qualitatively, the relationship of faith-based development organizations with churches will be not so much instrumental or transactional as organic and long term. All faith-based development organizations need to act with a generous ecumenism, recognizing that no one church can fully reflect God's mission.

The relationship of faith-based development organizations with churches will also be marked by the acceptance of significant risks. In order to be most effective, fundamental attitudinal shifts may be needed. This may make the case for a deeper and more careful engagement with churches rather than a stepping back. The kinds of risks involved include those having to do with the charitable mindset of many churches, the dangers of passive funding relationships, theological positions that may create tensions with some development goals, the misuse of relationships, and co-option. It is important for faith-based development agencies to consider how they can capture and leverage the huge advantages of their church relationships while minimizing the very real risks.

In some cases this will entail helping churches to break out of social passivity and pietism. The resurgence, or rediscovery, of diaconal ministry in development is a very welcome prospect. An important area for practical research is the kinds of due diligence protocols to follow before entering into church relationships, as well as ways of monitoring and improving the effectiveness of those relationships over time. It is abundantly clear that a priority must be building the capacity of churches to help them engage more effectively and sympathetically in carrying out development work. This will require a willingness to invest in new skills and approaches.

CHAPTER 13

Implications

Since its inception, development as a profession has been heavily influenced by modernity. Its canons aspire to strengthen and sustain human society and help people all over the world to experience fullness of life and opportunity. As a profession, development deals with people; more particularly, its focus is on people living in the Majority World for whom religion is of central importance. Historically, however, international development as an academic discipline has tended to marginalize religious viewpoints. The significant gaps in understanding about the role of religion in development must be closed. In particular, this book highlights that what faith-based development organizations believe deeply influences the way they do their work. This can imbue a distinctive and effective praxis.

Theology reconsidered as a development asset

An implication of this analysis is that Christian theology should not be seen as something that necessarily stands apart from development. It is not simply a source of motivation for a cohort of Christian development practitioners. Nor is it inimical to development scholarship to consider how Christian theology informs the work of specific agencies.

Although some of the world's largest faith-based development organizations have been engaged in development work for more than half a century, scant attention has been paid to how their theology influences their organizational objectives. There has been an assumption of influence and benefit, which has seldom been tested. English theologian Stephen Plant argues: "My contention is that in spite of half a century of post-war development and relief—and two millennia of charitable service—the churches and their agencies are still *theologically* unsure of *why* they do *what* they do."[1] In his view, a regrettable consequence "is that the rich resources of Christian theology fail to have much if any discernible bearing upon the policies and practices of church-based development agencies. Christian theology has available to it a palate of rich color; but many Christian development practitioners, in making social justice their only rationale, seem content to paint in monochrome."[2] This book has tried to look more closely by describing how theologically derived beliefs or motifs impact the attainment of the organization's social purpose. This moves the discourse to an applied or concrete level.

The analysis also shows how some theological positions pose real risks for development work. Several examples emerge from the data including:

- how programmatic evangelism can limit access to communities or stir up conflict

- how a commitment to work through churches can mean engaging with organizations often stuck in a charitable mindset

- how more liberal ideas about staffing can promote inclusion but dilute organizational distinctiveness.

These brief observations indicate that an organization's theological positions are not neutral, and they influence development work in both positive and negative ways.

Organizational effectiveness and fidelity

The boards of faith-based development organizations should be vitally interested in the theological foundation and positions set out in their core documents and constitution. In this regard, the phenomenon of organizational drift is well known. Chapter 16 offers some ideas about how to maintain faith in the life of FBOs so that they can hold onto their distinctiveness.

Arguably, faith-based organizations should work much harder at understanding how their beliefs impact their work. At times, this may require an honest "reality check," because operational practices and activities may differ greatly from formal positions. The best organizations will have a clear organizational theology that motivates and supports the attainment of their social objectives.

A culture of honest reflection and transparency will help governors to better do their job. Ideally, the board and senior management of faith-based development organizations should strive to more carefully articulate and understand their beliefs as a source of both strength and risk. This kind of reflective process is part of achieving the "faith literacy" that Rick James has spoken of.[3] It will add to the body of shared learning, which in turn may benefit other organizations.

One encouraging development has been the Australian government-funded Church Partnership Program (CPP) in Papua New Guinea, which will be referred to later. The case study report on this program describes how this project has provided a forum for different church denominations to overcome differences of opinion in their work.[4] The report noted: "This result has been particularly evident in the articulation of the Theology of Development which refers to the dialogue around the core religious rationale that motivates and guides all seven churches and the partner Australian church-based NGOs in their development work."[5] In this case, the clarity of theological understanding resulting from that dialogue provided the basis for the churches' ongoing co-operation.

Engagement with anti-development views

The detailed studies of demographers of religion has shown that religious belief is growing, especially in the Global South, and that religious beliefs are a basic prism through which people engage the world.[6] This raises an important question: what if those religious beliefs include beliefs that are anti-development?[7] Religious beliefs may be sexist, parochial, judgmental, excluding, stigmatizing, or discriminatory. Such attitudes may be an ingrained part of the inherited culture.

This presents a challenge for faith-based development organizations. Where these kinds of beliefs are part of the inherited social *milieu*, there may be an opportunity to present fresh biblical or theological understandings. The best examples from the data concerned Christian attitudes to people with HIV and AIDS and the subordination of women through traditional gender roles. Specific programs are being developed on the basis of scripture and theology to present fresh understandings of these issues. There is, of course, a range of opinion within most religious traditions, and some opinions will be more conducive to the attainment of development goals than others.

It must be acknowledged that an honest reconciliation of views is not always possible. Nevertheless, a faith-based development agency may be able to isolate points of difference or identify areas of consensus that can serve as a platform for program activity. The existence of particular attitudes that may create tensions within some faith traditions is not a valid reason to avoid or disparage the role of religion in development.[8] On the contrary, it may provide a strong reason to engage. Side-stepping contentious issues does not change opinion; a well-constructed theological appeal might. There was evidence of this happening in the data in relation to people with HIV and AIDS. There, the position in some communities moved from judgment and stigmatization to acceptance on the basis of longer-term theological reflection.

Resurgent interest in faith-based approaches to development

At the outset of this book, the systemic bias against any serious consideration of the role of faith within development work was outlined. The academic literature reflects more than sixty years of neglect.[9] Its overriding emphasis has been on scientific empiricism. This literature has emerged largely from Western academic environments, which have been reluctant to recognize any public or social role for religious faith within professional development activity.

Some remain highly skeptical about the resurgent interest in the role of religion within development. One commentator has suggested that it is really about serving a deeply political purpose.[10] The resurgent interest in religion on the part of the World Bank has been criticized as enlisting religious institutions in an instrumental agenda to assist it in meeting its own objectives—while leaving mainstream conceptions of development largely unchallenged.[11] In short, the debate has been conducted in a way that allows the mainstream development sector to see itself as entirely normative, which then justifies using religion in a highly utilitarian way.[12]

Religions should not be "used" in the pejorative sense of that word.[13] Researchers like Katherine Marshall have contended that partnerships with religious institutions can involve a true mutuality, and this should be the goal. There is certainly no shortage of anecdotes about secular NGOs engaging with faith institutions in highly transactional ways (although some good may still result from this).

One example from the data was an anecdote about the domestic savings scheme in Rwanda. In that case, a secular agency wanted to implement a domestic savings program in a strongly Christian Rwandan village with a social tradition of living from day to day. The local Anglican priest warned that the program would gain no traction unless it was grounded in the community's religious values. Accordingly, the program was "translated." This meant that it was launched at the local Anglican church, maximizing attendance. It started with a one-hour teaching session on biblical principles of stewardship (run by the priest), moved to the secular workshop, then concluded with an extended time of public prayer in which the priest prayed for villagers to take personal responsibility.[14]

The best faith-based development organizations aspire to a highly consultative, community-based, and long-term view of development, and they set up local structures to ensure the ongoing participation of churches. This helps to overcome skepticism about city-based NGOs that make fleeting visits. Some organizations involve themselves in the training of clergy in development-related areas and set up church-based partnerships and structures. Overall, it seems to me that Marshall's ideal is achievable. It is clear that all NGOs can risk treating religious institutions in an instrumental way. The data from this research, however, shows that faith-based development organizations are well positioned to engage more deeply with counterpart religious institutions, especially where they have put in place localized and longer-term structures from the outset.

Implications for instrumental approaches

Religion has shown remarkable resilience and the evidence shows that theistic belief is strengthening around the globe.[15] In 2010, 12 percent of the world's population claimed no religious affiliation compared with 20 percent in 1970. Religious affiliation is highest in developing countries, and the most recent statistics confirm a strong shift in the center of gravity for Christianity to the Global South.[16]

While in 1910 Christians in the Global North comprised 80 percent of all Christians, by 2010 that figure had fallen to less than 40 percent. Christians of all denominations comprise 33 percent of the world's population, and Muslims 22 percent. In Africa, "religion shows no sign of disappearing or diminishing in public importance, as development theorists have generally supposed."[17] In fact, Christian faith has risen there from 9 percent to 47.9 percent over the last one hundred years. It has been reported that, for the first time, the rise in Christian affiliation in the Global South is outpacing the decline in the North, fuelling a global net growth in Christianity.[18]

This landscape has important implications for the development profession, which is heavily influenced by modernity thinking. It has to wrestle with how it can best serve the Majority World, which sees religious faith as its primary source of meaning. While development practice has espoused working in a close and participatory way with communities, the place of religion has been awkward and unsettling. Some parts of the development sector have responded by treating religious institutions in a transactional way, for example, by rolling out workshops, training, or services that they have not been involved with in assessing, shaping, or designing.

This approach merely recognizes religion as an "unavoidable" feature of the development landscape. Critics argue that such an approach is "based on normative assumptions in terms of how both religion and development are conceptualized: religion is understood to be apart from 'mainstream' development, while development is defined as that thing that development agencies do."[19] This kind of thinking has not optimized the constructive role that religion can play in securing development outcomes.

There are many disadvantages to instrumentalism. It is a type of approach that uses faith institutions in an episodic way as a delivery channel. However, the literature suggests that development programs are more effective when reinforced *from within* communities. Where a development project or message is experienced as something from the "outside" that has been projected upon a community, it will be much harder for it to take hold. Wendy Tyndale cautions, "The reduction of relationships between people as merely instrumental to the aim of attaining maximum economic efficiency has often led to a breakdown of solidarity..."[20] Again, "When genuine participation is sacrificed...the sense of common ownership is soon lost and with it, the motivation to make a contribution."[21]

At its worst, instrumentalism reduces the relationship with the faith institution or community to one of convenience. The underlying assumption in some cases is that externally produced pre-packaged messages or projects can be neatly received and socialized. The data casts serious doubt on that assumption, illustrating that the church or faith institution can be left with the task of translating or reframing the project. The real cost of development work includes the cost incurred by the religious institution in undertaking this important contextualization. It can be argued that co-creating with the community provides greater ownership from the outset and is more respectful. It builds capacity, shares knowledge, draws on local input, and promotes goodwill. In this regard, Denis Goulet has noted that religious beliefs, "when properly respected, can serve as the springboard for modes of development which are more humane than those drawn from outside paradigms. When development builds from indigenous values it extracts lower social costs and imposes less human suffering and cultural destruction than when it copies outside models."[22]

An enlightened secularism?

As Western donor governments have sought to affirm their secular underpinnings, this has led to a hesitancy in recognizing the positive role that religious faith and faith institutions might play in carrying out development work. One bureaucratic response has been to avoid or filter out faith-related elements from government-funded development programs. An example is the stance taken by some European governments who will not fund development projects that are co-located with faith institutions. Another has been the historical resistance of multilateral agencies to engage with faith-based institutions. In development work, this may be seen as a kind of neo-colonialism that is disrespectful to local culture.[23] When Western governments and donor agencies avoid engaging with faith institutions, they may, by default, export a particular view about development. Over time, the exclusion of faith elements from government-funded development programs may suggest that there is no valid role for faith-based approaches.

An implication of this book is that consideration should be given to how religious beliefs can be positively used to reinforce the government's own goals for development. A recent Australian funded program in Papua New Guinea (PNG) recognized at an early stage the need to increase and strengthen the role of the local church.[24]

This contrasts with the more traditional approach, which attempts to separate religious belief from development as if they were mutually exclusive worlds. The rationale for the PNG partnership is compelling:

> Working with the churches in PNG is highly relevant for the PNG context. With strong legitimacy among the population, which is more than 95% Christian, churches can contribute to public policy in PNG, enhance government transparency and accountability, support social justice and peace building and develop social capital. In addition the churches in PNG play a crucial role in service delivery—some 50% of health services and 40% of the schools in PNG are run by the churches. In the context of PNG, where the government is relatively fragile with very little capacity, the role of the churches is especially important. The churches themselves have strengths in their legitimacy, widespread presence and ability to shape social capital but can benefit from stronger structures, systems and development practice. Such capacity development is the highly relevant focus of the CPP [Church Partnership Program].[25]

I would argue that this type of partnership is not inconsistent with the responsibilities of secular government and should be encouraged. Properly understood, secularism is about being neutral about religion, not anti-religious. As such, it involves balancing competing viewpoints—including the freedom of religious expression and conscience; the equality of people with religious, non-religious, or anti-religious consciousness; and creating an open public forum where people can speak on behalf of these different points of view.[26] In this way, secular government is a helpful system of government that seeks to accommodate diversity and pluralism.

At times, secularism has been misunderstood as a position of entrenched suspicion or antagonism toward religious viewpoints, and this has influenced the willingness of some actors to engage with it. Anne-Marie Holenstein reminds us that "the secular system of a State does not necessarily presuppose a non-religious society or the exclusion of cooperation between Government Donor Agencies and Faith-Based Organizations. A secular system frees the State from being patronized by religion, but it also frees religion and religious communities from patronization by the State."[27]

One commentator who has been cautious about the resurgent interest in the role of faith in development is Gerard Clarke. He points to the dangers of proselytizing and the denigration of faiths in poor and culturally sensitive areas. At the same time, Clarke recognizes an organization such as the Department for International Development (DFID)

> must revise its secular and technocratic vision of development
> ... Operationally, it must develop a more coherent corporate position on faith and development, promote faith literacy among staff, adjust its funding modalities to better accommodate FBOs, and diversify its engagement with FBOs beyond the mainstream Christian churches, while working to build their capacity and their inclusion in key development partnerships."[28]

This encapsulates something of the dilemma facing policymakers.

Both the benefits and the risks of greater engagement with faith institutions and faith-based methodologies are real. Holenstein acknowledges this highly ambiguous position: "Religion and faith communities can be effective as 'angels of peace' and as 'warmongers.'"[29] They can legitimize the use of force and demonize people of other faiths.[30] Religious NGOs can exacerbate conflicts by setting up exclusionary boundaries in favor of their co-religionists and engaging in proselytism.[31] While noting the attempt to mitigate risk through the development of codes of conduct,[32] she recommends that critical questions be framed as a reference point to test relationships. Some of the questions she proposes include:

- Does the program contribute to faith harmony beyond its own faith community?

- Does the program strengthen group solidarity exclusively within its own faith community or does it have a socially integrating effect? In other words, do others outside that faith community really benefit?

- How is a local FBO seen by the local population?[33]

This seems to be a very constructive approach that could be considered by governments to help reconcile their dilemma.

It should be noted that the risks are not all one-sided. There are also very real risks for religiously based institutions in dealing with governments, especially the risk of being co-opted into political or other agendas. There is evidence to indicate that the effectiveness of development programs is compromised when this occurs.[34]

The conversation about "development"

It is important for the church and other faith institutions to have a voice in contributing to the discussion about the nature of "development." The last two decades have seen a fragmentation in development studies and a move away from classical economic and rationalistic approaches, opening up space for religious viewpoints.[35] Some argue that this opening up should move beyond a narrow consideration of how religion can be enlisted to serve development agendas to a broader conversation about what development is. The narrow approach "misses something of the plurality of positions within development studies. Development as a concept has always been contested, and development studies remains an interdisciplinary field, reflective and heterodox in its epistemological orientation, drawing from a continuum of social science theory and methods."[36]

Too often the question of engaging with religious NGOs is judged according to the interests of the mainstream development industry.[37] In this respect I agree with Philip Fountain who seeks to turn the question on its head: "Rather than asking how religion may align with our (secular liberal) priorities, attention should be turned to the more interesting and important question as to how development came to be seen among mainstream actors as distinctly secular, universal and [a] virtually unquestionable moral good such that religious involvement could be imagined as an abnormal intrusion."[38]

There is clearly work to be done in establishing the legitimacy of faith perspectives in the sector. It is important that faith leaders inject a spiritual perspective. For the Majority World, spirituality is an important part of human experience, and any concept of development that is dismissive of this perspective will be deficient.

More positively, for many practitioners and some institutions, development has come to mean *human* development. There has been a movement away from narrower material and technocratic aspects. According to the United Nations Development Program website, human development "is about creating an environment in which people can develop their full potential, and lead productive, creative lives in accordance with their needs and interests."[39] As early as 1980, Goulet described development experts as "one-eyed giants" who "analyse, prescribe, and act as if man could live by bread alone, as if human destiny could be stripped to its material dimensions alone."[40] Twenty years later, Tyndale echoed that flaws in the development process can be referenced to the failure to consider metaphysical questions concerning human life.[41] During the last ten years, there has been a dramatic surge of interest. It has taken a long time for these more holistic conceptions of development to gain any real traction. The voice of religious leaders may help ensure that this shift in emphasis does not dissipate.

There are a number of reflections arising from this book that suggest that a long-term holistic approach to development must consider spirituality. First, in many of the communities covered by the data, spiritual beliefs were strong and pervasive, consistent with worldwide data on increasing religiosity in the Majority World. Second, in some places, faith and daily life were inseparable, so that development activity divorced from a religious worldview was seen as culturally anomalous.[42] Third, some societies expressed their faith in a very communal manner, rather than seeing religion as a private choice. This led to spiritual expectations with regard to such things as prayer being projected upon the development agency in order to achieve local acceptance.

It is important for faith institutions to represent their constituencies in the conversation about the development process. In short, spiritual beliefs and practices are central to many people's understanding of what it means to be human, and faith institutions have a legitimate voice in the development dialogue.

In recent years, these conversations have begun to be formalized. The first initiative was the Development Dialogue on Values and Ethics sponsored by James Wolfenson of the World Bank in conjunction with George Carey, the then Archbishop of Canterbury. This evolved into the World Faith Development Dialogue, again facilitated by the World Bank, which established a secretariat under the leadership of Katherine Marshall. In addition, there has been a formal dialogue between faith leaders and DFID[43] and the establishment of the University of Birmingham's Religions and Development Programme.

Some faith leaders—including Archbishop Rowan Williams[44] and Pope Benedict XVI, through his papal encyclicals—have also made strong personal contributions that have touched upon important development themes.[45] These conversations have been highly beneficial in opening up a broader set of ideas about development.[46]

New kinds of development practice

The recognition of a greater role for faith within "development" may alter the boundaries of development work itself. It may call for the acknowledgement of an additional set of methodologies used by faith-based agencies, even if those methods seem strange. It may also result in a broader sphere of activities that may be considered under the rubric of "development."

One of the potential strengths of faith-based approaches to development is their strong ethics and values framework. This can be an advantage in helping communities frame development messages that are in sympathy with their religious teaching. Marshall has plainly stated that "the arguments for engaging in an active dialogue between institutions of faith and development turn around the growing appreciation that there are enormous areas of overlap, convergence, shared concern and knowledge, and a core purpose."[47] That overlap provides a positive foundation for mutual action.

A defining feature of religions is that they are concerned with transcendent or ultimate truths. These truths may be based on revelation, sacred sources, or traditional beliefs that are handed down from one generation to the next. Although religions vary from one another, most are concerned with an unseen, unprovable world:

> For most people in the world, including Africa, "religion" refers to the belief in the existence of an invisible world, distinct but not separate from the visible one, which is home to spiritual beings that are deemed to have effective powers over the material world. For people who hold this point of view, the invisible world is an integral part of the world, which cannot be reduced to its visible or material form only.[48]

Many religions hold that the spiritual world is linked to the material world through prayer and cultic practice, and that one influences the other.

When it comes to faith-based development practice, the data indicated a wide range of spiritual or faith-related methodologies. These included corporate devotional practice, private and public prayer, a more embedded longer-term relationship with churches, a positive role for discernment in decision-making, the role of faith in inculcating social values, building up churches' capacities to strengthen civil society, using religion to help form social identity, and the use of scripture in designing programmatic tools. These methodologies clearly recognized an active role for religious faith within "development."

Moving beyond these categories, the data traversed more explicitly "spiritual" territory by recognizing spiritual influence within the broader penumbra of wellbeing. The data showed that staff responded to perceived malign spiritual influences through prayer, including prayers of deliverance. This poses something of an intellectual dilemma. While the social consequences of all belief systems can be observed and mapped to some degree, spiritual knowledge of this kind is esoteric and cannot be tested. At this deeper spiritual level, there can be a clash of worldviews.

According to the data, some traditional religious practices had strongly negative consequences. They were seen as oppressive and socially debilitating, and in some cases were linked with so-called witch-craft killings and the stigmatization of widows. It is important to note that some commentators like Kurt Ver Beek, and Gerrie Ter Haar and Stephen Ellis[49] have identified some positive features of traditional belief systems that can be used in pursuing development goals. Namawu Alolo and James Connell have also given a largely sympathetic account of African Traditional Religion (ATR), without denying its more sensational and negative aspects.

The lines are blurry and to some extent subjective. If it is accepted that development should be more holistic, in recognition that for most people spiritual beliefs are an important aspect of their human experience, then in some concrete settings there may be a contest of spiritual ideas. It was in this area that the data raised the prospect of religious imperialism in opposition to aspects of ATR.

The implication from this research for the sector is not to deny the role of religion in development, which can be positive, but to ensure that the manner of engagement around spiritual topics is respectful, ethical, and non-coercive. This is the key. While spiritual belief is an important part of human existence, freedom of conscience is a non-negotiable development norm. This lies at the heart of all truly participatory development approaches. As the role of faith gains greater legitimacy in development work, faith-based methodologies and the scope of development practice will come under closer scrutiny. What must not change, however, are the accepted norms of respectful community engagement.

Overview

This book illustrates the way the beliefs and religious motifs of FBOs can play out in their development work. This reveals a distinctive praxis that can lead to very sympathetic and effective engagement within developing communities.

More broadly, I argue that there are strong reasons for a much greater engagement between the development sector, governments, and religious institutions. In relation to faith-based development organizations, the data has shown that the nature of their engagement with religious institutions does not need to be instrumental or transactional, but can be pursued in a much more positive way.

Historically, the literature indicates that the systemic anti-religious bias in development has operated to the detriment of the world's poor. This research supports the renewed impetus to examine the role of religious faith within development practice and to flesh out potential areas of comparative advantage. The more traditional dichotomous approach of the sector, and of Western governments, which attempt to sever "faith" from "development," are retrograde because they will fracture the integrated values base of communities and organizations.

The dangers for governments and policymakers of greater engagement with religious organizations are very real, and it is suggested that the way forward lies in establishing clear protocols, review mechanisms, and administrative safeguards. There are also real risks of *not* engaging more deeply if governments are to fulfill their development objectives.

It has been demonstrated that faith-based development does have some unique strengths to offer. It can be very hard, however, for these organizations to maintain their faith and preserve their integrated values base. The next section reflects on how accountability is understood by faith-based development organizations and the factors that conspire to suppress their religious identity.

PART THREE

Faith, Development, and Accountability

CHAPTER 14

Accountability for Faith-Based Development Organizations

Why should Christians care about accountability?

Christians are a people who live for God in the world. This dual axis is evident in the two great commands: to wholeheartedly love God and neighbor. Karl Barth puts it this way: "First and supremely it is God who exists for the world. And since the community of Jesus Christ exists first and supremely for God, it has no option but in its own manner and place to exist for the world. How else could it exist for God?"[1] Anything that helps the Christian community to more diligently serve God in the world must be embraced. This is why Christians should care about accountability.

At a personal level, a sense of being accountable strengthens discipleship. For this reason the Christian faith has a strong tradition of encouraging penitential self-reflection. This kind of thinking helps Christians to be honest about their failings and to be better directed in their future efforts. The assurance of God's grace helps individual Christians to continuously recommit to his service. This is equally true of Christian organizations. Yet this abundant grace should never be taken as an excuse for inaction or lassitude.[2] Well-developed notions of accountability provide a renewed focus on Christ's mission and guard against carelessness and presumption.

Why should faith-based development organizations care about accountability?

Faith-based development organizations exist for public purposes. Their ministry objectives and continued effectiveness depend on the support offered by diverse stakeholders. The public nature of this kind of mission, both in inspiration and execution, requires a commensurate level of accountability.

When an organization identifies itself as "Christian," this imbues a special responsibility. The adjective "Christian" speaks not only of the self-giving love and compassion of Jesus but also of the obedience and faithfulness in the way mission is carried out. God commands his people not to take his name in vain. Faith-based development organizations do take God's name, whether expressly or implicitly. It is unclear whether such a thing as corporate blasphemy exists, but this is worth reflecting on.

In addition to the responsibility to honor God's name through conduct there are responsibilities owed to all who uphold the organization's work and mission: its leaders, employees, volunteers, donors, partners, and beneficiaries. Whenever an FBO slips from the highest standards, multiple stakeholders are affected.

Faith-based development organizations require strong leaders who can clearly articulate the responsibility of ministering in Christ's name. Nothing can substitute for this kind of leadership, yet it can be reinforced by embedding organizational practices that underscore the responsibilities of Christian ministry. Well-thought-out accountability measures fall into this category.[3]

Faith-based organizations must be honest in their intent. Where they have signed up for a range of accountability measures, such as charters of best practice, their "Yes" should be a "Yes"[4] and not a qualified "maybe." A "Yes" in name only would leave the organization open to a charge of hypocrisy.[5]

To whom are faith-based organizations accountable?

Ultimately, accountability is directly to God for the organization's work.[6] While this is true, it requires unpacking, for a narrow emphasis on an ultimate obligation to God can be misused to avoid responsibilities of a more intermediate and temporal nature.

The biblical position is that accountability and responsibility are intertwined. Faith-based development organizations are responsible to a broad range of stakeholders. These include employees, governments, funding bodies, donors, church bodies, partner agencies, other development organizations, and most important, the world's poor and disenfranchised. To say that an organization is responsible to these stakeholders means that it is accountable to them, albeit in different ways. The ultimate responsibility to God can be discharged only by taking these more particular responsibilities seriously.

What does accountability to different stakeholders look like?

Every FBO has accountability to different groups, and the nature of that accountability is contextualized. The Bible indicates that the way accountabilities are discharged must be ethical and carefully considered. As one example, the gospels teach that where a brother is caught up in error, the fault must be brought to his attention gently and privately in the first instance. In that way the brother may be restored without humiliation. And yet a persistent failure does require an escalation.[7]

In the area of disclosure, which is only one aspect of accountability, the competing interests of stakeholders may need to be balanced. For example, faith-based development organizations must comply with government obligations to report the level of donated funds, but that must be done in a way that does not breach the privacy or trust of individual donors. And while an organization may disclose general information to donors, ethical considerations apply when it comes to disclosure of personal information or stories about beneficiaries in programs, such as, for example, their HIV status. The point is that the extent of disclosure must be sufficient to help ensure accountability to the particular stakeholder while balancing the interests of others.

Leaving aside the complexities of particular cases, the general trajectory of scripture is clear. The people of God are to be light on a hill,[8] known by their love[9] and their good citizenship.[10] They are to work hard, infusing the world with their goodness and service. Secrecy and obfuscation are anathema to the collective calling to shine *and be* the light of Christ.

Scripture and accountability

The New Testament was not set in a corporate or highly institutionalized environment. There are no first-century organizations comparable to modern faith-based development organizations. Perhaps the closest are early church communities that were struggling to serve God in the world. Nonetheless, there are some general principles that emerge that can help inform the nature of accountability to particular types of stakeholders. Some key accountabilities are discussed below.

Accountability to the poor

Faith-based development organizations must remain vigilant in their mission to poor communities, for that is the godly calling for which they were created. This fundamental accountability must be discharged diligently and faithfully. As organizations become larger and more complex, this original sense of call can become lost. It is easy for organizations to become more concerned about institutional preservation than the communities they purport to serve. Some of the factors that can place an organization's sense of identity at risk are discussed in chapter 16.

In this context it may be helpful for the organization to remind itself of the rich and varied sources of its mission. One is the prophetic call to care for widows and orphans,[11] which echoes across both Old and New Testaments.[12] Another is the consciousness of all humans being made in God's image.[13] This stamps every human being with an intrinsic dignity that should be upheld. Being made in the image of God goes further than establishing global fraternity, for humans are also made in the *relational* image of the Godhead, and that invites every human into a fellowship of self-giving love.

The Golden Rule[14] instills empathy and reminds us that we can serve God only by serving each other.[15] Jesus' transcendent teaching about *neighbor* breaks through our ethnic and familial narrowness.[16] His solidarity with the poor shows us what an authentic love in action looks like.[17] Scripture consistently teaches that we should never tire of doing good, especially for the poor. Jesus' incarnational presence discredits our feeble attempts at serving God while neglecting the least of Jesus' brothers and sisters.[18] And his instruction to pray for his kingdom come on earth does not allow us to outsource personal responsibility.[19] These and other sources were discussed in chapter 2.

By deep and frequent reflection on the biblical and theological foundations of mission, faith-based development organizations can resist the temptation to become pious, lazy, and self-serving.

A related mistake is to ignore "inbound" accountability. Development practitioners should listen and learn from the poor. The Good News of Jesus implores his followers to seek the best for others. Ministry approaches that breed dependency, or that are patronizing, or paternalistic, or that treat the poor as "clients" diminish the Good News. The global family includes the poor who must be respectfully and sensitively engaged. It has been observed that "The Christian gospel has sometimes been made the tool of imperialism and of that we have to repent."[20] A frequent assumption in the West is that we know best.

In this light an important accountability is the accountability *to listen*. This must not become a pretense or a tick-the-box process. For a Christian development organization the listening must signify a genuine willingness to learn. Development workers should try and empathize deeply with those cast out by unjust systems: "We can find ourselves learning about such struggles from those whom we tried to charitably help before. They can become our teachers, rather than we theirs."[21] The poor are constantly evangelizing us; they are a "living appeal for our conversion to the gospel."[22] And this appeal is not a timid gospel that evokes merely shallow pity. It is nothing less than true liberation of our selves. The lives of the poor challenge, confront, and yet ultimately liberate those who respond in spirit with the listening love of Christ.

Accountability to donors

Christians should be beyond reproach in their financial dealings. There must be proper oversight mechanisms for the application of both donated goods and funds.

In the Old Testament we see an instructive account of how community finances were applied in the repairing of the temple.[23] This involved placing donated monies in a secure chest in a guarded location, the counting of the funds by responsible persons in the presence of each other, recording the account taken, the placing of the money in smaller bags, and then passing on the sums to overseers. Funds received in this way were not used for any other purpose and were not co-mingled with other offerings belonging to the priests.[24]

In Acts 6:1–4 we read about a specific group of disciples being appointed to oversee the daily distribution of food in the community. This was to ensure that there was no discrimination in the way those resources were applied, especially against the interests of widows of a certain ethnic origin.

And in 2 Corinthians 8, Paul relates a program where the church in Corinth was going to contribute to care for the needs of the church in Jerusalem. The trusted disciple Titus, and another brother beyond reproach, were appointed to accompany the offering from Corinth and to personally oversee its distribution. Their intention was that "no one should blame us about this generous gift that we are administering, for we intend to do what is right not only in the Lord's sight but also in the sight of others."[25]

Some clear and common themes emerge from these brief references. In short, God expects, and scripture applauds, the highest standard of probity in dealing with donated resources. This includes proper security of all funds received, open and transparent accounting, the application of funds only for their intended purpose, careful oversight, and the need to establish processes that are right in the sight of both God and the community.

Accountability regimes that give effect to these principles are consistent with the witness of scripture. But they are only half the story. The other half is maximizing the effectiveness of God-given resources. There is little credit in transparent accounting for a harmful or ineffective program.

In Matthew 24 Jesus tells a searching parable about the return on investment of another's funds.[26] This sobering parable is set in the context of the dawning of the kingdom of God. In the parable, a man goes on a journey and entrusts his servants with his property. To one he gives five talents, to another two talents, and to a third one talent, each according to his ability. The first two servants invest their talents wisely and produce a great return. The third servant buries his talent in a hole in the ground. The master returns from his journey and demands an account from each servant. The third servant is condemned as lazy and wicked.

The parable commends those who take initiative and who produce a return for the sake of the kingdom. It equally condemns the wasting of opportunity. The express teaching of scripture is that of those to whom much has been given, much will be expected.[27]

It is vital that faith-based development organizations have in place mechanisms to track their ministry effectiveness. Tracking *efficiency*, that is, the cost of raising and administering funds, is relatively easier— but such tracking proceeds on an underlying assumption that the work funded is effective. That assumption cannot go untested. While efficiency is an important aspect of stewardship, scripture places a greater emphasis on the *effectiveness* of what we do. Christ's teaching consistently focuses on how fruitful disciples are in his service.[28]

Any accountability initiatives that promote greater fruitfulness are to be welcomed. A relevant question for a faith-based development organization to ask is whether it is a good and faithful servant, or whether it is digging a hole in the ground?

Accountability to governments

The general rule is that Christians, as far as possible, are to respect government authorities. Romans 13:1 urges: "Let every person be subject to the governing authorities; for there is no authority except from God." The application of this rule is expanded in verse 7: "Pay to all what is due to them—taxes to whom taxes are due, revenue to whom revenue is due, respect to whom respect is due, honor to whom honor is due."

This principle has been regarded as problematic for Christians living under tyranny or despotism, or where the specific demands of conscience have come into conflict with an obligation owed to the state. Christians have qualified Paul's teaching to the extent necessary to fulfill the higher duty of loving God with all one's heart, and soul, and mind.[29] In some contexts, nonviolent resistance has been the path followed. In others, there has been conscientious objection to military service.

In most cases the obligation of submission to state authorities will cause no problem. In a regulatory sense, faith-based development organizations must comply with laws about taxation, fundraising, and employment. The way in which they pursue their advocacy, however, may need to be carefully nuanced in some jurisdictions. It is noted that submitting to a governing authority does not preclude trying to change its viewpoint.

There may be situations in which an organization may be unable to reconcile its presence in a country with the attitudes and behavior of the government concerned. In these cases, faith-based development organizations can be expected to act in the company of others, whether the UN, or faith communities, or other NGOs. It is difficult to conceive of a faith-based development organization taking other than nonviolent action. It will take special care to ensure that it is not inadvertently drawn into politico-military alliances that compromise its ability to fulfill its mission.

In those countries where faith-based development organizations operate it may be appropriate to ask whether *minimum compliance* with regulatory regimes is the best expression of Christian discipleship. There is an ethic Jesus teaches about going the extra mile. Perhaps in a regulatory context this means seeking to influence government policy in a more positive way to achieve better systems. Christians, and faith-based development agencies, should stand ready to do even greater good wherever they can.

Accountability to the development sector

A posture of operational humility should characterize the way faith-based development organizations engage with others. This is especially important for larger, better resourced, and more prominent organizations. Arrogance of any kind must be eschewed, because every agency knows that God works through a variety of other agencies, both faith-based *and* secular.

Unlike private commercial organizations, faith-based development organizations do not seek financial returns for shareholders. On the contrary, they seek social returns and the creation of social wealth and opportunity. This understanding must influence the way organizations interact; it dictates that relationships with other agencies should primarily be collegial rather than competitive. They should be open to sharing their experiences in relief and development work, those things that have been successful, and those that haven't.

Many FBOs will understand their mandate in terms of living for the kingdom of God. As Christian organizations they will recognize that they do not exist for themselves. Instead they will be inspired by "the sovereignty of the risen Lord and the coming sovereignty of him who has conquered death and is bringing life, righteousness, and the Kingdom of God."[30] That understanding leaves them seeking God's horizon, looking for new and better ways to serve him. Their responsibility is to lead, behave collaboratively, and embrace those initiatives that instill greater accountability to God and each other. Faith-based development organizations will disparage narrow self-interest and try and work collegially, for the very heart of Jesus' message (and action) is radical love expressed in the service of others.[31]

Accountability to the Church Universal

No faith-based development organization is the bride of Christ.[32] The fellowship of faith-based development organizations unites around a narrower, though God-inspired mission. That mission is to reach out in Christian love to the world's poor and marginalized through community development, to respond with Christian compassion to humanitarian disasters, and to advocate against injustice. While not the bride of Christ, faith-based development organizations will be anxious to help and support the bride in ways appropriate to their mission.

Three types of accountability spring to mind. The first is to ensure that the behavior of faith-based development organizations does not dishonor the church universal. There are many rich and divergent traditions of Christian faith: Roman Catholicism, Protestantism and the reformed churches, the Orthodox faith, Pentecostalism, and many locally constituted independent churches. Faith-based development organizations require a generous ecumenism. They must not behave in a way that discredits the extended Christian family, or disparages any part of it.

Second, faith-based development organizations have a responsibility to help churches everywhere understand and live out their mandate for social justice. A holistic gospel calls the followers of Jesus to transformative social action. Faith-based development organizations may properly conceive their work as a *diaconal*[33] ministry of service. This service witnesses to the servanthood and compassion of Christ, and in so doing inspires Christians and people of goodwill everywhere.

Third, faith-based development organizations have an accountability to speak prophetic words that will often challenge church communities in the West and encourage those in the Global South. Churches are built up by gaining a broader and deeper understanding of God's work in the world. Speaking into the life of congregations helps guard against insularity and pietism and contributes to a sense of global fellowship. Luke reminds us that "people will come from east and west, from north and south, and will eat in the kingdom of God."[34] This sweeping vision of grace pushes aside the dull parochialism sometimes present within congregational life.

Disclosure as an aspect of accountability

One aspect of accountability is the transparent disclosure of information, good and bad. Faith-based organizations are public organizations, and they must be accountable to their stakeholders. But what if the information disclosed is potentially damaging to the organization? Should bad news be disclosed? To some degree, this question is academic because there are many existing professional charters that cannot be lightly ignored.

It is nonetheless worth reflecting on human reluctance to disclose bad news. It can cause embarrassment, humiliation, and disappointment. Such disclosures can lead to donor disenchantment and revenue impacts. So why would any sensible organization apparently act to its own detriment?

A relationship of *trust* is forged by the kind of honesty that leads to vulnerability. Supporters and other stakeholders[35] should be taken seriously and not patronized. Many supporters will understand the complexity of development work. Taking supporters on a more realistic journey is about honesty. Development work is not risk-free and simple. A greater loyalty can come from treating supporters with respect and intelligence.

Bad news tends to leak out anyway. Any sense of cover-up can be far more damaging. Attempts to cover up by some religious organizations have profoundly compromised their reputation and moral authority. It has also aggravated damages in legal actions.[36]

While it may seem counterintuitive, the making of difficult disclosures is exactly what is required. This can be done in an appropriate way, time, and place to allow no space for those who allege cover-up or conspiracy and to speed organizational learning from such experiences. An attitude of openness is therefore highly protective. Experience shows that it will benefit organizations in the longer run.

Like individual Christians, organizations can also benefit from the discipline of self-reflection. God knows all our secrets already.[37] There is discomfort when we confront organizational failure head-on, but there is also grace, assurance, and time for learning. Critically, the discipline of facing up to and disclosing bad news creates a positive incentive for internal change. When matters are kept hidden, this advantage is lost, and the organization's light before the broader community will surely dim.

CHAPTER 15

Accountability for Crosscutting Themes

Since its inauguration, the UN and its various agencies have promulgated many charters and protocols that indirectly affect the work of NGOs. The principles set out in these instruments have been adopted by many countries and are now reflected in their official aid policies. FBOs receiving government funds may be required to adhere to these standards. In addition, governments are also free to impose their own priorities on aid programs that they support. This process has shaped the thinking and policy directions of the whole sector.

A long list of topical issues has emerged which are sometimes called "crosscutting themes." This term refers to topics that are considered so important that they ought to be "mainstreamed" in the design and implementation of development programs. Some common themes are: gender equality, child rights, the incorporation of minorities, indigenous culture and heritage, sustainability, community participation (including complaints and feedback mechanisms), human sexuality, human rights more generally, disability inclusion, environmental protection, and child protection. This list is by no means exhaustive.

In many areas, government requirements and sector trends will not cause any offense to FBOs. Some areas, however, may be more problematic. For example, in areas like reproductive health and sexual ethics tensions can arise. This underscores the need for FBOs to be very clear about what they think, and this requires careful and sustained theological reflection.

It is impossible to properly consider all of the potential issues in a book of this kind. I have, however, prepared a very brief overview of four areas that I have had to consider in my own professional experience. I recognize that this is scarcely adequate, but have concluded that some illustration is better than none. The four issues selected are: disability inclusion; gender equity; care for the environment; and child protection. What follows contains my own personal reflections.

Disability inclusion

Issue

In developing countries, people with disabilities live not just with the challenges of poverty but also with additional layers of disadvantage. There is a "bidirectional link" between poverty and disability: "disability may increase the risk of poverty, and poverty may increase the risk of disability."[1] In the case of women and girls with disabilities, the suite of problems can be compounded.

People with disabilities may be regarded as a burden to their families or to their society more generally; be denied educational opportunities; be seen as cursed or as having incurred some kind of divine punishment; be hidden away or isolated out of a sense of personal or family shame; be denied social opportunities; be tied up and restrained; be subject to physical or sexual abuse; and be denied any kind of voice or representation.

Reflection

While there are many emerging theologies of disability, there are also many aspects on which Christians can wholeheartedly agree. The starting point is that God loves and affirms all people. His grace is limitless, and this is scandalous in any society where there is an inherent tendency to judgment and exclusion. People living with a disability are not cursed, nor is their disability a product of sin. This idea was specifically repudiated by Jesus in John 9 when the disciples questioned the reason behind a case of congenital blindness.[2] That said, it is understandable how people living with disabilities may feel cursed, given their experience of a lack of human acceptance and generosity.

Living with disability can add to a person's vulnerability in a given social context. From ancient times God has sought protection for people with disabilities. For example, Leviticus 19:14 says: "You shall not revile the deaf or put a stumbling-block before the blind; you shall fear your God: I am the Lord." While it is appropriate to seek protection for people living with disabilities, their vulnerability does not diminish their humanity.

For this reason, people living with disabilities should not be seen as objects to be pitied or treated with condescension. It is very unfair to define or stereotype people because of their disability. Treating people as fellow humans means putting assumptions to one side. Affirming the humanity of others means that, to the extent possible, people living with disabilities should have agency over the decisions affecting them and be active, contributing members of society. This is about preserving human dignity.

For Christians there can be no link between "cure" and acceptance of people with disabilities. A fixation on cure, which is often well intended, can present as a lack of acceptance. It may equate people with disabilities as "sick" people who need to be "fixed." Again, this defines people by their disability and ignores their present capacities and giftedness.

Redemption for people living with disability is no different from redemption for anyone else. People with disabilities are in need of God's grace. There is perhaps one point of difference. Social redemption for people with disabilities requires something important that lies beyond their control; a reform of prevalent attitudes that obscure and deflect from their humanity.

The topic of disability raises many theological questions that cannot be explored here. One is, what does it mean for a person with disabilities to be made in the image of God? If the image of God is about love and service, then people living with disabilities are both affirmed in love and called in service. People with disabilities have a great deal to teach the body of Christ. In weakness the strength of Christ is most clearly shown.[3] For many, their disability imbues a strong sense of vocation.

God takes joy in all his creation, which he has declared to be good. When it comes to disability, it is contested whether disability is in fact a consequence of the Fall or simply an expression of diversity in God's creation. Some people living with a disability argue that their disability is an inherent part of who they are, and that it will have continuity for them in the resurrection. In this view, idealized notions of physical or mental perfection are set aside. These questions raise more broadly the nature of bodily resurrection and its continuity with earthly experience.[4]

Having said that, there are some passages in the Old Testament, especially those about the exclusion of people with disabilities from cultic service, that on the surface are very difficult to understand.[5] One thing, however, is abundantly clear. Christ has come to establish a new temple in his own resurrection life. Through the Spirit we live in him and he in us. The fellowship that Jesus Christ offers is open and free for all, and that inclusiveness should be emulated in our human fellowship and service.

Response

The principal UN involvement in this area is the Convention on the Rights of Persons with Disabilities. The World Health Organization is also vitally interested in responses to disability and in 2011 released its inaugural World Report on Disability, which found that the proportion of people living with a disability was as high as 15 percent, much higher than previous estimates. One reason for the under-reporting of disabilities is that in many cultures people with disabilities are kept "out of sight, out of mind." This highlights the importance of the intentional inclusion of people with disabilities in development programs.

Although there is an important place for disability-specific programming, the greater need is for mainstreaming of disability inclusion as an aspect of all programs. Ultimately, inclusion in a formal sense is not enough to meet the aspirations of the Christian gospel. Only appreciation and a sense of true belonging will do that.

Gender equality

Issue
Women are marginalized and disadvantaged within many developing communities. A contributing factor is the inherited gender roles that limit participation and opportunity for women. This impedes economic, social, and civic engagement. A focus on creating specific opportunities for women and girls can help reverse entrenched disadvantage. It has also been shown over many decades that creating such opportunities for women is one of the best ways to achieve general uplift within a community.

Reflection
It may be helpful for FBOs to reflect on their own theological understanding about the role of women in society and the hermeneutical processes that have been involved, explicitly or implicitly, in reaching these positions. Verses are sometimes taken and used inappropriately to assign a subservient and diminished role to women in both the church and broader society. For example, there are particular verses in Paul's letters indicating that women should cover their heads for worship (indicating submission), keep silent, and submit to their husbands.[6]

Any view of scripture that sees spousal relationships as "proprietorial" is abhorrent and inconsistent with the freedom promised in Christ. Again, any view that sees violence against women as acceptable within domestic relationships cannot be considered Christian. It is sobering to realize that some of the most devout developing communities also have among the highest rates of domestic violence.[7] It is well to remember that Paul's advice about wives submitting to their husbands is *mutual* (Ephesians 5:21). Husbands are specifically enjoined to love their wives as Christ loved the church (Ephesians 5:25)—in other words, with a limitless, sacrificial, and honoring love, one in which abuse, neglect, or violence is completely anathema.

It is suggested that a more nuanced and critical scholarship leads to different understandings. Not everything Paul says can or should be given a universal application. On the contrary, there are aspects of Paul's teaching that are culturally conditioned and are of little value in establishing a godly view of contemporary social norms.

At a more general level, it must also be acknowledged that patriarchy was present in the formulation of the Christian sacred texts.[8] Most scripture was written by men, and the early church councils were comprised exclusively of men. It is important to appreciate this background in making sense of the scriptures.

Despite this background, Jesus' more liberating approach to gender relationships does insinuate its way into the gospels. Jesus, as a man, offers an alternative picture of how men may relate to women. There are a number of subtly subversive stories including, for example, the famous exchange with the Samaritan woman at the well. This encounter was scandalous in its particular social context, but was affirming, revelatory, and life giving for the woman.[9]

It is clear that Jesus has a close relationship with women. They were close friends, he healed them, they supported his ministry financially (Luke 8:3), they were the only ones to stand with him at his crucifixion (when others abandoned him) (Mark 15:40–41), they were present at his burial, and they were the first to discover the empty tomb and see Jesus after the resurrection. As Elisabeth Moltmann-Wendel has pointed out, it is women who were the bearers of the actual traditions about the death and resurrection of Jesus.[10]

Jesus accepts women as they are. He breaks social taboos. For example, he touches Jairus's daughter when raising her, becoming "unclean" in doing so. Jesus also vigorously debates women like Martha, and he receives the ministry of Mary in anointing his body before death.

From a development perspective, Jesus' ministry is vitally concerned with the poor, and he lived his life in solidarity with the poor. Then, as now, women are massively overrepresented among the world's poor. It follows that Jesus has a special empathy for vast numbers of the world's women. A common ground between gender inequality as a development issue and the Christian gospel is that both aspire to greater freedom. There is no longer Jew nor Greek, male nor female (Galatians 3:28).

In the Old Testament, there are stories that reveal how God uses women in the most extraordinary ways. An incident that sticks in my mind is from Exodus 2:1–9. The background to the story is that Pharaoh was starting to worry about the increasing number of Hebrews in Egypt. He saw them as a threat and responded by issuing an edict that every newborn Hebrew male was to be drowned at birth (Exodus 1:22). Moses has an absolutely pivotal place in God's story of redemption for his people. He rescues them from Egypt, receives God's

Law, and then journeys with Israel toward the Promised Land. Before any of that can happen, Moses needs to be rescued *himself*. Who contributes to this rescue?

First his mother hides him, and then places him in a basket in the reeds by the edge of the Nile River (Exodus 2:3). Then the baby's older sister carefully stands watch (Exodus 2:4).

Next, Pharaoh's daughter sees the basket (Exodus 2:5). Her maidservant then steps into the river to retrieve it (Exodus 2:5). On cue, Moses' sister intervenes and offers to find a Hebrew woman to look after the baby (Exodus 2:7). Conveniently, the baby's actual mother is given official responsibility to look after him (Exodus 2:8–9). Finally, Pharaoh's daughter adopts Moses into the royal house (Exodus 2:10).

What does this episode tell us? Every person involved in the rescue of Moses was a woman. God's plans, and figuratively his covenant through Moses, are rescued by a group of clever and compassionate women (some of whom are outside the Hebrew faith!). In the middle of a very patriarchal world, a story appears that offers a very telling glimpse of how God relies on and values women in a most fundamental way.

Response

Development is not a narrow construct that is just about physical deficits, like access to food and water (as important as that is). It is also about human development more broadly, and this may include challenging the highly gendered social relationships that exist in some communities, including many Christian contexts. Women in most developing communities do not experience life in its fullness, and the example of Jesus can offer inspiration, support, and encouragement to development programs run by FBOs that have this aim. The example of Jesus is especially relevant to other men.

Care for the environment (including climate change)

Issue

Development programs should seek to bless creation as well as people. There is a growing realization about the interconnectedness of the whole created order. When unsustainable demands are placed on the environment, this exposes both human communities and the natural world to unacceptable risk.

Reflection

Right from the beginning, God's injunction to humans to exercise dominion over the created world came with significant responsibilities. A laissez faire exploitative attitude is completely contemptuous of God's plan:

"The land, the creation, was understood to belong to God, not us. We are not free to use the land as we wish... We ought to relate to the land (not use it) in a way that guarantees justice and preserves righteousness, the right order of creation. This is what having dominion is all about."[11] As good stewards, humans should be curators of what God has provided, thinking in terms of relationships and responsibilities, not merely unrestrained consumption or profit.

"Development" is not about repeating mistakes made in the West. Rampant consumerism, waste, pollution, and the despoiling of natural environments is not a model to be commended to anyone. On the contrary, there is a great deal that traditional and indigenous cultures can teach others about the sensitive use of land. These are lessons that should be heeded. Walter Brueggemann warns, "The staggering discernment is that death comes not only to the weak and poor [from unjust exploitation of the land] but eventually death reaches even into the life of the powerful and affluent who are not immune to death when it comes to the community."[12]

Our theology of creation needs to be carefully thought through. The much-lauded idea of "progress" requires very careful unpacking and scrutiny. Current patterns of consumption are demonstrably unsustainable. Consumerist gluttony, wherever it takes place, can have adverse global impacts felt disproportionately by the world's poor. A strong case can be made for rebalancing the relationship between humans and their physical environment. This is not a new call but one that is becoming increasingly urgent. Thirty years ago we were reminded: "Our human vocation is not to despoil, plunder and pillage, but to foster nurture, bless and give thanks. This sense of vocation emerges from our growing realization that human beings and the rest of creation grow together and share a common destiny."[13] Perhaps inspiration can be drawn from earlier theological traditions, such as the richness of Franciscan spirituality, which offers a far more appreciative view of the natural world.[14]

Christian theological responses that see salvation in pietistic terms, divorced from God's concern for the world, are unhelpful, unbiblical, and inadequate. The fact is that redemption does not stand apart from creation. A particularly dangerous stream of thought concerns "the rapture," a popular thesis that suggests that humans will be teleported from this earth as Armageddon approaches. Scholars like N. T. Wright have performed a great service in meticulously debunking this theory.[15] It matters because the unfortunate corollary of this line of thinking is that humans can treat the earth any way they please because God's elect are, literally, taking off. The Lord's Prayer is a sufficient corrective to this viewpoint. Our Savior has taught us to pray, "Thy Kingdom come, *on earth*" (Matthew 6:10, emphasis added).

An illustration of human sinfulness concerning creation is the phenomenon of climate change. It is now incontrovertible that the world is heating up due to carbon emissions. A substantial part of those emissions comes from the burning of fossil fuels to support industrialized economies. These economies are driven by the incessant demand for consumer goods. While this activity provides employment and a degree of material affluence, it also comes with a serious cost to creation that is felt most acutely in poor communities. The papal encyclical *Laudato Si'* thoughtfully addresses the issue of climate change in the context of both a theology of creation care and of justice.

There are multiple concerns confronting development practitioners as a result of climate change as the world heats up. Some of those concerns include:

- an acceleration of desertification into areas that could previously sustain productive agricultural activity

- the spread of mosquitoes carrying viruses such as malaria into areas that were previously unaffected; these areas are now becoming warm enough to sustain mosquitoes as carriers

- more prolonged and more frequent droughts; this places stress on vulnerable farming communities and contributes in a major way to the problem of food insecurity

- the prospect of low-lying coastal and delta communities facing rising sea levels as polar and glacial ice melts

- transmigration due to environmental change.

Another concern is the emerging link between climate change and more extreme weather events. Many FBOs engage in both longer-term development activities and humanitarian and emergency responses. Climate change will impact this mix. In short, there will be fewer resources for ongoing development work as climate-related emergencies increase. Development gains are also placed at risk when these disasters strike.

Response

FBOs can respond to the theme of care for creation in a variety of ways. An assessment should be undertaken of the environmental footprint of proposed development programs to ensure that they are sensitively designed to mitigate adverse environmental impacts. Programs that minimize their carbon footprint, emphasize renewable energy sources, respect ecological diversity, and adopt sustainable agricultural practices are to be commended. In some instances, the preservation of a community's natural heritage can become the basis of its economic development through eco-tourism and traditional arts and crafts.

In relation to climate change, FBOs should consider the ways in which they might influence energy policy on behalf of the world's poor. As is often the case, those most affected are least able to be heard in these debates. For many FBOs this will be properly seen as a question of justice. In developing communities, the important priority of disaster risk reduction (a term that refers to the ways in which communities can better prepare themselves for anticipated climate-related disasters) will become all the more pressing. In many contexts, churches—as grassroots and locally embedded organizations—are especially well placed to serve their communities in this way.

Child protection

Issue

In recent decades there has been a series of widespread and egregious scandals involving the abuse of children by clergy and other persons in positions of authority. These appalling abuses have been brought to light by well-publicized investigations and government enquiries around the world. The inestimable harm caused to children has been compounded by additional factors. For example, the abuse has not been isolated or opportunistic. On the contrary, it has been systemic and predatory. Even when alerted to abuse, the comprehensive pastoral response that might have been expected from church authorities has instead taken the form of obfuscation and institutional self-interest.

In carrying out development programs, FBO staff may have a continuous and direct exposure to children. An effective and transparent system of child protection is required to prevent, detect, and respond to instances of abuse. This is both a regulatory priority and an urgent theological imperative.

Reflection

The starting point in reflection on child protection is that God is a God of love. This is his overarching and preeminent characteristic. God is overwhelmed by nothing except love. Love is so ingrained in the Divine that, in God, that adjective becomes noun. God is not just loving, he *is* love. In relation to children this love is expressed in many ways.

Protection: The consistent witness of scripture is that God has a protective heart toward vulnerable groups. There are numerous references to caring for "widows and orphans," and this catch phrase reflects a constant and tender concern. In relation to vulnerable children God sees himself as a divine parent, exercising protective oversight. Not only does God understand himself in this way but Jesus encourages all his followers to relate to God as "Abba" or Father. This posture is invitational and relational, offering shelter to those experiencing the fragility of life.

Justice: God's fiercely protective stance demands justice for those who have no voice. He repeatedly urges his people to speak up for the fatherless and to defend their cause.[16] In other words, God expects his people to heed the prophet's call and advocate on behalf of all those who are in need of protection and who cannot protect themselves. Defending their cause may require comprehensive reform of the systems that expose children to risk.

Rights: Children bear the image of God and are imbued with a sacred dignity because of this. Development programs should be especially mindful of the rights of children and cultivate ways for their healthy participation and growth. Those who stand in a relationship of care toward children are duty bound to uphold their rights.

Acceptance: Jesus welcomes and accepts children. They are not to be regarded as a nuisance or a distraction but as individuals cherished by God. Jesus repudiates the cultural norms of his day by welcoming and openly engaging with children. Even more significantly, Jesus chooses to use children as the metaphor for acceptance into his kingdom: "Truly I tell you, unless you change and become like children, you will never enter the kingdom of heaven" (Matthew 18:3). Given that the kingdom of God is the endpoint of Jesus' ministry, this reference is powerfully affirming of children.

Sacredness of life: All human life is precious to God. Children offer blessing and the hope of new possibilities. They should not be exploited in any way. The sacredness of life requires special care for those who are at risk. Christian ethics insist that power is to be used for good. Jesus warns: "Whoever welcomes one such child in my name welcomes me. If any of you put a stumbling-block before one of these little ones who believe in me, it would be better for you if a great millstone were fastened around your neck and you were drowned in the depth of the sea" (Matthew 18:5–6). As fallen creatures, humans have a tendency to use power in ways that are selfish and exploitative. There is an unequivocal pastoral responsibility to guard against this in areas of known risk.

In relation to children, the distortion and abuse of relationships will not endure forever. A time is coming when God's model will prevail.

> The wolf shall live with the lamb,
> the leopard shall lie down with the kid,
> the calf and the lion and the fatling together,
> and a little child shall lead them (Isaiah 11:6).

The propensity for harm is overcome in this striking glimpse of God's kingdom. The shocking and egregious abuse of children will end, and right and harmonious relationships will be established.

Response

Churches have often failed miserably to live up to their responsibilities. FBOs have an opportunity to show best practice and lead the way. A practical start is to ensure that staff, partners, and communities are familiar with the UN Convention on the Rights of the Child.

A level of intentionality and unflinching resolve is required for the sake of children in programs. This should always be the first and primary driver. That said, neglect of child protection is not only damaging to children but will inevitably rebound to damage an organization's reputation and its stakeholders. A theology of safeguarding involving elements of love, protection, shelter, justice, and sanctity should drive child protection at every FBO with children in their programs.

Conclusion

Christian theology provides an impetus for action in some of the most important and challenging themes of program design. FBOs have an accountability to reflect on the crosscutting themes such as those highlighted in this chapter and to consider how their theological convictions inform programmatic responses. To be able to do this, theology needs to be taken seriously in the first place. In this light, the next chapter examines those factors that can help or hinder FBOs in becoming more faithful in their mission.

CHAPTER 16

Becoming a Faithfully Based Organization

Development is a systematic process, generally long-term, of working with communities. The goal is to help communities to empower themselves to overcome the factors they recognize as diminishing their human life. Development is not solely about physical or economic deficits, although these are important. Humans cannot live by bread alone, but nor can they live without it. Poverty comprises a complex suite of issues that may be described as anti-human because they deny people the achievement of what they were created to be. The denial of basic freedoms, respect, opportunities, self-expression, health, security, participation, and self-determination all diminish human life.

The gospel is meant to be transformative, involving important questions about life before death and the search for justice.[1] At its heart is the call to actively seek that God's will be done on earth as it is in heaven.[2] Jesus speaks of a new way of living because the kingdom of God is at hand.[3] God is understood to be immanent, active, and present. Transcendent living means working with God to bring the kingdom forward, in hope and power.[4] The gospel must not be allowed to become insipid and detached, which would be to parody its true essence.

This book has argued that Christian faith and development ideals are largely sympathetic to each other. A renewed appreciation of the role of faith within development is essential. Throughout history, a great impetus for compassionate action and justice has been Christian faith, and this faith has led to the formation of many of the world's largest development organizations. In the Majority World, served by those organizations, theistic worldviews are pervasive and growing. Yet the modern world has arguably persisted in a false self-confidence, which at times has been to the detriment of developing communities.

I share this lament: "The systematic omission or devaluing of religion in scholarship is a form of cultural imperialism which could result in the reduced effectiveness of development research and potentially damaging interventions."[5] It certainly impedes efforts to improve the lives of the poor by denying their reality.[6] This book has attempted to redress this imbalance in a small way by showing how religious motifs inform the work of faith-based development organizations. I have attempted to describe an approach that is very resonant with the poor and that provides a basis for comparative advantage in some settings.

But there is one critical topic left to explore. What are the factors that contribute to the marginalization of Christian faith within faith-based development organizations? These "dis-integrative" factors make it harder to keep Christian faith at their heart and place their distinctive contribution at risk. This chapter talks about some of those factors, and what can be done about them.

The faithfully based organization

The label "faith-based organization" (FBO) is frequently used to distinguish between organizations having some connection with a religious worldview, on the one hand, and secular organizations on the other. I believe the term FBO is generally unhelpful and sometimes misleading. It is a crude and dichotomous label. It says nothing about how real or vital or integrated faith is in the life of an organization. For this reason, I will argue for the term "faithfully based organization" as a better internal descriptor. This at least gives an organization something to aim for.

Being "faithfully based" is not about achieving a "generic" look. It is, however, about being dedicated and intentional in bringing faith to bear on organizational life. Christian faith should not sit awkwardly and hesitantly at the margins, but should shine at the center. It must find its expression, not in nostalgic reflection, but in present inspiration and empowerment.

When a Christian development organization is tightly aligned around its perceived purpose, then this cohesion will help secure organizational effectiveness. In this way, a specific religious identity can be a powerful asset in furthering the organization's goals.[7] While religious identity can be understood as a matter of external brand or reputation, its greatest contribution exists in understanding how faith integration can help achieve organizational effectiveness. Anecdotally, there is evidence that secular development NGOs envy the role faith can play in building a shared sense of purpose among employees and stakeholders and a sense of organizational cohesion. They certainly have fewer tools to work with in seeking to positively reinforce their organizational values.

The bad news is that many "Christian" development organizations are not cohesive or aligned in their organizational purpose. They are, in fact, deeply confused and conflicted. In Europe especially, many organizations have distanced themselves from their faith origins to accommodate an increasingly hostile external environment. A heightened sensitivity to church and state relationships, pluralism, church scandals, and an antagonistic media have caused these FBOs to significantly downplay their religious identity and to become quasi-secular.[8] The management challenge of trying to reassert the Christian identity of an organization that has lost its center of gravity is enormous. Prevention is better than cure, and that is the thrust of this reflection.

It is a matter of deep regret that many FBOs find it hard to articulate what faith actually means to them. They will not have engaged in the process of self-reflection recommended earlier. In short "They find it hard, inconvenient or unnecessary to draw upon Christian scripture and tradition to *shape* rather than merely *decorate* [their activities]..."[9] Against this background, attempts to address Christian identity are often ill considered and can marginalize the role of faith even further. One common mistake is to *departmentalize* faith, rather than to *integrate* faith. Compartmentalization is destined to fail: "When it looks like an organization may be drifting away from its original faith position, people of faith will often respond by establishing special programs to protect the organization's spiritual heritage. However, if these programs are separated from the main activity of the organization, they become irrelevant and fall away over time."[10]

The faith element of a Christian development organization is not something that can be kept to one side. It is foundational and should infuse the whole operation. Another form of sidelining is *ex post facto* blessing. This happens when Christian faith is used to legitimize actions already taken. It has been reported that in mainstream Protestant FBOs in Europe "theology has predominantly played a peripheral and secondary role—one which has tended more to confirm actions already taken. It has tended to follow rather than map out. Most staff believe that theological reflection has little or nothing of substance to add to the work being done and to the ordering of priorities."[11] This kind of shallow formalism completely misunderstands the essentialist nature of faith in faith-based development.

The literature discloses a diverse range of factors that tend to marginalize the role of faith in faith-based development organizations over time. Those factors have allowed for the progressive dis-integration of faith and practice. It is important that these factors are well understood if dis-integrating tendencies are to be named, resisted, and overcome.

The rising tide of secularism

Secularism is alluring and powerful. To be secular is to be seen as modern, relevant, professional, scientific, neutral, inclusive, and easier for government to deal with. To be secularized is, in a sense, what it means to be modern. Conversely, to be explicitly faith-based risks being seen as outdated, unscientific, amateurish, captive to mixed-motives, and more problematic for governments. To be secular also means having a legitimate place in the formation and implementation of public policy. With these considerations in mind, some organizations may come to doubt the value of their Christian heritage.

In the post-modern world too, secularism can be seen as more inclusive. A feature of post-modern thinking is the uncritical acceptance of diverse practices and beliefs and the subjective validation of diverse moral and ethical positions. The idea of a Christian meta-narrative in history is seen as arrogant. Secularism, on the other hand, provides a platform that has the appearance of neutrality. This is attractive because it is less likely to offend, alienate, or exclude.

Secularism is a term with differing meanings. The traditional rendition of secularism is of a more inclusive variety which does not object to religious symbols and religious expressions taking an inclusive place within state sponsored activity.[12] In more recent decades, however, secularism is far more likely to refer to a more strident and exclusively anti-theistic stance that objects to any representation of religious faiths within public life. The term "secular" is used in the second sense here, especially with reference to American commentators who reflect a more strict separation of church and state as required specifically by their Constitution.

The general point for consideration is to understand "how faith-related organizations respond to competing—and perhaps conflicting—institutional environments: one characterized by professionalization, bureaucratization, and secularization, and the other characterized by religious traditions, beliefs, and practices."[13] It is suggested that many Christian organizations have not been able to negotiate these tensions well. They have not understood how to anchor themselves in a rapidly changing world, and they have been weakened by a secularizing external environment.

In Europe, Australia, and North America fewer people claim a religious affiliation than ever before. This is not the case in developing communities, as noted elsewhere. Secularism is still, however, a relatively recent phenomenon, only taking hold in the West in public policy since World War II. This is significant because most of the world's major development organizations were either formed, or grew rapidly, during this period. Community development, as a professional discipline, has emerged entirely as a child of the secular era.

It is queried, however, whether secularism does in fact represent a more neutral or inclusive position. Every system of thought is filled with its own assumptions, beliefs, and values. Neutrality is a myth. The excision of all trace of religion from public life does not leave behind neutrality. Stephen Monsma explains that: "When all religious references, acknowledgements, ceremonies, and beliefs have been carefully removed from an activity or institution one does not end up with an activity or institution that occupies a neutral, middle ground between religion and secularism. One ends up with an activity or institution that, for most intents and purposes, is secular, not religious."[14]

When public service and public institutions are pursued without any reference to religious views, this is not "neutrality" but secularism. Secularism should be understood as itself a viewpoint in a contested marketplace of ideas. The end result of stripping religious preference from public policy is to produce by default, "a generic, secular, cultural ethos."[15]

These arguments, while persuasive to Christians, do not change the reality of the external environment in which FBOs operate, especially in Western countries. Secularism is now firmly rooted as the public policy position of most Western governments. It is also the personal conviction of a growing and substantial cohort in Western populations, especially among younger people. The age of Christendom is dying. Christian development organizations may be seen as anachronistic and are likely to meet "an increasingly indifferent, if not hostile, reception."[16]

One response is for an organization to distance itself from its Christian past. Another is to embrace its Christian foundation with a renewed vitality as a point of difference. Again, organizations have found it hard to know how to proceed down the latter path, even if there has been a will to do so. Their attempts have sometimes been faltering. Core documents, even those speaking of faith foundations, are sometimes steeped in a rationalistic worldview. Staff can end up being highly cynical about a faith that proposes to "offer people 'life in its fullness' but [which] in form and content is limited by its one dimensional captivity to rational thought."[17] The substance of integration is therefore critical in the healing and restoration of identity for Christian organizations.

A stunted view of governance

Governance includes the responsibility of making sure that an organization remains true to its underpinning faith modality. Boards are, in a sense, the guardians of organizational integrity. In commercial organizations a primary concern of every board is to maximize the long-term financial returns for investor/shareholders. Not-for-profit boards, however, must oversee both the promotion of the objects and the philosophical or religious stance of the organization. In this regard, they function more like trustees.

As an organization grows, the role and responsibility of boards is invariably tested. Well-meaning volunteers need to face up to the realities of governing complex organizations, large balance sheets, demanding regulatory environments, and the circumstances where personal liabilities can accrue. Against this background, there can be a bias in favor of recruiting experienced, commercially minded board members. Thomas Jeavons warns, however, that:

> [a] pressure contributing to the tendency of Christian service agencies to adopt secular, for-profit management practices—and, through this mechanism, to absorb and assimilate secular values—is the presence of large numbers of businesspeople on their boards. These people fail to see the significant differences between the character and the mission of non-profit, especially religious, organizations and those of business organizations.[18]

The *spiritual* governance for FBOs must be a priority. The board of a Christian organization is the primary sponsor and protector of its faith identity, and this is a much broader remit than that promoted by most governance consultants. Equal attention should be paid to what the organization *is* as to what it *does*.[19]

Board members are not simply bean counters, risk managers, and target setters. Arguably, their most significant contribution will be modeling the desired culture.[20] An overly narrow focus on technical competencies can put the organization's longer-term identity at risk.[21] Boards must be good stewards and properly discharge all their formal regulatory responsibilities. But they are stewards of identity and culture too. When these aspects are neglected, FBOs begin to drift away from their original purpose.[22]

As one study of Christian aid and development organizations specifically noted: "In every instance, among the most effective organizations studied, there was evidence that the board regularly returns to examinations of the organization's basic mission, either as an exercise undertaken for the board members' own sake as part of a board retreat or some other occasion, or in relation to their efforts to resolve specific policy or program issues."[23]

Boards must learn to continually reflect on the "why" question. This question forces a reconsideration of the organization's purpose, its original vision of ministry, and the sustaining presence of God who called it into being.[24] Boards should "provide an example to the rest of the organization of seeking God's direction and following the guidance of the Spirit in decision-making."[25] Likewise, Jeavons warns against an uncritical managerialism that is slowly corrosive of an organization's faith identity. He argues that program choices "should grow out of a sense of spiritual leading and giftedness, as well as the more usual analysis of strengths and opportunities."[26]

Some helpful disciplines at board level include prayer, devotion, and dedicated times for reflection and retreat. Investing in the development of board members and executive staff by training them as Christian thinkers and leaders will assist that envisioning process. In the end, executive leadership, consisting of both the board and senior management, should articulate the organization's goals in a way that is clear and compelling in terms of faith.[27] Undoubtedly, intentional governance processes around faith issues will help to secure longer-term identity. Without this commitment, boards and managers may increasingly find it much harder to resist "the pressures of contemporary economic, social and political idols."[28]

The subversive influence of money

Governments have consistently looked to the private sector in delivering their foreign aid and social programs. There has been a growing realization that in many cases private actors have the ability to deliver services more cheaply and efficiently through their own networks. A very serious theoretical concern has accompanied this development, namely, the cooption of organizations so that they become a quasipublic adjunct to government agendas. Dependence on government funds causes organizations to become instruments of wider public policy goals so that the organizations lose their own autonomy and distinctiveness.[29] There is a particular concern in the case of FBOs because of the policy desire to separate church and state in many jurisdictions. Despite this, governments have continued to provide, and have actually increased, funding to private operators, including faith-based development organizations.

In speaking about the U.S. context, Monsma cautions that government always has "the upper hand in the relationship . . . thus gradually moving the private agencies in directions they otherwise would not have gone."[30] Some commentators fatalistically assert that a loss of religious freedom to some degree is nearly always inevitable. The receipt of government funds compromises the character of the organization by leading it to make different choices.[31] In relation to faith-based development organizations, Rick James reports that the desire to attract secular funding sources "encourages FBOs to dis-integrate their faith from development work."[32] In particular, notions of secular government make European countries very sensitive to any charge of propagating a faith position.

The potential corrupting influence of external funding is summed up in Resource Dependency Theory (RDT). The basic idea is that organizations supposedly behave in a manner that maximizes their inputs. To this end "they alter their structures and goals in order to obtain the external resources they require."[33] RDT is based on the pioneering work of Jeffrey Pfeffer and Gerald Salancik.[34] In summary, their thesis can be articulated as follows:

- The environment contains scarce resources.

- Organizations are dependent on the environment for survival.

- Dependencies create external control situations.

- Asymmetric dependencies create power.

- Power goes to those who control resources.

- The magnitude, criticality, and alternative availability of exchange affects dependency.

Organizational behavior reflects this pattern of influence. Government funding does represent a threat to religious identity, so that in Europe "many FBO recipients of government money feel they have to separate out the spiritual dimension in their mission."[35] James notes that "proselytising may be seen by some [governments] as worse than corruption," and accordingly organizations suppress their religious identity out of fear of losing funding streams.[36]

One particular issue is the impact that receiving government money may have on public advocacy. Faith-based development organizations may desire to advocate against government policies that are perceived to harm the interests of the poor. For example, Western governments may be criticized for inadequate public expenditure for aid and development, perpetuating domestic agricultural subsidies which are damaging to the global poor, inadequate climate policies, and being harsh creditors of developing countries. One the one hand, receiving government funding offers the benefit of greater scale, which means that organizations can do more good in the world, at least in the short-term. On the other, there is a concern that receiving large amounts of government money may be a disincentive to public advocacy. It can be very hard to tell whether a large government grant is an insidious threat to religious identity or an expression of God's providence.[37]

The literature suggests that the influence of receiving government funding can also be indirect. The receipt of government funding may impact the deeper question of organizational identity. Some researchers

have linked the receipt of government funding to the sociological phenomenon of "isomorphism." For example, Paul Di Maggio suggests:

> Government funding of organizations causes "isomorphism,"
> that is, a self-understanding by a group of organizations that
> they are in the same "industry" (for example, social care) and a
> consequent professionalization of activity and growing similar-
> ities between organizations in the "industry," whatever their
> origins or histories. Thus public sector organizations and orga-
> nizations that were originally "voluntary" come to look very
> much like each other.[38]

When there is a change in self-understanding, there can also be a
change in mission and values.

Restrictive and distortive?

While the sources of funds can influence how an organization's work is
done (for example, by separating out faith elements), it can also shape
what types of activities an organization may choose to pursue. In short,
external sources of funding can both suppress religious identity *and* dis-
tort program choices. This is not simply a debate about the strings attached to government grants: "More subtle but equally important are the
instances in which organizations may alter program choices or designs,
or fund-raising techniques, in order to draw more material support."[39]
How readily will an organization choose the path of opportunistic
growth at the expense of integrity of mission? Will it be *mission-driven* or
funding-driven?[40]

The potential adverse impact of sources of funding is not restricted
to government. Mass market private donors can also steer an organization in a particular direction. For example, an organization may refrain
from asserting its Christian identity out of fear of alienating "mainstream" retail supporters in a post-Christian market. Larry Reed describes a typical trajectory:

> As a social service organization grows, it needs to acquire more
> sources of funds. It often outgrows the funding capacity of the
> church or denomination that got it started. It begins attracting
> funding from donors that support specific activities of the or-
> ganization, but don't buy into the overall mission of the orga-
> nization. As this source of funding grows, the organization
> begins to modify its message to appeal to more donors.[41]

In his research Jeavons recounts how one evangelical organization
altered the way it would present information and frame its appeals so as

to achieve growth beyond its usual constituency. This kind of market-driven pragmatism introduces a trade-off between the short-term growth and longer-term identity.[42] The integration challenge here is learning how to tell an attractive and compelling story about Christian identity and ministry in an increasingly skeptical post-modern environment.

The power of religious dollars

The underlying assumption that funding sources impact organizational identity can have a positive flip-side. This is an important but often overlooked corollary. One criterion for defining a FBO is to consider whether an appreciable amount of financial support comes from religious sources. This turns the assumption into a defining proposition. Because agencies will reflect the interests of their sources of financial support, then faith-based organizations should theoretically be very active in seeking out support from religious adherents and institutions.

There is some evidence that a relatively small proportion of church-based funding can go a long way to preserving a distinctly religious identity. One study reported by James Vanderwoerd noted that "The most important dollars we have in our budget are Lutheran dollars—the smallest dollars, but the most important dollars because they define who we are and why we do what we do. They're Lutheran. We are Lutheran. They define who we are. Those dollars may be small but in a sense they control the board. They're very important."[43] In another case study an organization refused to seek funds beyond its traditional base, even though its excellent reputation would have allowed it to easily do so. The reason for this was an organizational desire "to draw our support from the people we represent. This requires us to remain accountable to them."[44]

The conclusion is that strategically placed sources of funds from churches, congregations, and individual Christians help to positively reinforce Christian identity.

Secular training, secular approach, secular staff

There will be a number of roles within the life of an organization where an active Christian faith is a prerequisite. Christian leaders are needed who are able to lead by example, providing a clear and consistent witness to the centrality of Christian faith to the whole organization. They will model passion, servant leadership, and dedication in following Jesus. The careful work of integrating Christian faith into field programming will require committed Christians with a capacity to pray, discern, and reflect theologically about their work. Christian personnel are needed who can work and pray together with local church leaders.

One problem is that many Christian development organizations are unwilling or unable to find competent Christian staff to fulfill these roles. Most development studies degrees are offered at secular universities that teach development from a secular paradigm. The culture of modernity has shaped the professional training of development practitioners. This culture is largely hostile to Christian faith and sees development as a career option to be pursued, rather than as a Christian vocation into which followers of Jesus are called. A lack of qualified Christian candidates may result in compromise appointments of people who are unable to live out the Christian faith and integrate the faith dimension into their work.

In some jurisdictions, there is also confusion and uncertainty about whether an organization can or should discriminate in hiring decisions. There is a tension that exists between the desire of many organizations to be as inclusive as possible while at the same time recognizing the need to employ Christians both to affirm the organization's faith basis and specifically to enable the integration of faith and development. For some organizations, an inclusive and gracious approach to hiring can itself be an expression of its Christian values.[45] For others, a permissive approach will be seen as placing its distinctive identity at risk. The integration of faith in development practice is a matter of fundamental importance and faith should not be considered simply as a matter of individual choice or preference.

In an attempt to be inclusive or address shortages of qualified Christian staff some organizations merely require staff to accept its values and ethos at a very general level.[46] This response raises important questions. Without Christian staff, how can the work of faith integration occur? And if the work of integration does not occur, in what sense is the organization undertaking development work that is distinctive? It is certainly the case that God can and does use the skills of those who do not profess the Christian faith in his service. That proposition can be strongly affirmed from within Christian theology. It is a vastly different proposition, however, to turn that into a normative assumption and argue that it makes no difference who an organization hires. It plainly does.

A false divide: professionalism over faith?

Another dis-integrating tendency is the preferencing of formal professional or business qualifications over Christian faith in hiring decisions.

In my view, both are clearly desirable. The uncritical reliance on social science theories can displace the role of faith and, over time, subvert the identity of the organization. In a similar way, a singular focus on material matters, such as revenue targets, can distract from broader questions of mission and purpose.

International development has been largely shaped by the cult of modernity. Practitioners are encouraged to pay obeisance to logframes, theories of change, or other tools of rationality. The root problem is the relegation of faith to the "spiritual" world. This perpetuates a central tenet of modernity, namely, the belief that work and faith, the material and the spiritual, need to be kept separate.[47] European FBOs have engaged in this kind of dichotomous thinking, allowing faith to dissipate so that they can become "more professional."[48]

This tendency is well documented in the literature. One hypothesis is that "when religious organizations operate in institutional conflicts characterized by high levels of professionalism and bureaucratization, they will inevitably become secularized."[49] Reed describes what amounts to a slow process of subversion: "When organizations find it difficult to find people with these [professional] skills among the Christian community, they begin to look outside... As these people move up the ranks in the organization and become leaders, they can move the organization from its Christian commitment."[50] There is a need for faith-based development organizations to be very careful in making senior appointments if they are to preserve their religious character.[51]

A further dimension is the progressive use of paid staff rather than committed congregationally-based volunteers can also contribute to the loss of an organization's Christian identity. At the heart of the issue is the automatic deference paid to formal professional qualifications at the expense of supposedly ignorant, though well-intentioned, Christian volunteers.

How then are these tensions to be avoided? I am reminded that Christians are expressly commanded to love God with all their mind. For this reason they must remain open to new techniques, systems, and approaches that can better serve God's purposes. These tools, however, must not replace God and become, as it were, well-intentioned idols. Professional skills and love of God are not incongruous. They go hand-in-hand and enter their proper relationship when the former serve the latter.

Hiring and Christian culture

The public demands, appropriately, greater integrity of religious or philanthropic organizations. There is an expectation that "such organizations should operate out of a different—'value base'—[and] of course, most religious organizations *explicitly claim* to be operating out of a different values base."[52] Faith-based organizations are joined in the expectation that they should honor, nurture, and promote specific moral and spiritual ideals—since those ideals provide the particular inspiration for their service.[53]

The executive leadership must try and build a culture that nurtures the ideals of Christian service and ethical behavior. By culture I mean the shared assumptions and beliefs that are taken for granted and that underpin a cohesive workplace.[54] These operate at an unconscious level. It has been argued that the only way to build a distinctive and cohesive culture is to recruit people whose primary commitments are to Christian assumptions and beliefs.[55]

A cohesive workplace culture is achievable only where there is a significant cohort of staff, especially among the leadership, who have a shared history and shared understandings. It is argued that "one of the most effective ways to ensure participants in an organization will contribute to fulfilling its mission is to select them with an eye toward the degree to which they share the 'cognitive premises' underlying the actions of the organization."[56] When key decision makers and culture-bearers do not have a Christian worldview then it becomes difficult or impossible for the organization to intentionally develop a culture that honors God and in which the integration of Christian faith and development activity is an organic and natural desire.

The recruitment of Christians will facilitate the integration of faith with development practice. Organizations must be very intentional in making hiring decisions to reinforce faith commitments and Christian values. This is important "because there are other 'cognitive premises' that participants may bring to these organizations that can operate at cross-purposes with those commitments and values. Most significant and insidious in this regard—because the conflicts are so subtle—are some staff members' professional commitments and values."[57]

The literature suggests that Christian development organizations should be closed, at least insofar as employing senior leaders and development practitioners is concerned, if a distinctively Christian culture and development praxis is to be achieved. Whether an organization employs *only* Christians, however, is likely to reflect particular theological understandings. Some understandings will value a shared Christian worldview at all employment levels and the greater sense of unity and shared purpose that can come from this. Other traditions or approaches will seek to give expression to the graciousness and inclusiveness of God and will value the opportunity to share their own spiritual journey with others.

Where a mixed workforce exists, it must be leavened by senior leaders who are active, strong Christians. Ideally, there should also be a significant cohort of Christians within the general complement of staff. Absent these measures, an organization's tone and culture are at risk. Once an organization loses its "center of gravity," it is very hard to recover.

In theory,[58] the likely advantages of hiring only Christians for a faith-based organization will include:

- a more cohesive staff group and culture to work with

- a relatively easier task in maintaining a clear Christian identity for the longer term

- an environment more conducive to integrating faith and development because of shared understandings

- the ability to be clearly and openly expressive of Christian faith within organizational life

- making a statement that faith is very important in work life.

The likely advantages of a more mixed work force include:

- benefiting from the skill sets others may have to offer

- being able to contribute to the spiritual growth of non-Christians

- being seen as more inclusive and welcoming

- being challenged by differing perspectives

- the ability to fill positions more easily.

Living naturally

Ronald Sider and Heidi Unrah observe that one of the characteristics of religious organizations is the participation of their staff in organized religious practices such as prayer, Bible studies, devotional meetings or chapel services.[59] Monsma points more broadly to the importance of symbols in the workplace: "If a religious non-profit organization should ever find that it must strip its facility of identifying religious pictures and symbols...or must hire persons in open disagreement with the religious background and mission of the non-profit, its religious autonomy would have been effectively destroyed."[60]

While internal organizational culture can reinforce Christian faith, this can be a very sensitive and divisive matter. One issue is the perceived need to be sensitive to the views of people of different faiths or no faith who may feel uncomfortable about taking part, or even being exposed to, alien religious traditions. The concerns are heightened in those jurisdictions where allegations of religious discrimination in the workplace can lead to legislative sanctions. One response is to discontinue religious practices in the workplace. This kind of sensitivity to a minority may be at the expense of the freedom of the majority.

A second issue is the more general principle about whether it is appropriate to undertake religious practices in the workplace at all. John Bottomley, in his study of church-based community service agencies, notes that some staff feel uncomfortable about how to do the "God" stuff.[61] Stephen Carter, speaking in a North American context, says:

> One sees a trend in our political and legal cultures towards treating religious beliefs as arbitrary and unimportant, a trend supported by a rhetoric which implies that there is something wrong with religious devotion. More and more our culture seems to take the position that believing deeply in the tenets of one's faith represents a kind of mystical irrationality, something that thoughtful public-spirited American citizens would do better to avoid.[62]

Jeavons believes that a level of intentionality is required to counter this type of thinking. He argues that:

> The most effective Christian service organizations reinforce participants' commitments and attention to those premises in the work situation by activities and procedures that lift up those ideas and values that are of central importance. So, in these organizations we find [*inter alia*] the heaviest emphases on worship and prayer as part of the work, [and] on articulation of basic values and beliefs in discussions of organizational priorities and plans.[63]

This should be practiced at all levels so that every individual is given opportunities to be involved in the spiritual dimensions of an organization's ministries—like prayer, worship, and discernment of organizational direction.[64]

In relation to workplace religious practices, Monsma takes a firm stand: "If one chooses to join one's self to a religious nonprofit, then one should be prepared to be required to take part in certain religious exercises that it may judge to be important to maintaining its religious character."[65] I disagree. I do not think anyone should be forced on matters of conscience. To my mind, a position that is invitational rather than coercive is preferable. While some non-Christian staff may be prepared to go on a journey with the organization in exploring questions of faith, others may feel inhibited and uncomfortable. In this regard, the stridency or triumphalism of Christian co-workers can be especially off-putting.

While compulsory involvement is hard to justify, Christians should certainly be actively encouraged to look to their faith as a source of constant inspiration and reflection in the workplace. Activities should be regular, well organized, and visible. Religious organizations themselves have been complicit in the historic post-Enlightenment split between public and private life, with some institutions timidly accepting that religion is for the home and private morality.[66] A misplaced sense of inclusiveness has in some cases led to the banishment of religious expression in the work environment. At the same time, there is a lingering, regretful lament. The disintegration of expressions "of worship in the life of agencies must eventually leave agencies at the risk of being disconnected to their founding vocation under God."[67]

Remembrance is a key way of reinforcing an organization's faith identity. Every organization will have its own story that can be shared and celebrated. Bottomley states: "The task of remembrance has firm roots in Christ's command at his Last Supper, and calls agencies to both individually and collectively strive to understand what they were created to be from God's goodness."[68] The learning and repeating of the organization's story is a way to develop a shared sense of journey and purpose. This renews the corporate sense of call and helps new employees to be inducted into that story and to draw strength from its legacy.[69] Unless there is a level of intentionality about this, the sense of being engaged in a godly mission will quickly dissipate. The role of leadership is critical here: "The good leader will be the one who knows their organization's narrative, inhabits it, and develops it as the world around changes."[70]

Knowing what to do

Christian development practice requires a commitment to biblical holism, and that requires programmatic responses of a different kind. For example, it may require working out ways to engage with and encourage local churches, connecting faith communities with each other, and bringing prayer and spiritual disciplines to development practice. This is a broader suite of skills that is not taught in secular development studies.

Employees and volunteers can offer only the skills they have. Staff who do not identify with the Christian faith may find it hard to embrace a distinctly Christian concept of development. For some, this may raise issues of integrity about working for a Christian development organization. At a personal level, an employee may not be able to bring the disciplines of Christian faith to the development task, although he or she may be able to bring other vitally important gifts and talents that can be used by their organization in the service of God.

For Christian staff too, it must not be assumed that there is an automatic familiarity with how to integrate faith with development practice.[71] Confusion and uncertainty may reign unless there is a firm organizational commitment to integration that is manifest in clear processes. Development is never an "off-the-shelf" process, and a Christian approach to transformational development requires, among other things, space for prayer, reflection, discernment, and personal discipleship. Equally important, however, is knowing how these elements fit within day-to-day practice.

While CEOs of most FBOs state that the integration of faith with professional practice is important, there is no real consensus about what that means.[72] Smaller organizations with a well-articulated sense of mission are best placed to develop a clear narrative about what faith means in their work. It does seem that as organizations grow, corporatized processes and systems may squeeze out the integration of faith. Commercial systems, processes, and key performance indicators (KPIs) that are more suited for commercial environments may begin to subtly shape and redefine the workplace along standard corporate lines.[73] On this point James reports: "Some staff now feel they are too busy with the demands of professional bureaucracy to integrate their faith. Heavy workloads with relentless deadlines make it difficult to be both professional and 'faith'-ful at the same time."[74]

Hard, careful, thinking is required about how to integrate faith in development. Even if there is a will to tackle this, there are capacity constraints, skill-set deficits, and systems and processes that are not conducive. Unless this broader suite of issues can be addressed, faith integration will remain illusory.

Choosing your friends

Another source of dis-integration of faith and development is the shaping of sector norms by non-Christian actors. As faith-based development organizations expand, they may become more involved with other players in the sector, peak bodies, and self-regulatory mechanisms. It has been cautioned that, "as organizations grow and become more sophisticated they become less accountable to the original group that got them started and more accountable to . . . their professional peers." Those peers may operate from a rigidly secular understanding of development: "Growing organizations are often taking on professional staff who have links with other organizations in the same field and thus draw the organization towards more secular ideologies and away from the specifically religious goals of the organization's founders."[75]

It is entirely appropriate that Christian development organizations should engage with their colleagues and contribute fully to the development of higher standards of accountability and governance. Indeed, there is a theological imperative to do so. Yet they must learn to do this with a clear and confident understanding of their own faith position, and with a cautious eye about accepting obligations with a potential to compromise their identity.

Partnering arrangements have a potential to put an organization's identity at risk. James notes that for some European FBOs the "increasing secularization of their partner portfolio has raised questions about their distinctiveness..."[76] Reed cautions that: "Often as a result of financial pressures organizations will develop alliances or merge with other organizations in the same field. If the different organizations do not share a common faith commitment the lowest common denominator will usually prevail."[77] It would be unwise, however, to generalize too freely. There is a vast difference between selecting a short-term project partner, with a limited remit, and conducting a merger. The research of Sider and Unrah has noted that a distinction needs to be drawn between funding and other partnering arrangements that impose project specific limitations and those that affect the identity of the organization as a whole: "An organization is more likely to accept funds that restrict the religious characteristics of a particular program than funding that alters the overall nature of the organization."[78] The same is true of partnerships. Every individual arrangement, and the cumulative effect of all arrangements, needs to be weighed.

A fundamental partnership for many faith-based development organizations will be its relationship with the church both locally and in the field. Some organizations see this relationship as so important that it defines their self-understanding. Where partners uphold the same religious convictions, they can learn from each other and hold each other to account in a spirit of love. This will reinforce identity at a general level, and will aid integration of faith into development by a mutual Christian framing of the development task. It is telling that "FBOs in Europe are more like secular NGOs than like churches."[79] The question arises, from whom have they taken their lead?

Faith-based or faithfully based?

The descriptor "faith-based" is inadequate. It refers to organizations in which the connection with faith is distant, tenuous, or vague. The adverb "faithfully" points to the ongoing and central role that faith should play in the life of a Christian organization. In the end, what matters is whether an organization is attempting to serve God in this world with diligence and passion.'

This chapter has attempted to explain the many factors that help marginalize or relativize Christian faith within faith-based development organizations. It is not healthy for the leaders of Christian organizations to develop a "siege mentality," nor do they need to do so. Every threat is also an opportunity. A renewed level of intentionality is required. While this can be difficult, the commitment to being faithfully based will ultimately grow vitality, distinctiveness, and a renewed sense of hope and power.

EPILOGUE

Getting to Know Your City

It is demonstrably the case that Christians have a long and proud history of being agents for social transformation in the world. Those who claim to follow Jesus but leave all the hard work up to God make it plain that they haven't really understood him. Hope for the world is found in the example of Christ, who was willing to become vulnerable and even to embrace suffering and death for the sake of others.

Christians are called to live out their purpose in blessing God's world. Geopolitical trends reveal that power and profit continue to be placed above people. For that reason, poverty continues to blight us all. International development work is a heroic and important undertaking, one that continues to grapple with intractable and complex issues of global poverty.

Faith-based development is a vital ministry that is inspiring, necessary, and enormously difficult. At its best it helps others to experience fullness of life while deepening our own humanity. Its heart is about striving to love our neighbors the way we should and learning to please God by leading more integrated lives. Faith-based development is not a theoretical exercise. It involves embracing the world's beauty and also its jarring ugliness. Sentimental notions of love quickly disappear when hope is incarnated through personal commitment. No matter what a person's role or responsibility, the acceptance of God's call to service always involves cost, inconvenience, and a deeper level of challenge.

To hallow the lives of others, as Christians affirm, means seeing all people as having an intrinsic dignity deserving of our respect. This requires a willingness to walk alongside, listening and learning, and moving beyond personal comfort zones. The closer the walk, the more there is to understand. At a basic level, faith-based development work is about ministering as friends because new life is experienced together in community.

Faith-based development recognizes that God is the ultimate change agent in the world, and that we are invited into his work. Christian theology affirms that God is already present and active in every community, and this means that engagement through development work can be truly reciprocal. Overarching the development task is the horizon and promise of the kingdom of God. This broken and hurting world is where the reign of God will eventually take hold and where every power that short-changes humanity will be confounded.

Finally, the dedication and care with which Christians serve in the world will point to greater truths. By communicating love through actions and presence, faith-based development can evoke richer meanings still.

These brief personal reflections indicate some of the guiding beliefs that have inspired me in development work and that no doubt have insinuated their way into this book. I suspect, however, that what others take away from its pages will differ according to the category of reader. What I hope others may draw from it is set out below.

For governors of FBOs

Responsible governors of faith-based development organizations will be properly concerned about the theological underpinnings of the organizations they serve. They should regularly return to the central question of the difference that faith makes in fulfilling the organizational mandate. A specific mapping of how Christian belief and practice contribute to the organization's mission can be very instructive. It is important to ask what trade-offs have been made, and whether or not they have been made intentionally. Does the organization want to affirm or re-affirm its religious identity, and if it does, then what changes are required?

Questions of funding and identity are tightly interlinked. Some organizations may trade off aspects of religious identity to obtain access to public funds. They may see the gaining of those funds as the greater good. For others, this approach will be anathema. Some organizations will try and manage questions of identity and public funding by holding them in tension. For these organizations, so-called "religious" dollars will be the most important dollars in their funding mix, because they will bring an accountability based upon identity. My central point is that questions of identity are far too important to be left to chance. Organizational cultures can change almost imperceptibly over time, and decisions that impact religious identity should be made explicitly and intentionally.

For churches interested in development

This book has presented relationships with churches as simultaneously representing both great strength and great risk in connection with development work. There are certainly unparalleled advantages in terms of the authoritative voice of churches, their geographic reach, permanent presence, and localized and embedded nature. They represent a repository of teaching that is largely sympathetic and reinforcing of development goals. Churches act as community gatekeepers, they have the ability to mobilize spiritual and social capital, and they can impart values and ethics that build up the social fabric. They can also provide important pastoral support and be a source of hope and resilience in times of crisis.

At the same time, churches can be socially passive, reflecting charitable rather than transformative models. They can be pietistic, inward looking, and in some cases they can hold anti-development views. Their call to justice and prophetic action may be muted. This book raises important questions for churches: Are church leaders equipped to serve their communities through knowledge of development principles and issues? How can Christian theology inform and better serve the goals of community development? And what innovative tools and approaches are yet to be imagined which will resonate with their constituencies? Undoubtedly, development work can help the church fulfill its true calling through diaconal ministry.

For the sector generally

There is a renewed cause for optimism as faith-based approaches to development are taken more seriously. It is important though that the level of engagement extends beyond mere transaction with faith-based institutions. There is so much more to learn, and in the end mainstream conceptions of development should be challenged by the things that matter to the communities they purport to serve.

First and foremost is the need to engage with religious views, which are the primary lens by which most people on the planet understand the world. When spiritual life is taken seriously, the concept of development will necessarily be broadened. It is argued that highly rationalistic views of development, steeped in modernity, present a narrow and decidedly Western view of what it means to flourish as a human.

My view is that development work should be seen as a shared undertaking that recognizes the skills, dedication, and goodwill of many. With this in mind, it is time for faith-based approaches to be accorded greater legitimacy and recognition.

For governments

The question is being asked more frequently about how secular governments can fulfill their development goals by engaging more constructively with churches and faith-based institutions. Western secular governments are understandably careful in how they engage with faith-based institutions. It is argued, however, that secularism, properly understood, is about recognizing a plurality of religious and non-religious positions in public life, rather than taking an anti-religious stance. An important question for governments will be the kinds of policies and protocols that can be adopted to help mitigate the risks to secular government from engaging with religious institutions and faith-based development organizations. What does a more "enlightened secularism" look like? The keeping of religious institutions and teachings out of the development programs they fund is ideologically arrogant and potentially damaging to the poor. It risks exporting a Western, modernist view of development which is dismissive of the role of faith in human experience. Such an attitude is doctrinaire and contrary to the views of most people in the world.

For NGOs

Every NGO working in international development has a worldview, whether it is acknowledged or not. That worldview will offer advantages or disadvantages, depending on the context. It is important to explore more fully what faith-based development can offer. In many communities these approaches will have strong resonance because of their spiritual underpinning, their localized and embedded nature, and the way in which love is communicated through action and presence. I would urge all NGOs to adopt a critically self-aware posture: What is the organization's worldview? How does that worldview help or hinder in a given context? And, finally, is the NGO guilty of "proselytizing" that worldview in a way that is insensitive or even harmful?

For Christian development practitioners

There are strong theological motivations that have introduced many organizations and Christians to a highly secularized profession. For some, international development work does represent a personal calling, and their exposure to the development profession may not be entirely comfortable. It is a matter of deep regret that faith-based approaches were sidelined for so many decades. This book has attempted to illustrate the distinctiveness and unique value-added dimension that can attend faith-based development.

I began this book by referring to a metaphor from the gospel of Matthew, and that seems an appropriate place to end. To my mind, faith-based development is like a city on a hill, offering a new light that is needed. It is a cause for celebration that there is a growing openness within the development sector to explore what is distinctive about these approaches. Importantly, however, Christian development practitioners themselves are yet to walk the streets and lanes of their own city to

fully understand the light it has to offer. My hope and my encouragement is that they get know their city better and be willing to record and
share what they learn.

Sadly, over time many cities end up looking very much like each
other. It is important that FBOs do not lose their distinctiveness. They
have something special to offer and are meant to be a source of light,
not a pale reflection or imitation of others. While Christians are commanded to love God with their whole mind, they should take all that is
good and helpful and noble and refract that knowledge in their own
authentic way. When this happens there will be a renewed confidence, a
greater appreciation, and a better understanding of how the light of
FBOs can be made stronger still.

APPENDIX

List of World Vision Evaluation Reports

Goode, A. *World Vision Evaluation Report: World Vision Georgia.* Christian Commitments Programme, June 2010.

———. *World Vision Evaluation Report: World Vision Tanzania.* Christian Commitments Programme, October 2010.

———. *World Vision Evaluation Report: World Vision Rwanda.* Christian Commitments Programme, October 2011.

———. *World Vision Evaluation Report: World Vision Senegal.* Christian Commitments Programme, October 2011.

Kilpartick, R., and A. Goode. *World Vision Evaluation Report: World Vision Bosnia and Herzegovina.* Christian Commitments Programme, July 2009.

Newmarch, A. *World Vision Evaluation Report: World Vision Lebanon.* Christian Commitments Programme, November 2009.

———. *World Vision Evaluation Report: World Vision Armenia.* Christian Commitments Programme, November 2010.

Newmarch, A., and A. Goode. *World Vision Evaluation Report: World Vision Albania.* Christian Commitments Programme, September 2008.

NOTES

Foreword

1. Bryant L. Myers, "Holistic Mission: New Frontiers," in *Holistic Mission: God's Plan for God's People*, ed. Brian Wollnough and Wonsuk Ma (Oxford, UK: Regnum Books, 2010).

2. Katherine Marshall, "Responding to the Ebola Epidemic in West Africa: What Role Did Religions Play?" (http://wvi.org: Berkley Center for Religion, Peace and World Affairs, Georgetown University, 2016).

3. Bryant L. Myers, "Progressive Pentecostalism, Development and Christian Development NGOs: A Challenge and an Opportunity," *International Bulletin for Missiological Research* 39, no. 3 (2015).

4. Dena Freeman, ed., *Pentecostalism and Development: Churches, NGOs and Social Change in Africa* (Basingstoke: Palgrave Macmillan, 2012), 25.

Introduction

1. Matthew 5:14: "You are the light of the world. A city built on a hill cannot be hidden."

2. A. Linden, "The Language of Development: What are International Development Agencies Talking About?" in *Development, Civil Society and Faith-based Organizations: Bridging the Sacred and the Secular*, ed. G. Clarke and M. Jennings (Basingstoke: Palgrave Macmillan, 2008), 90.

3. B. Jones and M. J. Petersen, "Instrumental, Narrow, Normative? Reviewing Recent Work on Religion and Development," *Third World Quarterly* 32, no. 7 (2011): 1293.

4. C. Curran, "The Catholic Identity of Catholic Institutions," *Theological Studies* 58 (1997): 92.

5. Ibid., 95.

6. G. Carbonnier, "Religion and Development: Reconsidering Secularism as the Norm," in *International Development Policy: Religion and Development*, ed. G. Carbonnier (Basingstoke: Palgrave Macmillan, 2013), 1–2.

7. Bibliographic details of these reports are set out in the Appendix.

8. J. Lunn, "The Role of Religion, Spirituality and Faith in Development: A Critical Theory Approach," *Third World Quarterly* 30, no. 5 (2009): 940.

9. D. P. King, "World Vision: Religious Identity in the Discourse and Practice of Global Relief and Development," *The Review of Faith and International Affairs* 9, no. 3 (2011): 23.

10. Jones and Petersen, "Instrumental, Narrow, Normative?" 1298.

11. K. M. Ferguson, Q. Wu, D. Spruijt-Metz, and G. Dyrness, "Outcomes Evaluation in Faith-based Social Services: Are We Evaluating Faith Accurately?" *Research on Social Work Practice* 17, no. 2 (2007): 265.

12. King, "World Vision," 26.

13. R. James, "Handle with Care: Engaging with Faith-based Organizations in Development," *Development in Practice* 21, no. 1 (2011): 109–17.

14. M. Clarke, "Understanding the Nexus between Religion and Development," in *The Handbook of Research on Development and Religion*, ed. M. Clarke (Cheltenham: Edward Elgar, 2013), 1.

15. Ibid.

Chapter 1: The Secularized Nature of the Development Profession

1. Jones and Petersen, "Instrumental, Narrow, Normative?" 1292.

2. A. F. C. Wallace, *Religion: An Anthropological View* (New York: Random House, 1966), 265.

3. N. Malcolm, *Thought and Knowledge* (Ithaca: Cornell University Press, 1977), 621.

4. D. J. Hufford, "The Scholarly Voice and the Personal Voice: Reflexivity in Belief Studies," in *Guide to the Study of Religion*, ed. W. Braun and R. T. McCutcheon (London: Continuum, 2000), 304.

5. K. A. Ver Beek, "Spirituality: A Development Taboo," *Development in Practice* 10, no. 1 (2000): 31–43.

6. Ibid., 32, 39.

7. Ibid., 31.

8. Ibid., 38.

9. L. Selinger, "The Forgotten Factor: The Uneasy Relationship between Religion and Development," *Social Compass* 51, no. 4 (2004): 523–43.

10. Ibid., 525.

11. Ibid.

12. Lunn, "The Role of Religion, Spirituality and Faith in Development," 937–51. Lunn writes from a critical theory perspective.

13. Ibid., 940.

14. See Jones and Petersen, "Instrumental, Narrow, Normative?"

15. King, "World Vision, 23.

16. Ibid.

17. J. L. Esposito and M. Watson, eds., *Religion and Global Order* (Cardiff: University of Wales, 2000), 18.

18. Ibid, 17.

19. Ibid.

20. W. Tyndale, "Faith and Economics in 'Development': A Bridge Across the Chasm?" *Development in Practice* 10, no. 1 (2000): 17.

21. Lunn, "The Role of Religion," 940.

22. R. Chambers, "NGOs and Development: The Primacy of the Personal," unpublished paper for the Workshop on NGOs and Development: Performance

and Accountability (Institute of Policy Development and Management: University of Manchester, June 27–29, 1994), 3.

23. Ver Beek, "Spirituality," 39.

24. Ibid., 540.

25. M. Clarke, "Understanding the Nexus between Religion and Development," 3.

26. N. Grills, "'Believing' in HIV: The Effect of Faith on the Response of Christian Faith-based Organizations to HIV in India" (PhD thesis, Oxford University, 2010), 71.

27. Ibid., 72.

28. Ibid., 88.

29. S. M. Thomas, "Taking Religious and Cultural Pluralism Seriously: The Global Resurgence of Religion and the Global Transformation of International Society," *Journal of International Studies* 29, no. 3 (2000): 815–841, discussed in N. Grills, "The Paradox of Multilateral Organizations Engaging with Faith-Based Organizations," *Global Governance* 15 (2009): 512.

30. Grills, "'Believing' in HIV," 88.

31. Ibid., 90.

32. One example identified is that of the Norwegian Mission Society. This organization claims that its strength is its Christian holistic approach to development. Yet external funding sources "require it to separate out faith practices such as communal prayers and undertake *pure* development work." This pressures the FBO to secularize and "behave contrary to its cultural identity." See Grills, "The Paradox of Multilateral Organizations," 515, and I. Hovland, "Who's Afraid of Religion? The Question of God in Development" (paper presented at DSA Conference, Milton Keynes, September 7–9, 2005).

33. Clarke, "Understanding the Nexus," 5.

34. K. Marshall, "Faith and Development: Rethinking Development Debates," Development Dialogue on Values and Ethics, The World Bank, 2005, http://web.worldbank.org.

35. G. Carbonnier, "Religion and Development," 1.

36. "Global Data Upend Usual Picture of Christianity Trends," Anglican Communion News Service, March 20, 2013, http://www.aco.org, citing the work of religious demographer Dr. Todd M. Johnson.

37. R. James, "What is Distinctive about FBOs," International NGO Training and Research Centre, Praxis Paper 22 (February 2009): 8.

38. D. MacLaren, "Putting the Faith Back into Development," *Eureka Street* (October 26, 2011).

39. R. Williams, "Relating Intelligently to Religion," *The Guardian* (November 12, 2009): 1. This article was based on a lecture given by Rowan Williams in the seminary series "New Perspectives on Faith and Development" in London in 2009, "A Theology of Development," http://clients.squareeye.net.

40. Selinger, "The Forgotten Factor," 524.

41. Marshall, "Faith and Development," 8.

42. Ibid.

43. Additionally, it has been claimed that "FBOs probably provide the best social and physical infrastructure in the poorest communities . . . because

churches, temples, mosques and other places of worship are the focal points for the communities they serve" (Kumi Naidoo of CIVICUS, quoted in James, "What is Distinctive about FBOs," 7).

44. James, "What is Distinctive about FBOs," 8.

45. Marshall, "Faith and Development," 8.

46. D. Narayan, *Voices of the Poor: Can Anyone Hear Us?* (Washington, DC: Oxford University Press, 2000).

47. M. Widmer, A. P. Betran, M. Merialdi, J. Requejo, and T. Karpf, "The Role of Faith-based Organizations in Maternal and Newborn Health Care in Africa," *International Journal of Gynecology and Obstetrics* 114 (2011): 222.

48. Lunn, "The Role of Religion," 944.

49. Ibid.

50. See also G. Hoffstaedter, "Religion and Development: Australian Faith-Based Development Organizations," Australian Council for International Development, *Research in Development Series* 3 (2011) 5, 7–8, for further examples of the reach and scope of religious infrastructure deployed in international development.

51. Thomas, "Taking Religious and Cultural Pluralism Seriously," 815–41.

52. J. Devine and S. Deneulin, "Negotiating Religion in Everyday Life: A Critical Exploration of the Relationship Between Religion, Choices and Behaviour," *Culture and Religion: An Interdisciplinary Journal* 12, no. 1 (2011): 59–76. M. Clarke states: "Religion . . . is not simply concerned with the private circumstances of an individual and their rightful relationship with a supernatural deity, but rather it has a social realm that has relevance for wider society" ("Understanding the Nexus," 1).

53. Jones and Petersen, "Instrumental, Narrow, Normative?"

54. King, "World Vision," 22.

55. G. Ter Haar and S. Ellis, "The Role of Religion in Development: Towards a New Relationship Between the European Union and Africa," *The European Journal of Development Research* 18, no. 3 (2006): 351–67.

56. King, "World Vision," 22.

57. Ibid.

58. A. Wrigley, "Who's Afraid of Holistic Development? Navigating the Interface Between Faith and Development" (dissertation, School of Oriental and African Studies: University of London, 2011), 11; see also P. Adams and N. de Bussy, "NGOs, Identities, and Religion: A Case of Split Personalities?" *Asia Pacific Public Relations Journal* 9 (2008): 87–101.

59. James, "Handle with Care," 5, 7.

60. Ibid., 4.

61. Ibid.

62. Ibid., 6.

63. Hovland, "Who's Afraid of Religion?" and see James, "Handle with Care," 7.

64. Devine and Deneulin, "Negotiating Religion in Everyday Life," 73.

Chapter 2: Some High-Level Theological Motivations for International Development Work

1. Bertrand Russell, *Unpopular Essays* (New York: Simon & Schuster, 1950), 92: "Infanticide, which might seem contrary to human nature, was almost universal before the rise of Christianity, and is recommended by Plato to prevent over-population"; and, at 137: "Christianity also did much to soften the lot of slaves. It established charity on a large scale, and inaugurated hospitals."

2. Stephen Monsma, *When Sacred and Secular Mix* (Lanham: Rowman & Littlefield, 1996), 8.

3. Virginia A. Hodgkinson, "The Future of Individual Giving and Volunteering: The Inseparable Link Between Religious Community and Individual Generosity," in *Faith and Philanthropy in America: Exploring the Role of Religion in America's Voluntary Sector*, ed. Robert Wuthnow and Virginia A. Hodgkinson (San Francisco: Josey-Bass, 1990), 285.

4. Acts 6:2–4.

5. See David W. Wilbur, *Power and Illusion: Religion and Human Need* (lulu.com, 2010), 90.

6. As an example, Stephen Monsma notes that "It was the Puritans in New England who founded Harvard and Yale" (*When Sacred and Secular Mix*, 8).

7. John Perkins (*Beyond Charity: The Call to Christian Community Development* [Grand Rapids: Baker Books, 1993], 70) recounts Wesley's startling contributions, and the impediment of racial prejudice in these social awakenings taking hold in North America.

8. Those interested in reading more about Christianity's general contributions to Western society may wish to read Rodney Stark, *For the Glory of God: How Monotheism Led to Reformations, Science, Witch-hunts and the End of Slavery* (New Jersey: Princeton University Press, 2003).

9. R. James, "What is Distinctive about FBOs," 8–9.

10. See the analysis of J. Berger, *Religious Non-governmental Organizations: An Exploratory Analysis* (International Society for Third-Sector Research and the Johns Hopkins University, 2003). Her analysis examines a cohort of religious NGOs affiliated with the UN.

11. See Episode 1 of *The Faith Effect* DVD series produced by World Vision Australia in which N. T. Wright is interviewed.

12. Isaiah 2:2–4.

13. Romans 8:22.

14. Isaiah 11:6–7.

15. N. T. Wright, *Surprised by Hope* (London: SPCK, 2007).

16. Dewi Hughes from TEAR Fund is an exponent of this view in his book *God of the Poor: A Biblical Vision of God's Present Rule* (Milton Keynes: Authentic, 1998).

17. J. Moltmann, *Theology of Hope* (London: SCM Press, 1967), 325; see also H. Küng, *The Church* (London: Burns and Oates, 1968), 79 ff.

18. Ibid., 327.

19. See Matthew 6:10.

20. M. Volf, "The Trinity Is Our Social Program: The Doctrine of the Trinity and Our Social Engagement," *Modern Theology* 14, no. 3 (1998): 403–23.

21. *Perichoresis* refers to the co-indwelling, co-inhering, and mutual interpenetration of the persons of the Trinity. The social relationships of the Trinity provide a paradigmatic pattern of service and love for humans.

22. Luke 4:18–19, quoting Isaiah 61:1–2.

23. The phrase "widow and orphan" can be understood as biblical code for any disenfranchised group.

24. Harvey Cox, at an early stage, stressed that "God is first of all present in political events, in revolutions, upheavals, invasions and defeats" since "it is the world, the political world...which is the arena of God's renewing and liberating activity" (H. Cox, *God's Revolution and Man's Responsibility* [Valley Forge: Judson, 1965] 23, 25).

25. Amos 5:15. The gate refers to the city gate, which was traditionally the place in ancient Israel where an aggrieved person could come to seek justice from the city elders.

26. Matthew 22:39.

27. D. Bonhoeffer, "Christ, the Church, and the World," in *Theological Foundations for Ministry*, ed. R. S. Anderson (Edinburgh: T&T Clark, 1979).

28. Luke 10:30. See K. E. Bailey, *Poet and Peasant* and *Through Peasant's Eyes*, combined ed. (Grand Rapids: Eerdmans, 1976), ch. 3 of *Through Peasant's Eyes*, 33ff.

29. Pope Benedict XVI, *Deus Caritas Est*, papal encyclical letter on Christian love, December 25, 2005, paragraph 22, Vatican website, http://www.vatican.va.

30. S. Deneulin, "Christianity and International Development," in Clarke, *The Handbook of Research on Development and Religion*, 51–65, 64.

31. L. Bertina, "The Catholic Doctrine of 'Integral Human Development' and Its Influence on the International Development Community," in Carbonnier, *International Development Policy*, 115–127.

32. Ibid., 118.

33. Ibid., 119ff.

34. Deneulin, "Christianity and International Development," 58.

35. Bertina, "The Catholic Doctrine," 120, referencing John Paul II, *Sollicitudo Rei Socialis*, paragraph 31 (1987).

36. Bertina, "The Catholic Doctrine," 120.

37. F. Schleiermacher, *Brief Outline of the Study of Theology* (Richmond: John Knox Press, 1983), 91–126.

38. D. S. Browning, *A Fundamental Practical Theology* (Minneapolis: Fortress Press, 1996).

39. 2 Corinthians 8:9.

40. Acts 11:27–29.

41. Acts 6:1–6.

42. For example, as expressed by the prophet Micah: "What does the Lord require of you but to do justice, and to love kindness, and to walk humbly with your God?" (Micah 6:8).

43. International development work involves complex logistics, support, and scale. It is invariably mediated through corporate structures. Those structures require management, governance, and policies informing various aspects of organizational life and culture. While broader theological motivations of the kind outlined will inspire development activity, particular theological motifs may be emphasized within organizational life. To complete the picture of the influence of theology on development work, it is necessary to examine how the specific theological motifs adopted by an organization can affect its work. This provides a positive theoretical reason for writing this book.

Chapter 3: Theological Reflection on Prevalent Theories of Change

1. L. Boxelaar, L. Mackinlay, and T. Dearborn, "Articulating Our Theory of Change" (discussion paper prepared for World Vision International, 2010).

2. Matthew 22:37–39.

3. B. L. Myers, *Walking with the Poor: Principles and Practices of Transformational Development* (Maryknoll: Orbis Books, 1999), 55.

4. Exodus 20:3.

5. For the Christian, this danger has existed from the earliest days of the Enlightenment. This was symbolized prophetically with the enthronement of the Statue of Reason in Notre Dame Cathedral in 1793.

6. H. I. Brown, *Perception, Theory and Commitment: The New Philosophy of Science* (Chicago: Precedent Publishing, 1977), 166.

7. Monsma, *When Sacred and Secular Mix*, 118.

8. R. Berstein, *The Restructuring of Social and Political Theory* (London: Methuen, 1985), 5. There the author notes that intellectual life was viewed as having passed "through the dark ages of theological, metaphysical, and philosophical speculation, only to emerge in the triumph of the positive sciences."

9. J. Bottomley, *In, But Not of the World* (St. Kilda: The Creative Ministries Network, 2008), 4.

10. D. J. Bosch, *Transforming Mission: Paradigm Shifts in Theology of Mission* (Maryknoll: Orbis Books, 1991), 274.

11. Ed Dayton, quoted in J. Steward, *Biblical Holism: Where God, People and Deeds Connect* (Melbourne: World Vision Australia, 1994), 90. Participatory approaches will help here.

12. Myers, *Walking with the Poor*, 54.

13. Bosch, *Transforming Mission*, 355.

14. See Myers, *Walking with the Poor*, 21. There is also a risk that the Christian development organization itself will be perceived by developing communities more as the champion of that false god and less as a fellowship of humans offering God's love in humility and service.

15. A lament attributed to Albert Einstein seems especially resonant: "The release of atom power has changed everything except our way of thinking . . . the solution to this problem lies in the heart of mankind. If only I had known, I should have become a watchmaker" (*New Statesman*, April 16, 1965).

16. Pope Benedict XVI, *Deus Caritas Est*, paragraph 28.

17. The term "critical consciousness" is also sometimes used. This concept was popularized in P. Freire's book *Pedagogy of the Oppressed*, originally published in by Herder and Herder in 1970 (New York: Continuum, 2007).

18. Hughes, *God of the Poor*, 13.

19. Bosch, *Transforming Mission*, 357.

20. Hughes, *God of the Poor*, 16.

21. L. Boff, *Good News to the Poor* (Wellwood: Burns and Oates, 1992), 80.

22. S. Corbett and B. Fikkert, *When Helping Hurts: How to Alleviate Poverty Without Hurting the Poor* (Chicago: Moody Publishers, 2009), 146.

23. Boff, *Good News to the Poor*, xi.

24. Chambers, *NGOs and Development*, 2.

25. Brian McLaren, quoted in S-C Rah, *The Next Evangelicalism: Freeing the Church from Western Cultural Captivity* (Downers Grove, IL: IVP Books, 2009), 125.

26. A. Wrigley, "Who's Afraid of Holistic Development?" 9.

27. Boff, *Good News to the Poor*, 30.

28. Corbett and Fikkert, *When Helping Hurts*, 136.

29. Boff, *Good News to the Poor*, 23.

30. Ibid., 22.

31. R. Williams, "Relating Intelligently to Religion," 2.

32. Corbett and Fikkert, *When Helping Hurts*, 147.

33. M. Edwards and G. Sen, "NGOs, Social Change, and the Transformation of Human Relationships: A 21st-century Civic Agenda," *Third World Quarterly* 21, no. 4 (August 2000): 605–16, online at http://www.futurepositive.org. The quote is from page 10 of the online version.

34. Williams, "Relating Intelligently to Religion," 3.

35. C. Boin, J. Harris, and A. Marchesetti, *Fake Aid: How Foreign Aid Is Being Used to Support the Self-Serving Political Activities of NGOs* (London: International Policy Network, 2009), 21.

36. For example, see K. Rasanathan, J. Norenhag, and N. Valentine, "Realizing Human Rights-based Approaches for Action on the Social Determinants of Health," *Health and Human Rights* 12, no. 2 (2010): 52. See also A. Palmer, J. Tomkinson, C. Phung, N. Ford, M. Joffres, K. Fernandes, L. Zeng, V. Lima, J. Montaner, G. Guyatt, and E. Mill, "Does Ratification of Human-Rights Treaties Have Effects on Population Health?" *The Lancet* 373 (June 2009): 1987–92.

37. S. Batliwala, *When Rights Go Wrong: Distorting the Rights Based Approach to Development* (Harvard University: Hauser Center for Nonprofit Organizations, 2010), 7.

38. Revelation 21:4. It should also be noted here that the UN Declaration on Human Rights had significant Christian input and reflects the Judeo-Christian heritage. Further information about this can be found at http://www.isaiahone.org.

39. R. Williams, "A Theology of Development," 7.

40. Genesis 1:26–27.

41. Luke 18:1–8.

42. J. Berger, *Religious Non-governmental Organizations: An Exploratory Analysis* (International Society for Third-Sector Research and the Johns Hopkins University, 2003), 18.

43. Ibid., 19.

44. J. Moltmann, *The Trinity and the Kingdom of God* (London: SCM Press, 1980).

45. Luke 4:18.

46. Matthew 16:24–25; Mark 8:34–35; Luke 9:23–24.

47. Matthew 5:41.

48. R. Amesbury and G. M. Newlands, *Faith and Human Rights: Christianity and the Global Struggle for Human Dignity* (Minneapolis: Fortress Press, 2008), 110.

49. Boxelaar, Mackinlay, and Dearborn, *Articulating Our Theory of Change*, 4.

50. Ibid.

51. Tyndale, "Faith and Economics in 'Development,'" 17.

52. Wright, *Surprised by Hope*, 192, analyzing 1 Corinthians 15:58.

53. It is argued that religion is not a "missing link" in development, it is an overarching frame or narrative that can incorporate the multiple visions of how change may occur in any given setting. Jones and Petersen, "Instrumental, Narrow, Normative?" 1302.

Chapter 4: The Big Picture Narratives

1. Bosch, *Transforming Mission*, 400.

2. In this regard, human community can look to the eternal self-giving love of the Holy Trinity as its inspiration. This is what it truly means to be made in the image of God (Genesis 1:26–27).

3. D. G. Groody, *Globalization, Spirituality, and Justice* (Maryknoll: Orbis Books, 2007), 23.

4. Bosch, *Transforming Mission*, 397.

5. Romans 8:22.

6. Bosch, *Transforming Mission*, 10. It is noted that anthropology and other social sciences recognize the critical role of religion in human culture and society. Culture is holistic. It is a system of elements that are interrelated and interconnected.

7. The verb σώζω, *to save*, is translated variously in English as to heal, to deliver, to make well, to survive, and to bring safely—among other uses.

8. Myers, *Walking with the Poor*, 7.

9. Boff, *Good News to the Poor*, 56.

10. Matthew 22:37.

11. T. A. Dearborn, "Unavoidable Witness in the Work of a Humanitarian Organization," unpublished monograph produced for World Vision International (2011), 7.

12. Boff, *Good News to the Poor*, 14.

13. Ibid., 17.

14. *Witness to Jesus Christ* (World Vision International 2006 policy document, September 16, 1995, rev. ed., September 14, 2006), clause 1.

15. Ibid., clause 2.

16. D. Edmonds, "An Incarnational Agency in an Evangelical World: A Theological Consideration of Anglicare's Role in Mission" (paper presented on September 2, 2008, at the Anglicare Australia 2008 Conference, Sydney, NSW; Launceston: Anglicare Tasmania, 2008), 4.

17. Key Informant Interview (KII) with a senior humanitarian and emergency aid manager, Lebanon.

18. Focus Group Discussion (FGD) with Pastors' Committee, Nyasa Area Development Program (ADP), Tanzania.

19. W. Wink, *Engaging the Powers: Discernment and Resistance in a World of Domination* (Minneapolis: Fortress, 1992), 83.

20. Wright, *Surprised by Hope* (London: SPCK, 2007).

21. Bosch, *Transforming Mission*, 397.

22. Ibid., 35.

23. Myers, *Walking with the Poor*, 15.

24. Boff, *Good News to the Poor*, 32.

25. Wright, *Surprised by Hope*, 204–5.

26. E. Lucas, "The New Testament Teaching on the Environment," *Transformation* 16, no. 3 (1999): 96.

27. Revelation 21:3–4.

28. John 10:10.

29. Matthew 6:10.

30. Mark 1:5; Matthew 3:2.

31. See Moltmann, *Theology of Hope*.

32. L. Abrams, "Faith, Development and Poverty—Reflections," April 24, 2013, www.thewaterpage.com.

33. Revelation 21:3–4.

Chapter 5: A Spiritual Worldview—Meeting Communities Where They're At

1. A comment made by Tim Dearborn during a private conversation.

2. Wrigley, "Who's Afraid of Holistic Development?" 6.

3. O. Salemink, "Development Cooperation as Quasi-religious Conversion," in *The Development of Religion, the Religion of Development,* ed. A. Kumar Giri, A. van Harskamp, and O. Salemink (Delft: Eburon, 2004), 121–30. Philip Fountain also points out market-driven and secular ideologies can be zealously applied so as to seek to change the attitudes of others (P. Fountain, "The Myth of Religious NGOs: Development Studies and the Return of Religion," in Carbonnier, *International Development Policy*, 26).

4. Hufford, "The Scholarly Voice and the Personal Voice," 297ff.

5. Ibid., 303.

6. Pew Forum on Religion and Public Life, "The Global Religious Landscape" (December 18, 2012), online at http://www.pewforum.org.

7. FGD with Bcharre ADP, Lebanon.

8. A. Goode, *World Vision Evaluation Report: World Vision Rwanda* (Christian Commitments Programme, October 2011), 12.

9. FGD with women from an ADP in the Beirut area, Lebanon.

10. KII with a senior Design Monitoring and Evaluation Advisor, Senegal—a Muslim.

11. Imam's emphasis; KII with a Muslim leader, Kaffrine, Senegal.

12. KII with a senior operations manager, Senegal.

13. KII with a senior national office executive, Senegal.

14. A. Goode, *World Vision Evaluation Report: World Vision Tanzania* (Christian Commitments Programme, October 2010), 18. Emphasis added.

15. KII with Zone Manager 1, Rwanda.

16. KII with a senior national office executive, Lebanon.

17. KII with a senior leader from the Armenian Apostolic Church.

18. A. Goode, *World Vision Evaluation Report: World Vision Georgia* (Christian Commitments Programme, June 2010), 9.

19. KII with Apostolic priest 1, Armenia.

20. E. Bornstein, *The Spirit of Development: Protestant NGOs, Morality, and Economics in Zimbabwe* (Stanford: Stanford University Press, 2005). She notes that "In African Christian faith, the realms of the spiritual and the material cannot easily be separated: development is both spiritual and material" (49).

21. See R. D. Putnam, *Bowling Alone: The Collapse and Revival of American Community* (New York: Simon and Schuster, 2000).

22. Specifically, Putnam recognizes the need for bonding capital (links between those in existing groups, such as co-religionists) and bridging capital (goodwill links between different groups).

23. P. L. Berger and R. W. Hefner, *Spiritual Capital in Comparative Perspective* (Boston University: Institute for the Study of Economic Culture, Institute on Religion and World Affairs, n.d.), online at http://metanexus.org.

24. R. J. Barro and R. M. McCleary, "Religion and Economic Growth," *American Sociological Review* 68 (2003), 760–81.

25. R. D. Woodberry, "Researching Spiritual Capital, Promises and Pitfalls," 2003, online at http://www.metanexus.net.

26. R. and T. Shah, "Spiritual Capital and Economic Enterprise," The Oxford Centre for Religion and Public Life, April 24, 2013, online at http://www.ocrpl.org. "If it were demonstrated that the poor can leverage their vast stocks of religiosity as economically beneficial spiritual capital, this could translate into a new paradigm for development practice and policy" (1).

27. Ibid.

Chapter 6: Living for the Kingdom: The Now!

1. Why do we repent? Mark provides the answer in 1:14: "Because the Kingdom of God is at hand!"

2. Norman Perrin notes: "The central aspect of the teaching of Jesus was that concerning the Kingdom of God. Of this there can be no doubt..." (N. Perrin,

Rediscovering the Teaching of Jesus [New York: Harper and Row, 1967], 54). Harvey Cox echoes: "It was the heartbeat of his life, his constant concern and preoccupation" (H. Cox, *The Future of Faith* [New York: HarperOne, 2009], 48).

3. J. D. G. Dunn, *Unity and Diversity in the New Testament*, 2nd ed. (London: SCM Press, 1998), 13ff; H. Küng (*The Church* [London: Burns and Oates, 1968], 88) notes that the phrase "the reign of God" is used about forty times in Luke.

4. Reformed theologian Jürgen Moltmann has written extensively about how the promise of God's coming kingdom should impact the lived present. He developed the term *presentative eschatology* to describe this relationship: "'Presentative eschatology' means nothing else but simply 'creative expectation,' hope which sets about criticising and transforming the present because it is open towards the universal future of the kingdom" (Moltmann, *Theology of Hope*, 335).

5. KII with a senior national office executive, Bosnia and Herzegovina.

6. FGD with Ministry Quality staff, National Office, Tanzania.

7. FDG with Poro and Oshetime villagers, Albania.

8. KII with Sponsorship/Office Administrator, Bosnia and Herzegovina.

9. KII with a non-Christian community leader, Beirut.

10. R. Kilpatrick and A. Goode, *World Vision Evaluation Report: World Vision Bosnia and Herzegovina* (Christian Commitments Programme, July 2009), 27.

11. KII with a senior Humanitarian and Emergency Assistance (HEA) manager, Lebanon.

12. KII with a program manager, Georgia.

13. KII with a World Vision Administration Manager, Bosnia and Herzegovina.

14. KII with Muslim leader, Kaffrine, Senegal.

15. J. Haynes, *Religion and Development: Conflict or Cooperation?* (London: Palgrave Macmillan, 2007), 99.

16. E. Kessler and M. Arkush, "Keeping Faith in Development: The Significance of Interfaith Relations in the Work of Humanitarian Aid and International Development Organizations" (The Woolf Institute of Abrahamic Faiths, 2008), online at http://www.woolf.cam.ac.uk. Consistently, this paper reported "If you go to a Muslim community and start saying I'm a person of the Book or I am a Muslim, people will be more accepting of you because of the faith element" (quote from Maki Mohamed, Islamic Relief).

17. D. Belshaw, *Enhancing the Development Capabilities of Civil Society Organizations, with Particular Reference to Christian Faith-based Organizations* (Global Poverty Research Group, 2005), 4.

18. A scripture passage of special resonance here is Revelation 21:3–5, which speaks of a time when God makes his home among his people, and there is no more death, or mourning, or crying, or pain.

19. KII with an evangelist from Serving in Mission (SIM), Senegal.

20. Kilpatrick and Goode, *World Vision Evaluation Report: Bosnia and Herzegovina*, 11.

21. FGD, Idjevan staff, Tavush ADP, Armenia.

22. KII with prelate from the Armenian Apostolic Church.

23. M. Maggay, "Justice and Approaches to Social Change," in *Micah Challenge: The Church's Responsibility to the Global Poor*, ed. M. Hoek and J. Thacker (London: Paternoster, 2008), 132. Referred to in Goode, *World Vision Evaluation Report: Georgia* 25.

24. FGD with National Office Staff, Georgia.

25. KII with ADP Manager 3, Tanzania.

26. FGD with ADP Buliza staff, Rwanda.

27. Belshaw, *Enhancing the Development Capabilities of Civil Society Organizations*, 4.

28. Narayan, *Voices of the Poor*.

29. K. Marshall, "Development and Religion: A Different Lens on Development Debates," *Peabody Journal of Education* 76, nos. 3–4 (2001), 8.

Chapter 7: Work as Ministry

1. Karl Barth, quoted in J. G. Flett, *The Witness of God: The Trinity, Missio Dei, and the Nature of Christian Community* (Grand Rapids: Eerdmans, 2010), 261.

2. Matthew 25:37–40.

3. J. G. Flett, *The Witness of God*, 234.

4. D. J. Bosch, *Transforming Mission*, 18.

5. R. James, "What is Distinctive about FBOs," 14.

6. Ibid., 20.

7. Pope Benedict XVI, *Deus Caritas Est*, paragraph 33.

8. T. Jeavons, *When the Bottom Line Is Faithfulness* (Bloomington: Indiana University Press, 1994), 70.

9. Ibid., 50.

10. British Overseas NGOs for Development (BOND), *A BOND Approach to Quality in NGOs: Putting Beneficiaries First*, report prepared by Keystone (2006), vi.

11. Ibid., vi.

12. Goode, *World Vision Evaluation Report: Rwanda*, 19.

13. A date commonly used to mark the commencement of the development profession is the inauguration speech of U.S. President Harry S. Truman in 1949. See M. Clarke, "Understanding the Nexus between Religion and Development," 2.

14. See M. Clarke, ed., *Mission and Development: God's Work or Good Works* (London: Continuum, 2012). This book helps document the outstanding contribution of missionaries to early development initiatives.

15. KII with a senior HEA manager, Lebanon.

16. KII with a Sponsorship/Office Administrator, Bosnia and Herzegovina.

17. F&A (Finance and Administration) Staff Focus Group Discussion (FGD), Tanzania.

18. FDG with National Office staff, World Vision Rwanda, and KII with Zone Manager 2, Rwanda.

19. A. Goode, *World Vision Evaluation Report: World Vision Senegal* (Christian Commitments Programme, October 2011), 22.

20. ADP Manager 3, Tanzania.

21. KII with a human rights advisor, UN Office for West Africa, Senegal.

22. Goode, *World Vision Evaluation Report: Senegal*, 23.

23. Pontifical Council for Justice and Peace, "Compendium of the Social Doctrine of the Church," 189 (Rome: 2004), online at http://www.vatican.va.

24. Cyrus the King of Persia (Ezra 1:1–4), Artaxerxes (Nehemiah 2:4–6), the Roman Centurion (Acts 27:30–32).

25. KII with a senior advocacy manager, Lebanon.

26. This concern was expressed in an interview with Muslim Leaders, Mswaki ADP, Tanzania.

27. Kilpatrick and Goode, *World Vision Evaluation Report: Bosnia and Herzegovina*, 8, 26.

Chapter 8: A Devotional, Reflective Culture

1. *Interfaith Relations* (World Vision International policy document, April 2, 2009) clause 2.5. See also *Witness to Jesus Christ* (World Vision International 2006 policy document, September 16, 1995, rev. ed, September 14, 2006), clause 26.

2. Edwards and Sen, "NGOs, Social Change, and the Transformation of Human Relationships," 605–16, online at http://www.futurepositive.org. The quote is from page 41 of the online version.

3. Ibid.

4. Ibid., 42.

5. Ibid.

6. R. Chambers, "NGOs and Development," 2.

7. Ibid., 3. He also finds it telling that psychologists are under-represented as development professionals.

8. It has been stated that "Christianity and most other world faiths stress a variant of the 'golden rule' (treat others as you yourself wish to be treated) as a guide to social relationships" (Belshaw, *Enhancing the Development Capabilities of Civil Society Organizations*, 4).

9. Ter Haar and Ellis, "The Role of Religion in Development," 353.

10. For example, texts such as J. P. Meier, *A Marginal Jew: Rethinking the Historical Jesus*, vol. 2, *Mentor, Message and Miracles* (New York: Doubleday, 1994); J. D. G. Dunn, *Jesus Remembered* (Grand Rapids: Eerdmans, 2003); D. C. Allison, *Constructing Jesus: Memory, Imagination, and History* (Grand Rapids: Baker Academic, 2010); and N. T. Wright, *Jesus and the Victory of God* (Minneapolis: Fortress, 1996). All address the hermeneutical issues in reconstructing and interpreting the Jesus story.

11. Matthew 19:14.

12. John 4:7–26.

13. Acts 2:42–47.

14. Acts 6:1–6.

15. Matthew 23:23–24.

16. Mark 1:40–42; Matthew 8:3.

17. James 1:27.

18. Concern for people with disabilities was one of the prominent notes of Jesus' earthly ministry. Persons with disabilities become witnesses for Christ, his healing of their bodies a sign of the spiritual healing he brought to all people (see Matthew 9:5ff).

19. Mark 7:37; Mark 10:46–52.

20. John 9:39–40; Acts 3:1–10.

21. Luke 18:18–23.

22. Romans 8:22–24; Psalm 24:1; Deuteronomy 10:14; Genesis 2:15.

23. Matthew 2:13–14; Luke 10:25–37.

24. Matthew 10:7–10.

25. For example, turning over the tables of the moneychangers in the temple (John 2:14–15). See also Matthew 26:52.

26. Matthew 5:9. Shawn Flanigan has noted the potential for religious actors to exacerbate conflicts, yet gives the following positive example of instances in which Christian faith helped to resolve conflict. She reports: "In the mediation process between the Nicaraguan government and the native peoples in the civil war in the 1980s, Mennonite negotiators focused on Christian ideals such as service, acceptance of suffering, the harvest of righteousness that awaits those who sow in peace, and the holy role of the peacemaker. Throughout negotiations, both sides turned to this religious symbolism to help create bridges..." (S. Flanigan, "Religion, Conflict and Peacebuilding in Development," in Clarke, *The Handbook of Research on Development and Religion*, 259).

27. Colossians 3:13; Matthew 18:21–22; Matthew 6:12.

28. Colossians 1:20; 2 Corinthians 5:18–19.

29. Luke 4:17–21.

30. Mark 2:15–17.

31. 2 Corinthians 8:21; Proverbs 6:16–20; Philippians 4:8–9; John 8:32.

32. Colossians 3:23; 2 Thessalonians 3:10–12; Proverbs 6:6–8.

33. Matthew 5:3–10; Revelation 21:3–5.

34. Matthew 9:10; Isaiah 58:10.

35. Ter Haar and Ellis, *The Role of Religion in Development*, 357–58.

36. KII with a Humanitarian and Emergency Assistance coordinator, Rwanda.

37. KII with a CEDC (Children in Especially Difficult Circumstances) program manager, Georgia.

38. FGD with Robero ADP staff, Rwanda.

39. Goode, *World Vision Evaluation Report: Rwanda*, 8.

40. KII with a Faith and Development coordinator, Bosnia and Herzegovina.

41. James, "What is Distinctive about FBOs," 20.

42. Jeavons, *When the Bottom Line Is Faithfulness*, 135ff.

43. James, "What is Distinctive about FBOs," 20.

44. KII with a Pastoral Carer, Senegal.

45. Goode, *World Vision Evaluation Report: Senegal*, 31.

46. Kessler and Arkush, "Keeping Faith in Development."

Chapter 9: Standing against Evil

1. Ter Haar and Ellis, "The Role of Religion in Development," 354–55.

2. For example, David King describes World Vision as an organization with an ability to reinvent itself over time. In particular, it changed from an evangelical organization to a development organization with a strong focus on professional methods and a commitment to advocacy and policy activism (King, "World Vision").

3. Myers, *Walking with the Poor*, 91.

4. Ibid., 15.

5. Ibid., 69. See also Chapter 7 of J. Christian, *God of the Empty-Handed: Poverty, Power and the Kingdom of God* (Monrovia: Marc Publishers, 1999) for a fuller explanation of the powers and principalities against which development work must contend.

6. Myers, *Walking with the Poor*, 99. See also P. Batchelor, *People in Rural Development* (Carlisle: Pasternoster Press, 1993), 85.

7. Preface to C. S. Lewis, *The Screwtape Letters* (London: The Macmillan Company, 1946).

8. Two useful books that have shed some light on this topic are Bryant Myers's *Walking with the Poor* and the important work by Indian theologian Jayakumar Christian, *God of the Empty-Handed*.

9. FGD with religious leaders, Tattaguine ADP, Senegal.

10. These examples taken from the FGD with the Children's Committee from the Kisongo Makuyuni ADP, Tanzania.

11. Goode, *World Vision Evaluation Report: Senegal*, 19.

12. Goode, *World Vision Evaluation Report: Tanzania*, 19; with reference to demonic possession, 33.

13. KII with a senior National Office executive, Rwanda.

14. KII with a senior operations manager, Senegal.

15. Goode, *World Vision Evaluation Report: Senegal*, 27.

16. N. A. Alolo and J. A. Connell, "Indigenous Religions and Development: African Traditional Religion," in Clarke, *The Handbook of Research on Development and Religion*, 138–63.

17. Ibid., 142.

18. Ibid., 145.

19. Ibid., 146.

20. Ibid., 138.

21. Ibid., 142–145.

22. Ibid., 151. *Muti* refers to murder or mutilation, often of children, to obtain body parts used for ritual purposes.

23. Ibid., 141.

24. Ibid., 161.

25. Ibid., 149, 152–53.

26. Ibid., 141.

27. A. Newmarch and A. Goode, *World Vision Evaluation Report: World Vision Albania* (Christian Commitments Programme, September 2008), 23.

28. ADP Team Leader, Albania.

29. KII with Zone Manager 1, Rwanda.

30. FGD Small Enterprise Development Agency, Tanzania.

31. H. Marquette, "Corruption, Religion and Moral Development," in Clarke, *The Handbook of Research on Development and Religion*, 220–37.

Chapter 10: The Imperative of Inner Transformation

1. W. Brueggemann, *Biblical Perspectives on Evangelism: Living in a Three-Storied Universe* (Nashville: Abingdon, 1993), 34.

2. Ed Dayton quoted in Steward, *Biblical Holism*, 89.

3. Hughes, *God of the Poor*, 2.

4. Flett, *The Witness of God*, 54.

5. Edwards and Sen, "NGOs, Social Change, and the Transformation of Human Relationships: A 21st-century Civic Agenda," 605–16, online at http://www.futurepositive.org. The quote is from page 39 of the online version. While not arguing from a Christian perspective, they do note that: "The goal of personal change must be a conscious and explicit element in all that we do" and that "even the socially committed will be unsuccessful if they ignore the inner basis of change" (44 and 41 respectively).

6. M. Parris, "As an Atheist, I Truly Believe Africa Needs God," *The Times Online*, January 8, 2009.

7. Groody, *Globalization, Spirituality, and Justice*, 185.

8. Ibid.

9. See, for example, Christian, *God of the Empty-Handed*, 147.

10. Groody, *Globalisation*, 186.

11. It is not correct to define "proselytism" as meaning any activity that may lead to conversion. It refers to violence, coercion, manipulation, or incentives being provided to induce someone to change his or her faith position.

12. Pope Benedict XVI, *Deus Caritas Est*, paragraph 31.

13. John Perkins puts it this way: "What separates Christian community development from other forms of social change is that we believe that changing a life or changing a community is ultimately a spiritual issue" (Perkins, *Beyond Charity*, 80).

14. Colossians 1:20; 2 Corinthians 5:18.

15. Goode, *World Vision Evaluation Report: Rwanda*, 5.

16. KII with a senior national office executive, Rwanda.

17. 1 Peter 3:15.

18. A. Newmarch, *World Vision Evaluation Report: World Vision Lebanon* (Christian Commitments Programme, November 2009), 13.

19. World Vision Human Resources coordinator, Bosnia and Herzegovina.

Chapter 11: Prayer and Spiritual Disciplines

1. Karl Barth, quoted in Flett, *The Witness of God*, 107.

2. Rick James notes that "Prayer expresses a human dependence on God" (James, "What is Distinctive about FBOs," 14).

3. The Apostle Paul also implores the followers of Jesus Christ to: "Rejoice always, pray without ceasing, give thanks in all circumstances; for this is the will of God…" (1 Thessalonians 5:16–18).

4. Myers, *Walking with the Poor*, 11.

5. Ibid.

6. KII with a Base Manager in Senegal.

7. Goode, *World Vision Evaluation Report: Rwanda*, 19.

8. KII with ADP Manager 2, Rwanda.

9. Goode, *World Vision Evaluation Report: Rwanda*, 18.

10. KII with ADP Manager 3, Rwanda.

11. KII with ADP Manager 2, Rwanda.

12. FGD with ADP Buliza staff, Rwanda.

13. KII with Zone Manager 2, Rwanda.

14. As outlined in chapter 9, the kinds of practices include referring sick people to traditional healers for illnesses needing serious medical attention, "cuttings," fetishes, oppressive cultic practices (the belief that "If I leave the spirits, they will kill me"), refusing to drink from certain wells, not building houses with iron roofs (for fear of spirit possession), not farming arable land (so as not to offend spirits), and stigmatizing vulnerable groups. Lesser concerns were the wearing of charms or the participation in rituals to ward off evil spirits.

15. The term "animism" has been used as per the World Vision evaluation reports, noting that some commentators prefer the term African Traditional Religion, which may have fewer pejorative connotations.

16. See Alolo and Connell, "Indigenous Religions and Development," 149: "The spirits of the living dead are regarded as ever-living, ever-watchful beings that possess the power to both help and harm their living relatives."

17. Goode, *World Vision Evaluation Report: Senegal*, 27.

18. KII with ADP Manager 3, Tanzania.

19. Muslims regard Jesus as one of the five main prophets in Islam. Hence it is acceptable to refer to Jesus as the Word of God. It is problematic, however, for Muslims to refer to him as the Son of God, because this would infer a divine status. For a comparison of the Lord's Prayer and the Muslim Fatiha, see Chawkat Moucarry, *Two Prayers for Today* (Tiruvella, India: Christava Sahitya Samithi, 2007).

Chapter 12: A Special Relationship with the Church

1. J. Moltmann, *The Church in the Power of the Spirit* (London: SCM Press, 1975), 83–85ff.

2. *Partnerships with Churches* (World Vision International policy document, September 16, 1995, rev. ed., March 13, 2003), clause 2.

3. Williams, "A Theology of Development," 5, Williams's emphasis.

4. Matthew 25:40.

5. Rah, *The Next Evangelicalism*, 50.

6. Cited in Myers, *Walking with the Poor*, 89.

7. M. Sharpe, "Name It and Claim It: Prosperity Gospel and the Global Pentecostal Reformation," in *The Handbook of Research on Development and Religion*, ed. M. Clarke (Cheltenham: Edward Elgar, 2013), 164–79.

8. Ibid, 164.

9. K. Marshall, *Africa: How and Why is Faith Important and Relevant for Development* (Georgetown University: Berkeley Centre for Religion, Peace and World Affairs), 10, online at http://www.vanderbilt.edu.

10. Goode, *World Vision Evaluation Report: Rwanda*, 14, 6.

11. Goode, *World Vision Evaluation Report: Georgia*, 9.

12. A senior bishop of the Armenian Apostolic Church, Armenia.

13. A. Ivereigh, "Religious Faith Builds a Civil Society in a Way Secularism Does Not," *The Guardian*, September 29, 2011.

14. Goode, *World Vision Evaluation Report: Rwanda*, 16.

15. Kessler and Arkush give an example of symbolic action in which a Christian bishop visited the work of Islamic Relief in Sudan and was so impressed by it that he made a personal donation. This was a powerful gesture in the Sudanese context (Kessler and Arkush, "Keeping Faith in Development," 9).

16. KII with a Public Health and HIV manager, Georgia.

17. KII with a Program Manager, Georgia.

18. Goode, *World Vision Evaluation Report: Georgia*, 18.

19. There are occasionally exceptions to this, as pointed out later in this chapter when discussing the risks of dealing with the church and its leaders.

20. D. Belshaw, *Enhancing the Development Capabilities of Civil Society Organizations*, 4.

21. Goode, *World Vision Evaluation Report: Rwanda*, 19.

22. Jones and Petersen, "Instrumental, Narrow, Normative?" 1300.

23. KII with a WCC Round Table representative, Armenia.

24. Goode, *World Vision Evaluation Report: Rwanda*, 16.

25. Ibid., 30.

26. Goode, *World Vision Evaluation Report: Rwanda*, 15.

27. KII with a senior executive, Senegal.

28. KII with a UN Advisor, Senegal.

29. KII with a senior advocacy manager, Lebanon.

30. Newmarch, *World Vision Evaluation Report: Armenia*, 10.

31. Ibid., 11; see also 16.

32. KII with a senior national office executive, Lebanon.

33. KII with a church pastor, Albania.

34. FGD with ADP Tattaguine religious leaders, Senegal.

35. KII with a senior operations manager, Senegal.

36. Newmarch and Goode, *World Vision Evaluation Report: Albania*.

37. Newmarch, *World Vision Evaluation Report: Armenia*, 11.

38. Ibid., 24.

39. The Georgian Orthodox Church and the Armenian Apostolic Church see themselves as having a legitimacy based on their antiquity, national dominance,

and rich cultural heritage. Other expressions of Christian faith may be seen by these groups as unnecessary and even subversive of religious and social cohesion. It is against this background that other denominations may be labeled "sects."

40. Kilpartick and Goode, *World Vision Evaluation Report: Bosnia and Herzegovina*, 26, referring to the Serb/Orthodox, Croat/Catholic, Bosniak/Muslim divide in Bosnia and Herzegovina.

41. KII with a CEDC Program Manager, Georgia.

42. Goode, *World Vision Evaluation Report: Rwanda*, 16.

43. Ibid., 6.

44. Goode, *World Vision Evaluation Report: Georgia*, 31.

45. Sharpe, "Name It and Claim It," 174.

46. Ibid., 175–76. Can a parallel perhaps be drawn with Max Weber and the so-called "Protestant work ethic," which he argued undergirded the development of capitalist economies?

47. Goode, *World Vision Evaluation Report: Georgia*, 13.

48. Newmarch and Goode, *World Vision Evaluation Report: Albania*, 24.

49. KII with Apostolic Priest 1 and colleague, Armenia.

50. KII with a sister from a religious order, Armenia.

51. W. Tyndale, "Key Issues for Development," World Faiths Development Dialogue, *Occasional Paper* 1 (November 1998).

52. Clarke, "Understanding the Nexus between Religion and Development," 6.

53. G. Clarke and M. Jennings, *Development, Civil Society and Faith-Based Organizations: Bridging the Sacred and the Secular* (Basingstoke: Macmillan, 2008), 16.

Chapter 13: Implications

1. Stephen Plant, "Does Faith Matter in Development?" (paper presented at Faith and Development Theory and Practice Forum, Cambridge University, November 26–27, 2004), 3.

2. Ibid.

3. James, "Handle with Care," 2.

4. J. Dart and J. Hall, "Church Partnership Program, Papua New Guinea," case study report (Canberra: AusAID, September 2010).

5. Ibid.

6. See, for example, the work of Dr. Todd Johnson, from the Center for the Study of Global Christianity.

7. For example, Deryke Belshaw has noted that "The general ethos of the dominant religion may be 'conservative' and anti-reform" (Belshaw, *Enhancing the Development Capabilities of Civil Society Organizations*, 5).

8. Matthew Clarke notes that while it is easy to find examples of stereotypes of religion as male dominated and hierarchical, there are also examples "where religious faith stands firmly in the corner of the oppressed and disad-

vantaged and where social justice is a core tenet" (Clarke, "Understanding the Nexus between Religion and Development," 11).

9. J. Lunn, "The Role of Religion, Spirituality and Faith in Development," 940; see also P. Fountain, "The Myth of Religious NGOs," 10.

10. Philip Fountain argues that "the prior exclusion of religion and the current celebration of its newfound celebrity status by development studies are plagued by an ongoing ideological bias apparent in the framing and deployment of the concept. Religion is not an object waiting to be discovered and analysed, but rather a domain constructed according to dominant modern presuppositions by the religion and development literature. Discourse relating to religion is, correspondingly, not neutral description but deeply political and should be analysed accordingly" (Fountain, "The Myth of Religious NGOs," 10).

11. Fountain, "The Myth of Religious NGOs," 11.

12. Ibid., 11–14.

13. "Fountain presents a rather suspicious even conspiratorial dissection of the approach that I (and my colleague Lucy Keough) are said to represent . . . at no stage, in any way, were we *thinking*, much less saying, that religion should be 'used'" (Katherine Marshall, "Revisiting the Religious Revival in Development: A Critique of Philip Fountain," in Carbonnier, *International Development Policy*, 37).

14. Example given during FGD, Rebero Inter-church Committee and ADP.

15. Anglican Communion News Service, citing the work of religious demographer Dr. Todd M. Johnson ("Global Data Upend Usual Picture of Christianity Trends," March 20, 2013, http://www.aco.org.).

16. Rah, *The Next Evangelicalism*, 13.

17. Ter Haar and Ellis, "The Role of Religion in Development," 351.

18. "Global Data Upend Usual Picture of Christianity Trends."

19. Jones and Petersen, "Instrumental, Narrow, Normative?" abstract.

20. Tyndale, "Key Issues for Development," 13.

21. Ibid.

22. D. Goulet, "Development Experts: The One-Eyed Giants," *World Development* 8, no. 6–7 (1980): 485.

23. Grills, "The Paradox of Multilateral Organizations."

24. Dart and Hall, "Church Partnership Program," executive summary, v.

25. Ibid., v.

26. C. Taylor, "Why We Need a Radical Redefinition of Secularism," in *The Power of Religion in the Public Sphere*, ed. J. Butler, E. Mendieta, and J. Van Antwerpen (New York: Columbia University Press, 2011), 34–59.

27. A-M. Holenstein, "Governmental Donor Agencies and Faith-Based Organizations," *International Review of the Red Cross* 87, no. 858 (2005): 370.

28. G. Clarke, "Agents of Transformation? Donors, Faith-Based Organizations and International Development," *Third World Quarterly* 28, no. 1 (2007): 91.

29. Holenstein, "Governmental Donor Agencies," 371. Shawn Flanigan also notes that "religion has the ability to stimulate militancy on behalf of the

other, as well as militancy aimed against the other" (Flanigan, "Religion, Conflict and Peacebuilding in Development," 252).

30. Holenstein, "Governmental Donor Agencies," 371.

31. Fountain, characterizing Flanigan's thesis, "The Myth of Religious NGOs," 19.

32. Holenstein references the Geneva Spiritual Appeal, which was launched in 1999 and was co-signed by the heads of several international organizations and religious leaders. The kinds of principles enshrined are: refusal to invoke a religious or spiritual power to justify violence of any kind; refusal to invoke a religious or spiritual source to justify discrimination and exclusion; and refusal to exploit or dominate others by means of strength, intellectual capacity or spiritual persuasion, wealth, or social status. Holenstein sees these principles as helpful, but insufficient.

33. Holenstein, "Governmental Donor Agencies," 372.

34. C. Candland, "Faith as Social Capital: Religion and Community Development in Southern Asia," *Policy Sciences* 33 (2001): 355–74. The article concludes that "NGOs that are rooted in religiously articulated programs for social reform can be particularly effective at community development and build social capital, especially in political environments in which the state does not promote civic religion" (371). However, the broader political context is highly relevant. Where the state has co-opted religious institutions for arbitrary or authoritarian political purposes, this can lead to a loss of credibility and damage the effectiveness of development programs.

35. Jones and Petersen, "Instrumental, Narrow, Normative?" 1293.

36. Ibid., 1300.

37. Fountain, "The Myth of Religious NGOs," 24.

38. Ibid., 25.

39. Ter Haar and Ellis, "The Role of Religion in Development," 353.

40. Goulet, "Development Experts," 481.

41. W. Tyndale, "Towards Sustainable Development," 1–4; see also Ter Haar and Ellis, "The Role of Religion in Development," 365.

42. For example, Ter Haar and Ellis in "The Role of Religion in Development" report that "In Africa, both illness and healing are generally viewed as holistic in nature, requiring attention to the spiritual as well as physical aspects of a person. For this reason, religion plays an important role in health care in Africa generally" (361). For this reason, they state, "should policymakers and development agents pursue a path of greater cooperation with religious networks, it will mean lending serious attention to religious world-views, with which they may be unfamiliar or even feel uncomfortable" (365).

43. Resulting in the launch of the Department for International Development's (DFID's) *Faith Partnership Principles*.

44. For example, "New Perspectives on Faith and Development," November 12, 2009, online at http://rowanwilliams.archbishopofcanterbury.org.

45. Especially, Pope Benedict XVI, *Caritas in Veritate*, papal encyclical letter on integral human development in charity and truth, June 29, 2009, http://w2.vatican.va.

46. For a brief overview of the evolution of these initiatives, see Jones and Petersen, "Instrumental, Narrow, Normative?" 1294.

47. K. Marshall, "Faith and Development: Rethinking Development Debates," 11.

48. From Ter Haar and Ellis, "The Role of Religion in Development."

49. Ibid., 358, concerning peace-building through traditional mechanisms; see also K. A. Ver Beek, "Spirituality: A Development Taboo," 31–43.

Chapter 14: Accountability for Faith-Based Development Organizations

1. Karl Barth, "The Community for the World," in Anderson, *Theological Foundations for Ministry*, 499.

2. Romans 6:1–2, 15.

3. Many NGOs are signatories to multiple accountability charters. These may include the Code of Conduct for the International Red Cross and Red Crescent Movement and Non-Governmental Organizations in Disaster Relief (1994); the Sphere Humanitarian Charter and Minimum Standards in Humanitarian Response; the Humanitarian Accountability Partnership Standard in Accountability and Quality (2010); NGO HIV/AIDS Code of Practice; the Core Humanitarian Standard on Quality and Accountability (2014); INGO Accountability Charter (2006–2014).

4. Matthew 5:37; Deuteronomy 23:22–23.

5. In New Testament terminology, ὑπ ὅκρισις, literally "under judgment."

6. 2 Corinthians 5:9–10; Colossians 3:23.

7. Matthew 18:15–17.

8. Matthew 5:14–16.

9. John 13:35.

10. Titus 3:1–2: "Remind them to be subject to rulers and authorities, to be obedient, to be ready for every good work, to speak evil of no one, to avoid quarrelling, to be gentle, and to show courtesy to everyone."

11. Which is code for any disadvantaged or marginalized group.

12. Exodus 22:22–23; Psalm 10:14; Psalm 68:5–6; James 1:27.

13. Genesis 1:26–27.

14. Matthew 7:12; Luke 6:31; Leviticus 19:18; Mark 12:31.

15. Matthew 22:39–40.

16. Luke 10:25–37.

17. Matthew 5:3–5.

18. Matthew 25:44–45.

19. Matthew 6:10.

20. Leslie Newbigin, *The Gospel in a Pluralist Society* (Grand Rapids: Eerdmans, 1989), 159.

21. Justo L. Gonzales and Catherine G. Gonzales, *Liberation Preaching: The Pulpit and the Oppressed* (Nashville: Abingdon, 1980), 27.

22. Alvaro Barreiro, *Basic Ecclesial Communities: The Evangelization of the Poor* (Maryknoll: Orbis Books, 1984), 36.

23. 2 Kings 12:9–11.

24. 2 Kings 12:16. Note, however, that lower down the funding chain it is reported that men in charge were judged "completely honest," so no one needed to keep track of the money. Perhaps this suggests that in some situations it is appropriate to balance more rigorous process with personal trust and autonomy.

25. 2 Corinthians 8:20–21.

26. Matthew 25:14–30, known as the Parable of the Talents.

27. Luke 12:48: "From everyone to whom much has been given, much will be required; and from one to whom much has been entrusted, even more will be demanded."

28. Matthew 3:10, 7:16–17, 12:33; Luke 6:43; John 15:1–5; Romans 7:4; Ephesians 5:9; Colossians 1:10; James 3:17, among many others.

29. Matthew 22:37.

30. Moltmann, *Theology of Hope*, 325.

31. John Bright reminds us "The purpose of God for us is not to give us fat bodies" (*The Kingdom of God* [Nashville: Abingdon, 1953], 270).

32. The imagery of Jesus as groom, and later the church as his bride, is a consistent metaphor in the New Testament: Matthew 9:15; John 3:29; Ephesians 5:25–27; 2 Corinthians 11:2; Revelation 19:7–9, 21:2.

33. From the Greek, διακονος, meaning "servant."

34. Luke 13:29.

35. In particular, there should be open dialogue with developing communities and opportunity for these communities to inform decision-making processes as key stakeholders.

36. The child abuse scandals involving pedophile priests in different parts of the world is one example where punitive damages have been awarded.

37. Luke 12:2–3.

Chapter 15: Accountability for Crosscutting Themes

1. World Health Organization, "World Report on Disability," 2011, 10, online at http://www.who.int/disabilities/world_report/2011/report.pdf.

2. John 9:3.

3. 2 Corinthians 12:9.

4. Terrence Ehrman, "Disability and Resurrection Identity," *New Blackfriars* 96, issue 1066 (2015): 723–38.

5. Leviticus 21:16–23.

6. 1 Corinthians 11:5; 1 Corinthians 14:34; Ephesians 5:22.

7. For example, in Melanesia and parts of East Africa.

8. E. Moltmann-Wendel and J. Moltmann, *Humanity in God* (London: SCM Press, 1983), 38.

9. John 4:4–26.

10. Moltmann-Wendel and Moltmann, *Humanity in God*, 39.

11. Dean Freudenberger, "Implications of a New Land Ethic," in *The The-*

ology of the Land, ed. Bernard F. Evans, (Liturgical Press: Collegeville MN, 1987) 74.

12. Walter Brueggemann, "Land, Fertility and Justice," in Evans, *Theology of the Land*, 59.

13. Sean McDonagh, *To Care for the Earth* (Geoffrey Chapman: London, 1986), 103.

14. Pope Francis, *Laudato Si'*, papal encyclical on care for our common home, 24 May 2015, paragraphs 10–12, http://w2.vatican.va.

15. Wright, *Surprised by Hope*, 145–46.

16. Deuteronomy 10:18; Isaiah 1:17; Psalm 82:3.

Chapter 16: Becoming a Faithfully Based Organization

1. John 10:10.

2. Matthew 6:10.

3. Mark 1:5; Matthew 3:2.

4. See Moltmann, *Theology of Hope*.

5. Lunn, "The Role of Religion," 940.

6. Clarke, "Understanding the Nexus," 6.

7. R. Vanderwoerd, "Religious Characteristics of Government-Funded Faith Related Social Service Organizations," *Social Work and Christianity*, 35, no. 3 (2008): 267.

8. Clarke and Jennings, *Development, Civil Society and Faith-Based Organizations*, 4–5.

9. Stephen Plant, unpublished paper, quoted in James, "What is Distinctive About FBOs," 11.

10. L. Reed, *Keeping the Faith* (Oak Brook, Illinois: Opportunity International, 2001), 2.

11. R. Ridell, cited in James, "What Is Distinctive About FBOs," 15.

12. The saying of prayers at the opening of parliament, or religious instruction in state schools (with optional participation) fits comfortably within this approach.

13. Vanderwoerd, "Religious Characteristics," 260.

14. Monsma, *When Sacred and Secular Mix*, 55.

15. Ibid., 56.

16. Jeavons, *When the Bottom Line Is Faithfulness*, 54.

17. Bottomley, *In, but Not of the World*, 20.

18. Jeavons, *When the Bottom Line Is Faithfulness*, 75.

19. Ibid., 122. Elsewhere, Jeavons observes: "Faith and works must be united, and for any Christian service organization that takes its scriptural heritage seriously that means there must be attention to the ways the organization's work conveys the values and ideals of the faith tradition its represents" (56).

20. Bottomley, *In, but Not of the World*, 28.

21. Ibid., 25.

22. Reed, *Keeping the Faith*, 2.

23. Jeavons, *When the Bottom Line Is Faithfulness*, 197.

24. Bottomley, *In, but Not of the World*, 29.

25. Reed, *Keeping the Faith*, 2.

26. Jeavons, *When the Bottom Line Is Faithfulness*, 211.

27. Ibid., 60.

28. Bottomley, *In, but Not of the World*, 29.

29. Vanderwoerd, "Religious Characteristics," 259.

30. Monsma, *When Sacred and Secular Mix*, 11.

31. Jeavons, *When the Bottom Line Is Faithfulness*, 129.

32. James, "What Is Distinctive about FBOs," 11.

33. Grills, "'Believing' in HIV," 78.

34. This theory was articulated in the book by J. Pfeffer and G. Salanick, *The External Control of Organizations: A Resource Dependence Perspective* (New York: Harper and Row, 1978).

35. James, "What Is Distinctive about FBOs," 11.

36. Ibid.

37. Monsma, *When Sacred and Secular Mix*, 98.

38. Paul DeMaggio, cited in M. Torry, *Managing God's Business: Religious and Faith-Based Organizations and Their Management* (Aldershot: Ashgate Publishing, 2005), 21.

39. Jeavons, *When the Bottom Line Is Faithfulness*, 127.

40. Ibid., 104.

41. Reed, *Keeping the Faith*, 1.

42. Jeavons, *When the Bottom Line Is Faithfulness*, 129.

43. Vanderwoerd, "Religious Characteristics," 269.

44. Jeavons, *When the Bottom Line Is Faithfulness*, 99.

45. Bottomley, *In, but Not of the World*, 21.

46. James, "What Is Distinctive about FBOs," 17.

47. Bottomley, *In, but Not of the World*, 6.

48. James, "What Is Distinctive about FBOs," 11.

49. Vanderwoerd, "Religious Characteristics," 260.

50. Reed, *Keeping the Faith*, 1.

51. Jeavons, *When the Bottom Line Is Faithfulness*, 79.

52. Ibid., 40.

53. Ibid., 58.

54. E. Schein, *Organizational Culture and Leadership* (San Francisco: Jossey-Bass, 1985), 82.

55. Jeavons, *When the Bottom Line Is Faithfulness*, 147.

56. Ibid.

57. Ibid., 126.

58. I use the phrase "in theory" as these advantages can remain elusive without humility and goodwill.

59. Ronald J. Sider & Heidi Rolland Unruh, "Typology of Religious Characteristics of Social Service and Educational Organizations," *Nonprofit and Voluntary Sector Quarterly* 33 (2004): 122.

60. Monsma, *When Sacred and Secular Mix*, 106.

61. Bottomley, *In, but Not of the World*, 23.

62. Cited in Monsma, *When Sacred and Secular Mix*, 54.

63. Jeavons, *When the Bottom Line Is Faithfulness*, 126.

64. Ibid., 215–16.

65. Monsma, *When Sacred and Secular Mix*, 186.

66. Bottomley, *In, but Not of the World*, 23.

67. Ibid., 24.

68. Ibid., 13.

69. One of the most effective organizations in Jeavon's case studies was one where "[the] senior executives to secretaries, could tell me about the history of the organization" (Jeavons, *When the Bottom Line Is Faithfulness*, 106).

70. Torry, *Managing God's Business*, 172.

71. The lack of Bible studies for field workers around crosscutting themes such as gender, disability, and care for the environment is one example.

72. Bottomley, *In, but Not of the World*, 23.

73. Jeavons, *When the Bottom Line Is Faithfulness*, 75.

74. James, "What Is Distinctive about FBOs," 11.

75. Torry, *Managing God's Business*, 119.

76. James, "What Is Distinctive about FBOs," 17.

77. Reed, *Keeping the Faith*, 2.

78. Sider and Unruh, "Typology of Religious Characteristics," 118.

79. James, "What is Distinctive about FBOs," 4.

SELECTED BIBLIOGRAPHY

Abrams, L. "Faith, Development and Poverty—Reflections." April 24, 2013, www.thewaterpage.com.

Adams, P., and N. de Bussy. "NGOs, Identities, and Religion: A Case of Split Personalities?" *Asia Pacific Public Relations Journal* 9 (2008): 87–101.

Allison, D. C. *Constructing Jesus: Memory, Imagination, and History.* Grand Rapids: Baker Academic, 2010.

Alolo, N. A., and J. A. Connell "Indigenous Religions and Development: African Traditional Religion." In *The Handbook of Research on Development and Religion*, edited by M. Clarke, 138– 63. Cheltenham: Edward Elgar, 2013.

Amesbury, R., and G. M. Newlands. *Faith and Human Rights: Christianity and the Global Struggle for Human Dignity.* Minneapolis: Fortress Press, 2008.

Anderson, R. S., ed. *Theological Foundations for Ministry.* Edinburgh: T&T Clark, 1979.

Bailey, K. E. *Poet and Peasant* and *Through Peasant's Eyes*, combined ed. Grand Rapids: Eerdmans, 1976.

Barreiro, Alvaro. *Basic Ecclesial Communities: The Evangelization of the Poor.* Maryknoll: Books, 1984.

Barro, R. J., and R. M. McCleary. "Religion and Economic Growth." *American Sociological Review* 68 (2003): 760–81.

Barth, Karl. "The Community for the World." In *Theological Foundations for Ministry*, edited by R. S. Anderson, 499–533. Edinburgh: T&T Clark, 1979.

Batchelor, P. *People in Rural Development.* Carlisle: Paternoster Press, 1993.

Batliwala, S. *When Rights Go Wrong: Distorting the Rights Based Approach to Development*. Harvard University: Hauser Center for Nonprofit Organizations, 2010, http://transparentsea.co.

Belshaw, D. *Enhancing the Development Capabilities of Civil Society Organizations, with Particular Reference to Christian Faith-Based Organizations*. Global Poverty Research Group, 2005.

Benedict XVI, Pope. *Caritas in Veritate*, papal encyclical letter on integral human development in charity and truth, June 29, 2009, http://w2.vatican.va/content/benedict-xvi/en/encyclicals/documents/hf_ben-xvi_enc_20090629_caritas-in-veritate.html.

———. *Deus Caritas Est*, papal encyclical letter on Christian love, December 25, 2005, http://www.vatican.va.

Berger, J. *Religious Non-Governmental Organizations: An Exploratory Analysis*. International Society for Third-Sector Research and the Johns Hopkins University, 2003.

Berger, P. L., and R. W. Hefner. *Spiritual Capital in Comparative Perspective*. Boston University: Institute for the Study of Economic Culture, Institute on Religion and World Affairs, n.d.

Berstein, R. *The Restructuring of Social and Political Theory*. London: Methuen, 1985.

Bertina, L. "The Catholic Doctrine of 'Integral Human Development' and Its Influence on the International Development Community." In *International Development Policy: Religion and Development*, edited by G. Carbonnier, 115–27. Basingstoke: Palgrave Macmillan, 2013.

Boff, L. *Good News to the Poor*. Wellwood: Burns and Oates, 1992.

Boin, C., J. Harris, and A. Marchesetti. *Fake Aid: How Foreign Aid Is Being Used to Support the Self-Serving Political Activities of NGOs*. London: International Policy Network, 2009.

Bonhoeffer, D. "Christ, the Church, and the World." In *Theological Foundations for Ministry*, edited by R. S. Anderson, 534–66. Edinburgh: T&T Clark, 1979.

Bornstein, E. *The Spirit of Development: Protestant NGOs, Morality, and Economics in Zimbabwe*. Stanford: Stanford University Press, 2005.

Bosch, D. J. *Transforming Mission: Paradigm Shifts in Theology of Mission*. Orbis Books, Maryknoll, 1991.

Bottomley, J. *In, but Not of the World*. St. Kilda: The Creative Ministries Network, 2008.

Boxelaar, L., L. Mackinlay, and T. Dearborn. *Articulating Our Theory of Change*. Discussion paper prepared for World Vision International, 2010.

Braun, W., and R. T. McCutcheon, eds. *Guide to the Study of Religion*. London: Continuum, 2000.

Bright, John. *The Kingdom of God*. Nashville: Abingdon, 1953.

British Overseas NGOs for Development (BOND). *A BOND Approach to Quality in NGOs: Putting Beneficiaries First*. Report, Keystone: 2006.

Brown, H. I. *Perception, Theory and Commitment: The New Philosophy of Science*. Chicago: Precedent Publishing, 1977.

Browning, D. S. *A Fundamental Practical Theology*. Minneapolis: Fortress Press, 1996.

Brueggemann, W. *Biblical Perspectives on Evangelism: Living in a Three-Storied Universe*. Nashville: Abingdon, 1993.

———. "Land, Fertility and Justice." In *The Theology of the Land*, edited by Bernard F. Evans, 41–68. Liturgical Press: Collegeville MN, 1987.

Butler, J., E. Mendieta, and J. Van Antwerpen, eds. *The Power of Religion in the Public Sphere*. New York: Columbia University Press, 2011.

Candland, C. "Faith as Social Capital: Religion and Community Development in Southern Asia." *Policy Sciences* 33 (2001): 355–74.

Carbonnier, G., ed. *International Development Policy: Religion and Development*. Basingstoke: Palgrave Macmillan, 2013.

Carbonnier, G. "Religion and Development: Reconsidering Secularism as the Norm." In *International Development Policy: Religion and Development*, edited by G. Carbonnier, 1–5. Basingstoke: Palgrave Macmillan, 2013.

Chambers, R. "NGOs and Development: The Primacy of the Personal." Unpublished paper for the Workshop on NGOs and Development: Performance and Accountability, Institute of Policy Development and Management, University of Manchester, June 27–29, 1994.

Christian, J. *God of the Empty-Handed: Poverty, Power and the Kingdom of God*. Monrovia: Marc Publishers, 1999.

Clarke, G. "Agents of Transformation? Donors, Faith-Based Organizations and International Development." *Third World Quarterly* 28, no. 1 (2007): 77–96.

Clarke, G., and M. Jennings. *Development, Civil Society and Faith-Based Organizations: Bridging the Sacred and the Secular.* Basingstoke: Macmillan, 2008.

Clarke, M., ed. *The Handbook of Research on Development and Religion.* Cheltenham: Edward Elgar, 2013.

———, ed. *Mission and Development: God's Work or Good Works.* London: Continuum, 2012.

———. "Understanding the Nexus Between Religion and Development." In *The Handbook of Research on Development and Religion,* edited by M. Clarke, 1–13. Cheltenham: Edward Elgar, 2013.

Corbett, S., and B. Fikkert. *When Helping Hurts: How to Alleviate Poverty without Hurting the Poor.* Chicago: Moody Publishers, 2009.

Cox, H. *The Future of Faith.* New York: HarperOne, 2009.

———. *God's Revolution and Man's Responsibility.* Valley Forge: Judson, 1965.

Curran, C. "The Catholic Identity of Catholic Institutions." *Theological Studies* 58 (1997): 90–108.

Dart, J., and J. Hall. "Church Partnership Program, Papua New Guinea: Case Study Report." Canberra: AusAID, 2011.

Dearborn, T. A. "Unavoidable Witness in the Work of a Humanitarian Organization." Unpublished monograph, World Vision International, 2011.

Deneulin, S. "Christianity and International Development." In *The Handbook of Research on Development and Religion,* edited by M. Clarke, 51–65. Cheltenham: Edward Elgar, 2013.

Devine, J., and S. Deneulin. "Negotiating Religion in Everyday Life: A Critical Exploration of the Relationship Between Religion, Choices and Behaviour." *Culture and Religion: An Interdisciplinary Journal* 12, no. 1 (2011): 59–76.

Dunn, J. D. G. *Jesus Remembered.* Grand Rapids: Eerdmans, 2003.

———. *Unity and Diversity in the New Testament,* 2nd ed. London: SCM Press, 1998.

Edmonds, D. "An Incarnational Agency in an Evangelical World: A Theological Consideration of Anglicare's Role in Mission." Paper presented on September 2, 2008, at the Anglicare Australia Conference, Sydney. Launceston: Anglicare Tasmania, 2008.

Edwards, M., and G. Sen. "NGOs, Social Change, and the Transformation of Human Relationships: A 21st-century Civic Agenda." *Third World Quarterly* 21, no. 4 (August 2000): 605–16, online at http://www.futurepositive.org.

Ehrman, T. "Disability and Resurrection Identity." *New Blackfriars* 96, issue 1066 (2015): 723–38.

Esposito, J. L., and M. Watson, eds. *Religion and Global Order*. Cardiff: University of Wales, 2000.

Evans, Bernard F. *The Theology of the Land*. Collegeville, MN: Liturgical Press: 1987.

Ferguson, K. M., Q. Wu, D. Spruijt-Metz, and G. Dyrness. "Outcomes Evaluation in Faith-based Social Services: Are We Evaluating Faith Accurately?" *Research on Social Work Practice* 17, no. 2 (2007): 264–76.

Flanigan, S. "Religion, Conflict and Peacebuilding in Development." In *The Handbook of Research on Development and Religion*, edited by M. Clarke, 252–65. Cheltenham: Edward Elgar, 2013.

Flett, J. G. *The Witness of God: The Trinity, Missio Dei, and the Nature of Christian Community*. Grand Rapids: Eerdmans, 2010.

Fountain, P. "The Myth of Religious NGOs: Development Studies and the Return of Religion." In *International Development Policy: Religion and Development*, edited by G. Carbonnier, 9–30. Basingstoke: Palgrave Macmillan, 2013.

Francis, Pope. *Laudato Si'*. Papal encyclical on care for our common home, May 24, 2015, http://w2.vatican.va/content/francesco/en/encyclicals/documents/papa-francesco_20150524_enciclica-laudato-si.html.

Freire, P. *Pedagogy of the Oppressed*. New York: Continuum, 2007. First published 1970 by Herder and Herder.

Freudenberger, Dean. "Implications of a New Land Ethic." In *The Theology of the Land*, edited by Bernard F. Evans, 69–84. Collegeville MN: Liturgical Press, 1987.

Giri, A. Kumar, A. van Harskamp, and O. Salemink, eds. *The Development of Religion, the Religion of Development*. Delft: Eburon, 2004.

"Global Data Upend Usual Picture of Christianity Trends." Anglican Communion News Service, March 20, 2013, http://www.aco.org.

Gonzales, Justo L., and Catherine G. Gonzales. *Liberation Preaching: The Pulpit and the Oppressed*. Nashville: Abingdon, 1980.

Goode, A. *World Vision Evaluation Report: World Vision Georgia.* Christian Commitments Programme, June 2010.

———. *World Vision Evaluation Report: World Vision Rwanda.* Christian Commitments Programme, October 2011.

———. *World Vision Evaluation Report: World Vision Senegal.* Christian Commitments Programme, October 2011.

———. A. *World Vision Evaluation Report: World Vision Tanzania.* Christian Commitments Programme, October 2010.

Goulet, D. "Development Experts: The One-Eyed Giants." *World Development* 8, no. 6–7 (1980): 481–89.

Grills, N. "'Believing' in HIV: The Effect of Faith on the Response of Christian Faith-based Organizations to HIV in India." PhD thesis, Oxford University, 2010.

———. "The Paradox of Multilateral Organizations Engaging with Faith-Based Organizations." *Global Governance* 15 (2009): 505–20.

Groody, D. G. *Globalization, Spirituality, and Justice.* Maryknoll: Orbis Books, 2007.

Haynes, J. *Religion and Development: Conflict or Cooperation?* London: Palgrave Macmillan, 2007.

Hodgkinson, Virginia A. "The Future of Individual Giving and Volunteering: The Inseparable Link Between Religious Community and Individual Generosity." In *Faith and Philanthropy in America: Exploring the Role of Religion in America's Voluntary Sector*, edited by Robert Wuthnow and Virginia A. Hodgkinson, 284– 312. San Francisco: Josey-Bass, 1990.

Hoek, M., and J. Thacker, eds. *Micah Challenge: The Church's Responsibility to the Global Poor.* London: Paternoster, 2008.

Hoffstaedter, G. "Religion and Development: Australian Faith-Based Development Organizations." Australian Council for International Development, *Research in Development Series* 3 (2011).

Holenstein, A-M. "Governmental Donor Agencies and Faith-Based Organizations." *International Review of the Red Cross* 87, no. 858 (2005): 367–73.

Hovland, I. "Who's Afraid of Religion? The Question of God in Development." Paper presented at DSA Conference, Milton Keynes, September 7–9, 2005.

Hufford, D. J. "The Scholarly Voice and the Personal Voice: Reflexivity in Belief Studies." In *Guide to the Study of Religion*, edited by W. Braun and R. T. McCutcheon, 294–310. London: Continuum, 2000.

Hughes, Dewi. *God of the Poor: A Biblical Vision of God's Present Rule.* Milton Keynes: Authentic, 1998.

Interfaith Relations. World Vision International policy document, April 2, 2009.

Ivereigh, A. "Religious Faith Builds a Civil Society in a Way Secularism Does Not." *The Guardian*, September 29, 2011.

James, R. "Handle with Care: Engaging with Faith-based Organizations in Development." *Development in Practice* 21, no. 1 (2011): 109–17.

———. "What is Distinctive about FBOs." International NGO Training and Research Centre, Praxis Paper 22, February 2009.

Jeavons, T. *When the Bottom Line Is Faithfulness.* Bloomington: Indiana University Press, 1994.

Jones, B., and M. J. Petersen. "Instrumental, Narrow, Normative? Reviewing Recent Work on Religion and Development." *Third World Quarterly* 32, no. 7 (2011): 1291–1306.

Kessler, E., and M. Arkush. "Keeping Faith in Development: The Significance of Interfaith Relations in the Work of Humanitarian Aid and International Development Organizations." The Woolf Institute of Abrahamic Faiths, 2008, online at http://www.woolf.cam.ac.uk.

Kilpatrick, R., and A. Goode. *World Vision Evaluation Report: World Vision Bosnia and Herzegovina.* Christian Commitments Programme, July 2009.

King, D. P. "World Vision: Religious Identity in the Discourse and Practice of Global Relief and Development." *The Review of Faith and International Affairs* 9, no. 3 (2011): 21–28.

Küng, H. *The Church.* London: Burns and Oates, 1968.

Lewis, C. S. *The Screwtape Letters.* London: The Macmillan Company, 1946.

Linden, A. "The Language of Development: What Are International Development Agencies Talking About?" In *Development, Civil Society and Faith-based Organizations*, edited by G. Clarke and M. Jennings, 72–93. Basingstoke: Palgrave Macmillan, 2008.

Lucas, E. "The New Testament Teaching on the Environment." *Transformation* 16, no. 3 (1999): 93–99.

Lunn, J. "The Role of Religion, Spirituality and Faith in Development: A Critical Theory Approach." *Third World Quarterly* 30, no. 5 (2009): 937–51.

MacLaren, D. "Putting the Faith Back into Development." *Eureka Street*, October 26, 2011.

Maggay, M. "Justice and Approaches to Social Change." In *Micah Challenge: The Church's Responsibility to the Global Poor*, edited by M. Hoek and J. Thacker, 126–32. London: Paternoster, 2008.

Malcolm, N. *Thought and Knowledge.* Ithaca: Cornell University Press, 1977.

Marquette, H. "Corruption, Religion and Moral Development." In *The Handbook of Research on Development and Religion*, edited by M. Clarke, 220–37. Cheltenham: Edward Elgar, 2013.

Marshall, K. *Africa: How and Why Is Faith Important and Relevant for Development.* Georgetown University: Berkeley Centre for Religion, Peace and World Affairs, 2005. http://www.vanderbilt.edu/csrc/PDFs%20and%20Jpgs/marshall-africa.pdf.

———. "Development and Religion: A Different Lens on Development Debates." *Peabody Journal of Education* 76, nos. 3–4 (2001): 1–27.

———. "Faith and Development: Rethinking Development Debates." Development Dialogue on Values and Ethics, The World Bank, 2005, http://web.worldbank.org.

———. "Revisiting the Religious Revival in Development: A Critique of Philip Fountain." In *International Development Policy: Religion and Development*, edited by G. Carbonnier, 31–40. Basingstoke: Palgrave Macmillan, 2013.

McDonagh, Sean. *To Care for the Earth.* London: Geoffrey Chapman, 1986.

Meier, J. P., *A Marginal Jew: Rethinking the Historical Jesus*, vol. 2, *Mentor, Message and Miracles*. New York: Doubleday, 1994.

Moltmann, J. *Theology of Hope.* London: SCM Press, 1967.

———. *The Church in the Power of the Spirit.* London: SCM Press, 1975.

———. *The Trinity and the Kingdom of God.* London: SCM Press, 1980.

Moltmann-Wendel, E., and J. Moltmann. *Humanity in God.* London: SCM Press, 1983.

Monsma, Stephen. *When Sacred and Secular Mix.* Lanham: Rowman & Littlefield, 1996.

Moucarry, C. *Two Prayers for Today: The Lord's Prayer and the Fatiha.* Tiruvalla India: Christava Sahitya Samithy, 2007.

Myers, B. L. *Walking with the Poor: Principles and Practices of Transformational Development.* Maryknoll: Orbis Books, 1999.

Narayan, D. *Voices of the Poor: Can Anyone Hear Us?* Washington, DC: Oxford University Press, 2000.

Newbigin, Leslie. *The Gospel in a Pluralist Society.* Grand Rapids: Eerdmans, 1989.

Newmarch, A. *World Vision Evaluation Report: World Vision Armenia.* Christian Commitments Programme, November 2010.

———. *World Vision Evaluation Report: World Vision Lebanon.* Christian Commitments Programme, November 2009.

Newmarch, A., and A. Goode. *World Vision Evaluation Report: World Vision Albania.* Christian Commitments Programme, September 2008.

Palmer, A. J. Tomkinson, C. Phung, N. Ford, M. Joffres, K. Fernandes, L. Zeng, V. Lima, J. Montaner, G. Guyatt, and E. Mill. "Does Ratification of Human-Rights Treaties Have Effects on Population Health?" *The Lancet* 373 (June 20090): 1987–92.

Parris, M. "As an Atheist, I Truly Believe Africa Needs God." *The Times Online,* January 8, 2009.

Partnerships with Churches, World Vision International policy document, September 16, 1995, revised edition March 13, 2003.

Perkins, John. *Beyond Charity: The Call to Christian Community Development.* Grand Rapids: Baker Books, 1993.

Perrin, N. *Rediscovering the Teaching of Jesus.* New York: Harper and Row, 1967.

Pfeffer, J., and G. Salanick. *The External Control of Organizations: A Resource Dependence Perspective.* New York: Harper and Row, 1978.

Plant, S. "Does Faith Matter in Development?" Paper presented at Faith and Development Theory and Practice Forum, Cambridge University, November 26–27, 2004.

Pontifical Council for Justice and Peace. "Compendium of the Social Doctrine of the Church." Rome, 2004, online at http://www.vatican.va.

Putnam, R. D. *Bowling Alone: The Collapse and Revival of American Community.* New York: Simon and Schuster, 2000.

Rah, S-C. *The Next Evangelicalism: Freeing the Church from Western Cultural Captivity.* Downers Grove, IL: IVP Books, 2009.

Rasanathan, K., J. Norenhag, and N. Valentine. "Realizing Human Rights-Based Approaches for Action on the Social Determinants of Health." *Health and Human Rights* 12, no. 2 (2010): 44–59.

Reed, L. *Keeping the Faith.* Oak Brook, IL: Opportunity International, 2001.

Russell, B. *Unpopular Essays.* New York: Simon & Schuster, 1950.

Salemink, O. "Development Cooperation as Quasi-religious Conversion." In *The Development of Religion, the Religion of Development,* edited by A. Kumar Giri, A. van Harskamp, and O. Salemink, 121–30. Delft: Eburon, 2004.

Schein, E. *Organizational Culture and Leadership.* San Francisco: Jossey-Bass, 1985.

Schleiermacher, F. *Brief Outline of the Study of Theology.* Richmond: John Knox Press, 1983.

Selinger, L. "The Forgotten Factor: The Uneasy Relationship between Religion and Development." *Social Compass* 51, no. 4 (2004): 523–43.

Shah, R. and T. "Spiritual Capital and Economic Enterprise." The Oxford Centre for Religion and Public Life. April 24, 2013, http://www.ocrpl.org.

Sharpe, M. "Name It and Claim It: Prosperity Gospel and the Global Pentecostal Reformation. In *The Handbook of Research on Development and Religion,* edited by M. Clarke, 164–79. Cheltenham: Edward Elgar, 2013.

Shutt, C. "Changing the World by Changing Ourselves: Reflections from a Bunch of BINGOs." Institute of Development Studies. *IDS Practice Paper* 3 (2009), 24, http://www.ids.ac.uk.

Sider, Ronald J., and Heidi Rolland Unruh. "Typology of Religious Characteristics of Social Service and Educational Organizations." *Nonprofit and Voluntary Sector Quarterly* 33 (2004): 109–34.

Stark, Rodney. *For the Glory of God: How Monotheism Led to Reformations, Science, Witch-hunts and the End of Slavery.* Princeton, NJ: Princeton University Press, 2003.

Steward, J. *Biblical Holism: Where God, People and Deeds Connect.* Melbourne: World Vision Australia, 1994.

Taylor, C. "Why We Need a Radical Redefinition of Secularism." In *The Power of Religion in the Public Sphere*, edited J. Butler, E. Mendieta, and J. Van Antwerpen, 34–59. New York: Columbia University Press, 2011.

Ter Haar, G., and S. Ellis. "The Role of Religion in Development: Towards a New Relationship Between the European Union and Africa." *The European Journal of Development Research* 18, no. 3 (2006): 351–67.

Thomas, S. M. "Taking Religious and Cultural Pluralism Seriously: The Global Resurgence of Religion and the Global Transformation of International Society." *Journal of International Studies* 29, no. 3 (2000): 815–41.

Torry, M. *Managing God's Business: Religious and Faith-Based Organizations and Their Management*. Aldershot: Ashgate Publishing, 2005.

Tyndale, W. "Key Issues for Development," World Faiths Development Dialogue, *Occasional Paper* 1. November 1998.

———. "Faith and Economics in 'Development': A Bridge across the Chasm?" *Development in Practice* 10, no. 1 (2000): 9–18.

———. "Towards Sustainable Development: A Shift in Values." *Commentary: International Movement for a Just World* 1, no. 8 (2001): 1–4.

Vanderwoerd, J. R. "Religious Characteristics of Government-Funded Faith-Related Social Service Organizations." *Social Work and Christianity* 35, no. 3 (2008): 258–86.

Ver Beek, K. A. "Spirituality: A Development Taboo." *Development in Practice* 10, no. 1 (2000): 31–43.

Volf, M. "The Trinity is Our Social Program: The Doctrine of the Trinity and Our Social Engagement." *Modern Theology* 14, no. 3 (1998): 403–23.

Wallace, A. F. C. *Religion: An Anthropological View*. New York: Random House, 1966.

Widmer, M., A. P. Betran, M. Merialdi, J. Requejo, and T. Karpf. "The Role of Faith-Based Organizations in Maternal and Newborn Health Care in Africa." *International Journal of Gynecology and Obstetrics* 114 (2011): 218–22.

Wilbur, David W. *Power and Illusion: Religion and Human Need*. lulu.com, 2010.

Williams, R. "A Theology of Development." Lecture delivered on November 12, 2009, at the seminar series "New Persepctives on Faith and

Development," sponsored by the Tony Blair Faith foundation, DIFD, Islamic Relief, World Vision, and Oxfam. http://clients.squareeye.net.

———. "Relating Intelligently to Religion." *The Guardian*, November 12, 2009.

Wink, W. *Engaging the Powers: Discernment and Resistance in a World of Domination*. Minneapolis: Fortress, 1992.

Witness to Jesus Christ. World Vision International policy document, September 16, 1995, revised edition September 14, 2006.

Woodberry, R. D. "Researching Spiritual Capital, Promises and Pitfalls." 2003. http://www.metanexus.net/archive/spiritualcapitalresearchprogram/pdf/woodberry.pdf.

World Health Organization. "World Report on Disability," 2011, 10, online at http://www.who.int/disabilities/world_report/2011/report.pdf.

Wrigley, A. "Who's Afraid of Holistic Development? Navigating the Interface between Faith and Development." University of London: School of Oriental and African Studies, 2011.

Wright, N. T. *Jesus and the Victory of God*. Minneapolis: Fortress, 1996.

Wright, N. T. *Surprised by Hope*. London: SPCK, 2007.

Wuthnow, R., and V. A. Hodgkinson, V. A., eds. *Faith and Philanthropy in America: Exploring the Role of Religion in America's Voluntary Sector*. San Francisco: Josey-Bass, 1990.

INDEX

academic bias against religion, 3–6, 9,
46–47, 119, 122, 155
accountability, 93, 125
between church and FBOs, 106,
142
crosscutting themes and
child protection, 152–54
concept, defining, 144
disability inclusion, 145–47
environmental care, 149–52
gender equality, 147–49
disclosure as an aspect of accountability, 142–43
FBOs and need for accountability,
135–37
identity, accountability based on,
176
key accountabilities, 137–42
personal accountability, Christian
understanding of, 65, 135
to the poor, 71, 137–39
Adam, Peter, 39–40
advocacy, x, 34, 111, 140
advocacy against injustice, 77, 88,
142
advocacy departments of FBOs, 82
charity as response to advocacy, 113
as expected by God, 153
funding sources, impact on public
advocacy, 162
as localized, 85
Africa, 91, 123
African Traditional Religion (ATR),
50, 87–88, 103, 130
East Africa, 41, 62, 73, 93, 102,
115
public expression of faith as
expected, 104

public prayer as effective, 99–101
South African Truth and Reconcilia-
tion Commission, 78
See also individual African countries
Alolo, Namawu, 87, 130
Amesbury, Richard, 34
Appreciative Inquiry (AI), 30
Armenia, 50, 61, 109, 116

Bailey, Ken, 17
Barth, Karl, 64, 98, 135
Belshaw, Deryke, 60, 111
Benedict XVI, Pope, 18, 28, 65–66, 91,
128
Berger, Julia, 33
Berger, Peter, 51
Bertina, Ludovic, 19
Bible study and reflection, importance
of, 76–77
Boff, Leonardo, 17, 29, 30, 38, 39, 43
Bonhoeffer, Dietrich, 17
Bosch, David, 27, 28, 37
Bottomley, John, 169, 170
Boxelaar, Lucia, 34
British Overseas NGOs for Develop-
ment (BOND), 66
Brown, Gordon, 13
Brown, Harold, 27
Browning, Don, 19–20
Brueggemann, Walter, 90, 150

Carter, Stephen, 169
Catholicism
Catholic identity, *xviii*
Catholic Social Teaching, *xi*, 18–19
ecumenical challenges, 114
HIV/AIDS patients, Catholic
Church serving, 8

nuns, extremist commitment of, 64–65

Chambers, Robert, 6, 29–30, 74

child protection in the development sector, 152–54

Christian, Jayakumar, 91

church, 15, 61, 124, 127, 152
  charitable mindset of, 113, 117, 118, 120, 177
  church capacity, FBOs helping to build, 41
  church universal, accountability to, 142
  as delivery channel/distribution system, *xxiii*, 8, 12, 20, 109, 125
  evangelization activities, 41, 42
  FBOs, relationships with, 96, 106–12, 114–15, 117–18, 122–23, 129, 172
  local church services, staff members encouraged to attend, 76
  national churches of the Balkans, 50, 61
  risks of church relationships, 113–16, 118
  spiritual capital, link with, 51
  William Temple on the Church, 12

Church Partnership Program (CPP), 121, 125

Clarke, Gerard, 117, 126

climate change, 151, 152

Connell, James, 87, 130

conscientization, 29, 91

conversion, 40, 41, 91, 95, 96, 114

Corbett, Steve, 30, 31

corporate devotions, 73–74, 129

corruption, standing against, 88–89

crosscutting themes. *See under* accountability

Dayton, Ed, 27

Deneulin, Séverine, 18–19

Department for International Development (DFID), 5, 31, 32, 126, 128

Development Dialogue on Values and Ethics, 7, 128

development studies, 50, 102
  crosscutting themes, 144, 145–54
  cultural relativism in development theory, 83, 88

development as a contested term, *xxii*

development journals and websites, 4–5

development practice, new kinds of, 129–30

development sector, accountability to, 141–42

empowerment of women as a development strategy, 116

formation period of major development organizations, 158

goal of development work, 155

history of development studies, 3–4

holistic approach to development, 49, 90, 128, 130

modernity thinking in development profession, 81, 119, 123, 165, 166, 177

professionalization of development work, 67, 99, 111, 119, 165

subsidiarity as a development principle, 70

theories of change used by development sector, 25–26, 26–35

Tyndale on flaws in development process, 127–28

See also faith-based organizations; religious aspects of development work; secular aspects of development work

devotional practices, 57, 73–80. *See also* prayer

Di Maggio, Paul, 163

disability inclusion in development sector, 145–47

dominant discourse theory, 6, 7

ecumenism, 57, 74, 114, 118, 142

Edwards, Michael, 74, 91

Ellis, Stephen, 130

environmental awareness in development sector, 149–52

environmental care, engaging in, 151–52

evangelism, 92, 138
  development work, problems resulting from forced ties with, 38
  evangelical denominations seen as sects, 40, 96, 114

negative reactions to, 57, 95, 115,
120
by proxy, 41
evil, countering, 81–82, 85–86, 88, 89
ex post facto blessing, 157

faith-based organizations (FBOs)
developmental focus, 6, 121, 144,
166
accountability measures, imple-
menting, 135–43, 154
advantages of FBOs, *xxiii*, 10,
117
Christians, hiring as staff, 168
defining FBOs, *xvii,* 164
development initiatives and
themes, 60, 111, 112
exercise of power, sensitivity
toward, 70–71
funding concerns, 161–62, 163
long-term commitment as a
strength, 62–63, 122
motivation for faith-based development work, 11, 39, 40
participatory approach to development, 30, 31
prayer as part of development
practice, 98–105
respect and trust for FBOs, 9,
49, 104
theories of change, use of main
approaches, 25, 35–36
local focus
DFID, working with, 126
enduring presence in local
communities, 69
health services, providing, 8
local culture and capacities,
honoring, 27–28
malign/oppressive local practices, non-acceptance of,
83–85, 86, 129
spiritual focus, 33, 44, 93, 167
churches, partnering with FBOs,
106–12, 114–15, 117–18,
122–23, 129, 172
devotional practices, FBOs
supporting, 73–75
evangelism and FBOs, 41, 95
faith, staff guided by, 65–66, 71,
76, 79
FBOs as faithfully based,
156–57, 172–73
interfaith harmony, advancing,
57–58
kingdom of God as goal, 43,
54–57, 88, 141
material and spiritual salvation,
dual emphasis on, 18, 37–38
organizational objectives, theology as influencing, 119–20
spiritual activities, normalizing,
49–50
spiritual governance as a priority,
160, 166
theological reflection required of
FBOs, 144, 154, 157
faith literacy, *xxi,* 10, 80, 120, 126
female genital mutilation, 85
Fikkert, Brian, 30, 31
Flett, David, 64
Fountain, Philip, 127
Freeman, Dena, *xi*
Freire, Paulo, 29, 91

gender equality in development sector,
147–49
Georgia, 50, 56, 73, 109, 110, 115
Goulet, Denis, 124, 127
governance and faith issues, 159–61
government authorities, respecting,
140–41
Groody, Daniel, 91

Hefner, Robert, 51
HIV/AIDS, 59, 137
Catholic Church, serving AIDS
patients, 8
FBOs, aiding in shifting attitudes
toward, 112
stigmatization of people with, 84,
86, 110–11
theological reflection as changing
attitudes towards, 121
Holenstein, Anne-Marie, 125–26
Hughes, Dewi, 29
humanitarian response work in New
Testament, 20
human rights, 25, 44, 86
Christian promotion of, 16
human-rights awareness, 31–34,
85

individualistic agenda, promoting,
    46
universal human rights, *xx*, 13
    See also advocacy

inner transformation
    church aiding in, 62
    development discourse, addressing,
        90–91
    devotional practices, inner regenera-
        tion through, 76, 78
    empowerment strategies, inability
        to make strong shifts in inner
        values, 31, 74
    FBOs, pursuing agenda of, 75,
        92–93
inter-ethnic relationships, 94–95
interfaith relationships, 47, 48, 50,
    56–59
International Policy Network, 32
Islam, 85, 115
    Christian organizations, coopera-
        tion in Muslim communities, 47,
        48, 86, 96
    conversion attempts on Muslims, 41
    Muslims as percentage of world's
        population, 123
    prayer in Muslim settings, 73, 101,
        104
    staffing of FBOs in Muslim areas,
        71
    World Vision, Muslim relations
        with, 58–59, 80
isomorphism, 163

James, Rick, 64–65, 79, 120, 162, 171,
    172
Jeavons, Thomas, 66, 160–61, 163–64,
    169
Jennings, Michael, 117
Jubilee movement, 13, 16

kingdom of God, 19, 39, 42, 111, 154
    Christian hope for, 90, 141
    development work as inspired by,
        14–15, 40, 43, 76, 78
    as endpoint of Jesus' ministry, 153
    evil, standing against, 81, 82, 88
    as global fellowship, 142
    holistic missiology, resonating with,
        18

human rights, realized in, 32
    kingdom values, 54–57, 60, 61–62,
        67, 83, 88
    local communities, inculcating hope
        for God's reign, 59, 60
    "now-and-not-yet" nature of, 35
    parable of Matthew 24 and,
        139–40
    prayers for, 138

Lebanon, 56, 59, 71, 113, 114
Lewis, C. S., 82
liberation theology, 16–17
love, development work as an expres-
    sion of, 67, 68

Marshall, Katherine, *x*, 7, 122, 123,
    128, 129
McLaren, Brian, 30
methodological atheism, 46–47
ministry and mission, 38, 79, 112, 138,
    160
    Barth on mission, 98
    charitable mode of missionaries,
        113
    church and FBOs, similarity in mis-
        sions, 107, 142
    corporate devotions and, 73–74
    development work as ministry, 69,
        70, 71, 72, 118
    diaconal ministry, 20, 118, 142, 177
    holistic mission, *ix–x, xii*, 17–18,
        40, 49
    intentionality, maintaining, 170
    of Jesus, 16, 37, 40, 54, 148, 153
    ministry as service, 64
    mission-driven *vs.* funding-driven
        FBOs, 163
    vocation for, 66–67
Moltmann, Jürgen, 15, 33, 44
Moltmann-Wendel, Elisabeth, 148
Monsma, Stephen, 159, 161, 168, 169
Moses, 148–49
Muslims. *See* Islam
Myers, Bryant, *ix–xii*, 26, 28, 38, 82

Narayan, Deepa, 8, 10
neutrality
    cultural relativism in development
        theory, 83
    myth of neutrality, 48, 158–59

science, assumed neutrality of,
26–27, 46
secular agencies, neutrality claims
of, 47–48, 48–49, 59, 157
Newlands, George M., 34
non-governmental organizations
(NGOs), *xi,*
Christian NGOs, *x,* 14, 66, 109, 122
confidence in, as less than in religious
organizations, 63
FBOs, similarities and differences,
xx, 69
homogenization of, 9–10
instrumental treatment of religious
institutions, 123
religious NGOs, 33, 126, 127
Rick James, research on, 64–65
secular NGOs as envying Christian
development organizations, 156
worldviews of, *xxii,* 178
See also World Vision

Papua New Guinea (PNG), 125
pastoral care as alternative to psycho-
social care, 96–97
Pentecostalism, *xi,*
perichoresis, 16
Pfeffer, Jeffrey, 162
philetism, 114
Plant, Stephen, 119
political engagement, 82
poverty and the poor, 29, 91, 102, 145,
155
accountability to the poor, 71,
137–39
anti-religious bias in development,
the poor hurt by, 131
the church, holding to account in
caring for the poor, 111
climate change, effect on poor
communities, 151
consumerism, the poor disproportionately affected by, 150
evil of poverty, FBOs working to
overcome, 81–82
government policies harming the interests of the poor, 162
identification of Jesus with the poor,
64, 148
poverty, defining, *xxiii,* 6
preferential option for the poor, 18

prosperity gospel, attraction of, 115
root cause of poverty as evil spiritual activity, 86
self-regard of the poor raised by
spiritual experiences, 60
social capital, importance to the
poor, 109
solidarity of God with the poor,
reminding churches of, 107–108
theologians on, 38, 44
Voices of the Poor research findings,
63
prayer, 70, 105, 128, 138, 165
corporate prayer, 73, 161, 169
evil, power of prayer as response to,
82
Lord's Prayer, 15, 42–43, 80, 150
meetings, prayers during, 76
Muslim respect for, 48
prayer requests by local communities, 96
public prayer, 99–101, 102–103,
104, 122
types of, 98–99
prophetic call, 16, 115, 138, 177
prosperity gospel, 108, 115
Protestant work ethic, 6, 52
Putnam, Robert, 51

Rah, Soong-Chan, 108
the rapture as a dangerous theory, 150
Reed, Larry, 163, 166, 172
religious aspects of development work
developmental focus, 121, 127,
129, 138
churches as development partners,
113, 118, 176–77
development as a work of salvation, 38, 40
development issues, religious
leaders, responding to, 110,
111, 112
local spiritual beliefs, development impact of, 84, 86
ministry, development work as,
64
role of religion in development,
121, 124, 129, 130, 170–71
scripture and development practices, resonances between,
76–78

theological reasons for Christian involvement in development, 12–14, 14–20, 21
spiritual focus, 79, 109, 126
  hiring practices and reinforcement of faith culture, 166–68
  instrumental perspective of religion, *xix, xxiii,* 5, 9–10, 109, 122, 123–24, 130
  local trust in religious institutions, 8–9, 101
  religion as a personal, private matter, 3, 6, 7, 50, 51, 76, 104, 128
  religion as source of conflict, data not supporting, 58, 59
  religious practices in the workplace, 169–70
  reluctance of support for religious institutions, 117, 124–25, 131
  utilitarian approach to religion, 9, 122
religious identity, *xix,* xxiii, 11, 164
  Christian identity and FBO staffing issues, 71–72
  downplaying of, in European agencies, 156–57, 162
  public funding, effect on, 176
  social identity, intertwined with, 83, 117
  suppression of, reasons for, 9–10, 163
Resource Dependency Theory (RDT), 162
"rice Christians," 38
Rwanda, 88, 109, 122
  Christian teaching, population disposed towards, 47
  development efforts, affected by social conflicts in, 94–95
  genocide, shifts in attitudes towards, 112
  interpersonal harmony as a development challenge, 75
  kingdom values, link with development work, 62
  prayer with local families, 101
  prophetic voice, local church not embracing, 113, 115

Salancik, Gerald, 162
salvation, 15, 42, 43
  development as a work of salvation, 38, 40
  judgment on the salvation of others, 39, 57
  pietistic view of, 150
  spiritual and material salvation, dual emphasis of FBOs, 18, 37–38
Schleiermacher, Friedrich, 19
science and technological in development sector, 26–29
secular aspects of development work, 87, 124, 127
  development as taught from a secular paradigm, 165
  development goals, secular governments fulfilling, 177–78
  economic growth as primary focus, 6, 8
  faith literacy as needed for secular donors, 10–11, 126
  narratives and worldviews of secular organizations, 44, 46
  neutrality and, 48–49, 125, 157, 158–59
  professional staff, drawing organizations towards secular ideologies, 171–72
  secular funding sources, desire to attract, 161
  secular management practices, 160, 166
  secular system of a State, defining, 125–26
  short-term projects, secular agencies suited to, 62
  skepticism towards secular NGOs, 69, 101
Sen, Gita, 74, 91
Senegal, 60, 85
  Christian organizations in Muslim communities, 47, 48
  local church as passive, 113
  traditional practices, discouraging, 86
  World Vision, work in, 58–59
Shah, Rebecca and Timothy, 52
Shalom defining, 43
Sider, Ronald, 168, 172

Sierra Leone, 78
social ethics, 17
social trinitarianism, 15–16
spiritual capital, growing appreciation
    for, 51–53
subsidiarity principle, 19, 70

Tanzania, 47, 49, 59, 62, 110–11
Temple, William, 12, 13
Ter Haar, Gerrie, 130
theology, 43, 108, 151
    Catholic theological tradition,
        xviii
    clergy, theological understanding of,
        110, 111
    as a development asset, xxi, 76,
        119–20
    development themes, theological
        understandings of, 112
    of development work, ix, xi, 102
    disabilities, theological reflections
        on, 145, 146
    FBOs, theological reflection re-
        quired of, 144, 154, 157
    kingdom-inspired theological imper-
        atives, 56, 57
    theologically-framed advocacy, 85,
        88
    theological reasons for involvement
        in development work, 12–14,
        14–20, 21, 178
    theological reflection on theories of
        change, 25–26, 26–35
    Theology of Development of CPP,
        121
    See also kingdom of God
theories of change, 25–26
    change as emergent and complex,
        34–35
    human rights, 31–34

participation and empowerment,
    29–31
science and technology, 26–29
transformational development, ix, x,
    xii, 26, 171
treaty of Westphalia, 7
Tyndale, Wendy, 35, 117, 124, 127–28

United Nations (UN), 5, 7, 127, 144,
    146, 154
universal values, 56, 75, 93
Unrah, Heidi, 168, 172

Vanderwoerd, James, 164
ver Beek, Kurt, 4–5, 130
Volf, Miroslav, 15–16

Weber, Max, 6, 52
Williams, Rowan, 8, 31, 32, 128
Wink, Walter, 42
Wolfensohn, James, 7, 128
women, role in church and society,
    147–49
World Bank, 5, 7, 8, 63, 122, 128
World Conference on Religion and
    Peace, 8
World Faith Development Dialogue, x,
    7, 128
World Health Organization (WHO), 7,
    146
World Vision
    as a case study, xvii, xviii
    data compiled by, 41, 181
    Evaluation Report on Rwanda, 47
    interfaith prayer, permitting, 80
    Senegal, work in, 58–59
    Tanzania, report on success of holis-
        tic approach, 49
Wright, N. T., 15, 42, 43, 150
Wrigley, Anna, 30, 46